T H E
ARCHAIC
REVIVAL

Also by Terence McKenna

The Invisible Landscape (with Dennis McKenna)
Food of the Gods (forthcoming)
True Hallucinations (forthcoming)

THE
ARCHAIC
REVIVAL

Speculations on
Psychedelic Mushrooms,
the Amazon, Virtual Reality,
UFOs, Evolution, Shamanism,
the Rebirth of the Goddess,
and the End of History

TERENCE McKENNA

Illustrations by Satty

HarperOne
An Imprint of HarperCollins*Publishers*

HarperOne

Credits appear on page 265.

HarperCollins books may be purchased for educational, business, or sales promotional use. For information, please e-mail the Special Markets Department at SPsales@harpercollins.com.

HarperCollins Web site: http://www.harpercollins.com

HarperCollins®, 📖®, and HarperOne™ are trademarks of HarperCollins Publishers.

Library of Congress Cataloging-in-Publication Data

McKenna, Terrence K.
    The archaic revival : speculations on psychedelic mushrooms, the Amazon, virtual reality, UFOs, evolution, Shamanism, the rebirth of the goddess, and the end of history / Terrence McKenna. — 1st ed.
        p. cm.
    Includes index.
    ISBN: 978–0–06–250613–9
    1. Mysticism.   2. Shamanism.   3. Hallucinogenic drugs.
4. McKenna, Terrence K.   I. Title.
BL625.M35   1992
001.9—dc20   91–55290

22 23 24 25 26 LBC 42 41 40 39 38

To my father,
Joe McKenna

Contents

Foreword

FROM my downtown Seattle apartment, a number of provocative neon signs are visible, silently reciting themselves like lines from a hot, jerky poem. Above the entrance to the Champ Arcade, for example, there flashes the phrase LIVE GIRLS, LIVE GIRLS, LIVE GIRLS, a sentiment that never fails to bring me joy, especially when I consider the alternative. Less jubilant, though more profound, is the sign in the dry cleaner's window. It reads simply, ALTER-ATIONS, but it always reminds me of Terence McKenna—not merely because Terence McKenna is a leading authority on the experiential aspects of mind-altering plants, or because his lectures and workshops have altered my own thinking, but because Terence, perhaps more than anyone else in our culture, has the ability to let out the waist on the trousers of perception and raise the hemline of reality.

Scholar, theoretician, explorer, dreamer, pioneer, fanatic, and spellbinder, as well as ontological tailor, McKenna combines an erudite, if somewhat original, overview of history with a genuinely visionary approach to the millennium. The result is a cyclone of unorthodox ideas capable of lifting almost any brain out of its cognitive Kansas. When Hurricane Terence sets one's mind back down, however, one will find that it is on solid ground; for, far from Oz-built, the theories and speculations of McKenna are rooted in a time-tested pragmatism thousands of years old. Many of his notions astonish us not because they are so new, but because they have been so long forgotten.

As the title, *The Archaic Revival*, implies, McKenna has found a key to the future in the dung heap of the past. (It is entirely appropriate to note that psychoactive mushrooms often sprout from cow pies.) During the European Renaissance, scientists, artists, and enlightened citizens turned back to a much older Greek civilization for the marble sparks with which to ignite their marvelous new bonfire. In more than one place in this collection of essays and conversations, McKenna is urging that we turn back—way, way back—to Paleolithic shamanism, to retrieve techniques that not only could ensure our survival, but could assist us in mounting a fresh golden age: in fact, *the* golden age, the one toward which the plot of all history has been building.

McKenna doesn't consider himself a shaman, although he has studied with shamans (and drunk their potent potions) in Asia and the Amazon. He says, however, that he is attempting "to explore reality with a shamanic spirit and by shamanic means." Indeed, the shaman's rattle buzzes hypnotically throughout these pages, although it is sometimes obscured by the whoosh of UFOs, for McKenna's imagination (and expertise) ranges from the jungle to hyperspace, and only a dolt would ever call him retro.

Here, let me squirt a few drops of Terence's essence into the punch bowl, so that we might sample the flavor and chart the ripples:

> My vision of the final human future is an effort to exteriorize the soul and interiorize the body, so that the exterior soul will exist as a superconducting lens of translinguistic matter generated out of the body of each of us at a critical juncture at our psychedelic bar mitzvah.

O

> The purpose of life is to familiarize oneself with [the] after-death body so that the act of dying will not create confusion in the psyche.

O

> I don't believe that the world is made of quarks or electromagnetic waves, or stars, or planets, or any of these things. I believe the world is made of language.

O

> There is a hidden factor in the evolution of human beings which is neither a "missing link" nor a telos imparted from on high. I suggest that . . . [the] factor that called human consciousness forth from a bipedal ape with binocular vision involved a feedback loop with plant hallucinogens.

O

> Right here and now, one quanta away, there is raging a universe of active intelligence that is transhuman, hyperdimensional, and extremely alien. . . . What is driving religious feeling [today] is a wish for contact [with that] Other.

O

I scoured India and could not convince myself that it wasn't a shell game of some sort or was any more real than the states manipulated by the various schools of New Age psychotherapy. But in the Amazon . . . you are conveyed into worlds that are appallingly different . . . [yet] more real than real.

These tiny sips from McKenna's gourd, served out of context and stripped of his usual droll garnishes, are nevertheless intoxicating and, to my mind, nourishing. In larger gulps, his brew may even heal the ulcers through which the modern world is bleeding.

Our problems today are more complex and more threatening than at any time in history. Sadly, we cannot even begin to solve those problems, because our reality orientations are lower than a snowman's blood pressure. We squint at existence through thick veils of personal and societal ignorance, overlaid with still more opaque sheets of disinformation, thoughtfully provided by the state, the church, and big business (often one and the same). The difference between us and Helen Keller is that she *knew* she was deaf and blind.

Radical problems call for radical solutions. Conventional politicians are too softheaded to create radical solutions and too fainthearted to implement them if they could, whereas political revolutionaries, no matter how well meaning, ultimately offer only bloodshed followed by another round of repression.

To truly alter conditions, we must alter ourselves—philosophically, psychologically, and, perhaps, biologically. The first step in those alterations will consist mainly of cutting away the veils in order that we might see ourselves for that transgalactic Other that we really are and always have been. Terence the Tailor has got the sharpest shears in town. And he's open Sundays and holidays. Once the veils are severed, we, each of us, can finally start to attend to our self-directed mutagenesis.

The flying saucer is warming up its linguistic engines. The mushroom is shoving its broadcasting transmitter through the forest door. Time for the monkeys to move into hyperspace! It's going to be a weird, wild trip, but, guided by the archaic, Gaia-given gyroscope, we can commence the journey in a state of excitement and hope. With his uniquely secular brand of eschatological euphoria, Terence McKenna is inviting us to a Doomsday we can live with. Be there or be square.

Tom Robbins
Seattle, Washington

Acknowledgments

WANT to thank the many people and organizations that have invited me to express my opinions in various forums over the years.
*Revision, Gnosis, L.A. Weekly, Mondo 2000, Critique, Whole Earth
Review, Magical Blend,* and the Australian journal *Nature and Health*
all cooperated in the reprinting of essays or interviews that originally appeared in their pages. Thanks to the fine journalists who conducted these interviews: Jay Levin, Will Noffke, Michael Toms,
David Brown, Rebecca McClen, and Neville Drury. Special thanks
to Faustin Bray and Brian Wallace of Sound Photosynthesis of Mill
Valley for recording and editing many of my lectures and events. And
special thanks to Diane and Roy Tuckman of Los Angeles; the hundreds
of hours of Southern California airtime that they have given to my ideas
has been invaluable in helping me reach a larger audience.

The ideas expressed here were formed and often recast in the environment of Esalen Institute, where I have done some of my best thinking; to the management, staff, and seminarians of Esalen I offer deep
appreciation.

Friends in the many dozens helped form these ideas. First among
these is my partner Kat Harrison McKenna, whose enthusiasm for the
joys of the imagination equals my own. Thanks to Peter Meyer, who
wrote the computer software that supports the Timewave. Thanks to my
brother Dennis and to Rupert Sheldrake and Ralph Abraham, all of
whom helped me clarify my ideas. And to Tom Robbins for his generous
foreword. Better friends than these no man could ask for.

And finally I owe a deep debt of gratitude to my editor, Dan
Levy, who believed passionately in these ideas and whose friendship
and humor made working on this book a sheer delight.

Introduction

The Archaic Revival

ELCOME to the Archaic Revival. Twenty-five years ago I began to grapple with the realization that exploring the "Wholly Other" was related to shamanism. Pursuing that insight led me to use plant hallucinogens as a means of probing the mysterious dimension this oldest of humanity's religions has always claimed to be able to access. Of all the techniques used by the shaman to induce ecstasy and visionary voyaging—fasting, prolonged drumming, breath control, and stressful ordeals—I now feel confident that the use of hallucinogenic plants is the most effective, dependable, and powerful. I believe that rational exploration of the enigma of the Other is possible and that the shamanic approach to hallucinogenic plants, especially those containing psilocybin and dimethyltryptamine (DMT), will be absolutely central to achieving that end.

These essays, conversations, and interviews, while they make forays far afield, always return to the theme of the Other and its mysterious interpenetration of our lives. It is this that I am concerned to communicate: both the nearness and the strangeness of uncharted realms of risk and beauty full of promise. My hope is that these pieces convey a sense of fun and excitement, of discovery, and of the true depth of the dark waters of mystery upon which the cheerful world of the everyday is no more than a cork bobbing in an uncharted ocean.

I am acutely aware, as many of my readers will be, of the surreal, prophetistic, and even grandiose aspects of many of these ideas. I have come to hold the opinions expressed here based on a lifetime of peculiar experiences. Those experiences occurred at the edge of sanctioned reality, and in the absence of those experiences there would be no basis for my heretical opinions. But I have found the universe of psychedelic shamanism to be a *corpus delecti* for those seeking evidence that all is not well with the sunny world of materialism and scientific rationalism.

In addition to choosing to repress the strange abilities of the shaman and the psychic potential of contact with the Other, Western tradition has a built-in bias against self-experimentation with hallucinogens. One of the consequences of this is that not enough has been written about the phenomenology of personal experiences with the visionary hallucinogens. The exceptions are noteworthy and entertaining. Fitz Hugh Ludlow and Aldous Huxley come to mind, and both seem to exemplify two rules operating in such situations: each appeared early in the wave of interest that attended the "discovery" of hashish and later mescaline by the literate bourgeoisie, and each was naive in terms of medical or psychopharmacological presuppositions. The hallucinogenic South American brew *yagé,* or *ayahuasca,* had its effects chronicled in a similar way by William Burroughs and Allen Ginsberg in *The Yagé Letters.* These early descriptions of the effects of hallucinogens are like the exaggerated and romantic accounts that European explorers carried home with them from the New World. The realms of adventurous fantasy only gradually gave way to the mapped and explored continents we know.

The Archaic Revival is my explorer's notebook, my journey of travel through time and ideological space. It stretches from the prehistoric veldt of Africa to the unimaginable world beyond the transcendental object at the end of history. *The Archaic Revival* is also a roadshow of new strains of thought: we can evolve no faster than our language evolves.

The Archaic Revival offers tonics for language and new health for our best old memes. Lift up the tent edge and scoot inside where there is light and action. Strike up the band. The elfclowns of hyperspace are already juggling in the center ring. Hurry! Hurry!

Terence McKenna
Occidental, California

In Praise of Psychedelics

ONCE upon a time, while on one of my rare excursions into hyperconsciousness (on this occasion via mescaline), someone played for me a Terence McKenna tape. I was transfixed. McKenna was one of the loveliest speakers I'd ever heard, with a lush Irish gift of gab and an extraordinary ability to turn difficult intellectual concepts into verbal poetry. That his subject matter was the evolution of consciousness of the human species, and particularly the role of psychedelics in that evolution, made the tape a particularly engaging experience in my elevated state.

But what truly converted me into a McKenna fan was the level on which he explored what had been for some time one of the major strains in my own thinking—that history as we know it and define it is ending. This was an awareness that I had arrived at early in my journalistic career while researching a magazine assignment on the new psychotherapies. On a mass scale, were people able to break free from the psychological patterns and deadlocks of history, I reasoned, then all our views of human history would change and history as we'd learned it—the battle of nation-states, the struggles between classes, the endless fight for human equality—would in fact become mere footnotes in the annals of the species. It seemed only a matter of a couple of centuries.

To this view McKenna resonated with extrapolations of molecular chemistry,

■■

This interview, done by Jay Levin, appeared in *L.A. Weekly*, May 20–26, 1988. Half of this interview was done in a Mexican restaurant in Malibu, the rest driving on the Pacific Coast Highway in Jay's sports car.

physics, ethnobotany, anthropology, the mathematics of chaos, Jung, McLuhan, and much more. And what made his talk most compelling, at least during my own mescaline meditation, was his argument that the species' ability (eventually) to transcend our own sick history stems chiefly from the impact throughout history of what McKenna called "botanical shamanism." In other words, God's own given psychedelics—mushrooms, peyote, ayahuasca, morning glories, and so on.

McKenna, as it turns out, has never met Tim Leary, whom, it seems, he is about to replace as the culture's foremost spokesperson for the psychedelic experience. Where Leary was brilliant and original in both his experimentation and his salesmanship, McKenna is brilliant, scholarly, and priestly (in the best sense of the word). In fact, though a child of the sixties, the forty-one-year-old McKenna came to his fascination with "ethnopharmacology," as he calls it, not through Leary but through the far more cautious and spiritual Aldous Huxley, whose Doors of Perception *he read when he was fourteen. The son of a traveling salesman for heavy-duty electrical equipment and of a "housewife-mother" in a small, largely fundamentalist Colorado town, Paonia, McKenna recalls that the book left him "completely swept away." "I remember following my mother around our kitchen, telling her that if one-tenth of what this guy was saying was true, then this was what I wanted to do with my life." What in fact he has done is spend twenty years studying the philosophical foundations of shamanism, the use of hallucinogens in spiritual transformation, and the enormous impact and potential of natural hallucinogens on our evolving planetary culture and emerging "metaconsciousness."*

McKenna took his first psychedelic—LSD—in the sixties at Berkeley, where he was a student activist in the free speech and antiwar movements. As an art history major at first, he participated in a special program for gifted students in which "the literature, art, science, mathematics, and what have you of different historical periods were studied in depth." This laid the groundwork for what he calls his broadbrush "approach to exploring the history of human consciousness."

Halfway through college, harassed by Reagan's cops because of his barricades-style political activism in the student strike of 1968 at San Francisco State, McKenna decided a sabbatical was in order and went off to work as an art historian in Nepal, where he tried "to integrate the psychedelic experience into a Buddhist model." This led him to the study of Tibetan shamanism. Both cultures, he discovered, used psychoactive drugs in their explorations of consciousness—hashish and a local herb called datura. Thus began his investigation into the true nature of shamanism. He later finished his degree at the Department of Conservation of Natural Resources at Cal Berkeley, where, he says, he was "a self-organized major in shamanism."

*Aside from his wide knowledge, what makes McKenna fascinating is that he
has himself experienced virtually every form of psychedelic and psychotropic
known to or devised by man, and yet, throughout all these experiences, he has
managed to retain the keen-eyed, scientific, intellectual observer part of his
consciousness, which, after the experience, is able to describe its nature in the
most extraordinarily lucid detail. He has thus experienced levels of awareness
described by some of the great mystics of the past, but unlike most of them he
can relate his experiences to the cultural and historical evolution of the
species.*

*These experiences have led him to one profound and overriding conclusion: the
human species has evolved to its present dominant state through the use of naturally occurring hallucinogens and will not advance past its current primi-
tivism and reach new dimensions of evolved consciousness without further use
of these nature-given means of expanded consciousness. According to
McKenna, no fan of the pop drugs—crack, smack, et al.—or pop drug use, the
pharmacology should be entrusted to specially trained psychotherapy professionals—the potential shamans of postmodern culture—and he is a happy cru-
sader for the expanded legalization of the use of such materials by professionals.*

*These days, when not out lecturing or searching for new natural hallucinogens
in the rain forests of the world, McKenna divides his time between his home in
Sonoma County and the Botanical Dimensions garden site in Hawaii—a nonprofit effort at preserving the natural medicinal and shamanically significant
plants of the earth from the ravages of civilization. He lectures frequently to
psychotherapists and is a personal consultant to some of them.*

—Jay Levin

JL: You've implied that LSD is not truly "shamanistic"; that is,
that it doesn't induce the higher forms of "hallucinations" or vision or
consciousness available from natural products like psilocybin mushrooms. How do you compare it to other psychedelics?

TM: When I was young, I would take LSD once a month or so,
but I wasn't that crazy about it. I found it abrasively psychoanalytical,
and I also found it very hard to hallucinate. My interest in mysticism,
art, and that sort of thing had caused me to put a very high premium on
hallucination.

Then I encountered DMT [dimethyltryptamine] in early 1967.
DMT, which is a natural plant compound that's been synthesized in the
laboratory, is the most powerful of the psychedelics and is extremely
short-acting. After one exposure to it, I said, "This isn't a drug, this is
magic! This is a dimension to reality that most people never even suppose exists."

It was really the DMT that empowered my commitment to the psychedelic experience. DMT was so much more powerful, so much more alien, raising all kinds of issues about what is reality, what is language, what is the self, what is three-dimensional space and time, all the questions I became involved with over the next twenty years or so.

And I saw the psychedelic experience as recovering our birthright. The number of people and cultures that have gone to maturity and then to death without an inkling of this is to me the most shocking thing about the human situation. Because you are not a fully matured human being in touch with the potential of reality unless you have had a psychedelic experience. You don't have to embrace it—or abuse it—but you have to know that it exists. And there's only one way to know that it exists, and that's to have it.

JL: Tim Leary was saying much the same thing in the sixties, and it got him into trouble. What's the difference with you?

TM: You know, I am very much at variance with the wisdom of hindsight in looking back at how Leary and Alpert and Ralph Metzner handled it in the sixties. But to try to launch a "children's crusade," to try to co-opt the destiny of the children of the middle class using the media as your advance man, was a very risky business. And it rebounded, I think, badly.

I think Huxley's approach was much more intelligent—not to try to reach the largest number of people, but to try to reach the most important and influential people: the poets, the architects, the politicians, the research scientists, and especially the psychotherapists. Because what we're talking about is the greatest boon to psychotherapy since dreaming. I often use the metaphor that psychedelics are to psychology what telescopes in the sixteenth century were to astronomy. If a person is not willing to look through the telescope he cannot call himself an astronomer. And if a person is not willing to learn the lessons of the psychedelic compounds, then any therapy he or she does—anything done about the human psyche—is sand-boxed. These are the most powerful agents there are for uncovering the structure and potential of the human mind.

JL: You've said psilocybin is the most important of the natural hallucinogens. What has been your experience with it?

TM: Actually my first experience with psilocybin was when I encountered it in South America, in the Amazon. The DMT experience had acted like a compass. It said, "Ah-ha! *That's* where we want to go." But the DMT flash only lasts about three minutes, and we had the feeling—

my brother and I—that if you could get in there for forty-five minutes, you could really learn something that would astonish people. And in fact there's no end to it. It introduces you to a world of infinite beauty that is cognizable by human beings.

JL: What was your first mushroom experience like?

TM: What was amazing about the mushrooms, and it continues to be amazing, is that it is *animate*, that there's someone *talking* to you. This was actually a voice in the head, making sense, speaking English, and addressing the concerns that were most important to me personally. I was not set up for this.

JL: Did you recognize the voice as being different from the voice with which you normally talk to yourself?

TM: Yes, and I recognized that the information was not something that I could have come up with. That was the proof of the otherness of the voice. And I think what's really happening is that a dialogue opens up between the ego and these larger, more integrated parts of the psyche that are normally hidden from view. Ego may be a fairly modern invention—meaning the last one or two thousand years—a fairly modern adaptation of the psyche to its environment. One of the things happening in the Amazon is that forest people say they enter into a group mind when they take *ayahuasca*, and on it they make decisions for the tribe—where to hunt, who to make war on, where to move to, these kinds of things.

JL: On a visionary or an oral basis?

TM: Visionary *and* oral. Collectively. They see collectively what is to be done. I think that this is a dissolving of the power of the ego, allowing it to contact what I call the Overmind, but what someone else might call the superego. In other words, this much larger, much wiser organizing force that we all carry around inside ourselves but, ordinarily, can access only under situations of extreme psychological pressure or crisis. And then there's a little flash of wisdom. Like a chemical habit, we are hooked on ego. And the psychedelic dissolves that chemical or psychological dependency and replaces it with the facts of the matter: how the individual fits into the life and organization of this planet, the vast amounts of time all these things have been in existence and have worked themselves to their present status.

It was my reading in Jung, which happened very early, that put me strongly in touch with this notion of the self as a larger and more inclusive mode of being than what the ego provides. I don't care to get into questions about "Is it the voice of God?" or "Is it an extraterrestrial?" I don't think that these things can be known at this stage. But what is important is that it knows more about one than one knows about oneself, and, consequently, it is a source of stability, a source of gnosis, a source of information, and this is what most people lack. They are only superficially in touch with their own destiny, their own birth, their own death.

JL: Let's go back to the ego structure. What is the empirical evidence of its being only two thousand years old?

TM: You must know this book by Julian Jaynes called *The Origin of Consciousness in the Breakdown of the Bicameral Mind*? Well, he makes a very interesting case. He says that even as late as Homeric time, people wandered around rather automatically, and when they got into a very tight spot, suddenly there would be a voice in their head saying, "You're in a tight spot. Here's what you should do." They called this God, or a god, or the king (living or dead). This became the ego, the voice we now call "me," something that has been assimilated in the wake of civilization as a necessary means of adapting to socialization. Now, coming out of the linear and dualist kinds of structures that were put on us by Christianity and print media and a number of cultural factors, we need to reconnect with the next level of the Overmind—a globally conscious, ecologically sensitive, balanced, human, caring kind of consciousness that we can access only with considerable effort, through self-discipline, psychotherapy, psychedelics, this kind of thing.

JL: In studying spiritual systems and drugs did you find drug taking among the Tibetan Buddhists?

TM: Not so much among the Buddhists, but I found myself spending more and more time with the pre-Buddhist shamans. And then I went to India. I had studied yoga, but what the yogic texts don't tell you is that almost all *sadhus*, all yogis, are inveterate hash smokers and/or users of datura and were at that time, in the late sixties, absolutely fascinated by LSD and the psychedelic drugs coming from the West.

JL: Among the pre-Buddhist shamans was there drug use?

TM: Well, I don't think that there is really any difference. That is, if you study shamanism carefully, most shamanism that is vital *is* hallucinogenic-plant shamanism.

JL: How did the level of mystical awareness and manifestation of the shamans compare with the ashram gurus of India?

TM: As an anarchist and skeptic, I saw India basically as a very stratified kind of con game. I am no fan of gurus. I think that they have done quite enough for us, thank you, and that it is nothing that sophisticated people need to have anything to do with. Now I am not saying that there aren't people who have the wisdom that life confers, who can tell you how to live, how to die, how to carry on a relationship, have a child, and so forth and so on. But psychedelics address the unseen side of reality, the utterly Other, the transcendentally alien, and that is what interests me. Because if you look at classical descriptions of God, whether you're talking about the Kabbalah or Christian mysticism or Sufi mysticism, what you're always talking about is the unspeakable. And psychedelics propel you through your local language and into this unimaginable realm.

People need to be empowered, and you're not empowered by placing your spiritual development in the hands of a guru. You're spiritually empowered by taking responsibility for your spiritual development, by looking around and seeing what can be done. In a way, I see the entire New Age as a flight from the psychedelic experience. People will do anything other than take a psychedelic compound. Be rebirthed, Rolfed, this, that, and the other thing. Because they instinctively sense that the psychedelic experience is real. It puts you on the line. It isn't like a five-hour drumming session, or deep-tissue work.

So the issue finally comes down to the citizen versus the self. The citizen is an extremely limited definition of human potential. The self is a definition of human potential so broad that it threatens the obligations of the citizen.

JL: What does life look like to the fully self-realized person?

TM: Well, I certainly don't consider myself to be one, so I can only begin to answer. To me life looks extremely hopeful. The human potential is so vast. We don't have any problems that we cannot solve by applying ourselves to them with open minds. Now, you see, the current theory of problem solving is that we must solve all our problems with solutions that make a buck. Well, it just may not be possible to solve the problems of the twentieth century and make a buck at the same time. But if we're willing to put aside that notion, then the human future appears endlessly bright, because the human mind appears to be a much more open pipeline to God than anyone who is outside the psychedelic experience could ever imagine. And God appears to be a much more benevolent and involved force in human affairs than the kind of image that we have inherited from Western religion.

Now, why should taking a natural psychedelic drug compound like psilocybin give you hope? It's because it connects you up with the real network of values and information inherent in the planet, the values of biology, the values of organism, rather than the values of the consumer.

JL: What are those planetary values?

TM: Well, life comes first. Death is nothing to be afraid of; it's a natural part of the process. Sexuality is the glory of the living experience, and so forth and so on. They are, in fact, the humane, caring, ecologically sensitive values that are attempted to be communicated by the New Age, by the ecology movement, and so on. The problem is that these movements politicize everything immediately, turn everything into agendas, turn the opposition into the enemy, then embark on the old-style primate politics that have led us into this impasse.

JL: Patriarchal politics?

TM: Patriarchal politics. The politics of propaganda. The politics of money. The politics of hopelessness. I am a political activist, but I think that the first duty of a political activist is to become psychedelic. Otherwise you're not making your moves cognizant of the entire field of action. This is the thing: the importance of human values has to be brought back into the discussion of political priorities. This was attempted in the sixties; now it's presented as a joke that people would ever stand up and say that love is the answer. It's inconceivable in the present milieu.

JL: It would be useful at this point if you would define shamanism.

TM: Okay. Shamanism is use of the archaic techniques of ecstasy that were developed independent of any religious philosophy—the empirically validated, experientially operable techniques that produce ecstasy. Ecstasy is the contemplation of wholeness. That's why when you experience ecstasy—when you contemplate wholeness—you come down remade in terms of the political and social arena because you have seen the larger picture.

JL: How is it manifested in shamanic acts?

TM: Through the ability to cure, the shaman can confer psychological wholeness on the people who come to him with problems. He acts as an exemplar. He is like a superhuman person, simply by virtue of the fact that he is together, he is not confused. He knows when to hang on and when to let go. What erodes hope is inertia and the momentum of negative psychological activity. What the shaman sees is that the momentum of negative activity is, in fact, an illusion. And by simply changing your mind, you just step aside and the momentum sweeps past you and you are transformed. So it is the form of the mind that the shaman works with: he has a larger view because he is not really in his culture. I found this over and over again. Each culture has its own peculiarities and assumptions and phobias and faux pas. The shaman may appear to be a member of the culture, but he's broader, deeper, higher, and wider than the culture that created him.

A great psychotherapist to my mind would be a great shaman—and there are some very good ones. I don't want to name names because I don't want to leave anyone feeling hurt. I admire transpersonal psychotherapists. I think they are trying to remake the shamanistic institution in a modern form. What they have to realize is that they're wasting their time unless they use the shamanistic tools. And the foremost tool of the shamans is the technique of ecstasy, and that means the hallucinogenic plants. If you suggested to a South American shaman that he could do without the plants, it would be absurd, like suggesting to a stunt flier that he do it without an airplane. And we are moving toward the brink of global catastrophe without using the tools present at hand that might save us. That's stupid. Plain and simple, stupid.

JL: What's your sense of Western culture now?

TM: Well, I think we're entering into a further narrowing of options. Eager as I am to put the Reagan era behind me, the first half of the nineties will be a further exploration of these screwy cultural modes: fundamentalist religion, sexual repression, collapse of central authority. The AIDS epidemic is playing right into the hands of the people who want to repress and distort human misery. I think that there is a New Age about to dawn. I think that it will come, but I think it will come in the late nineties, that we still have much to go through. Because the cultural institutions will not reach for the emergency brake until things are really cracking to pieces. Because, you know, the present form of civilization represents a sinking ship.

JL: On the other hand, one could argue that the collective mind has already made collective decisions about collective healing, that the healing process and the climb toward collective consciousness is already going on. In other words, that the psychoanalytic movement, the spiritual movement (such as it is), the ecology movement, the cultural rebellion—all this, in fact, is the basis for profound positive change. Psychedelics played a part in this, and they continue to play a role, but you can't expect this culture to move into mass psychedelics.

TM: I think that's true. I'm not concerned. I think we're fine. Everything is right on track, developing the way that it should. The trick is to know that, so that one can contribute to it, rather than being frozen by anxiety. I make the analogy to a birth. A birth looks like something unnatural; somebody's being split apart, and there's a lot of blood, guts, and gore. You'd swear that this is death, not life. But in fact, it's a completely natural process. The goal then is to reassure the mother so that she realizes this is natural, this is going to have a termination, that it is part of the plan.

JL: How many times have you taken LSD?

TM: Well, if you put them all together . . . I don't know, maybe 150 times when I was young. Not a lot. I think that if you do these things right, they give you plenty to think about. One thing that people do that I'm definitely opposed to is to *diddle* with it. If you're not taking so much that going into it you're afraid you did too much, then you didn't do enough. Not the way people will take it to go to the movies, go to the beach, this and that. No, I talk about what I call "heroic" doses and "committed" doses. And if you only do heroic doses, then every trip will count. You won't have to do it more than three or four times a year to feel fully psychedelic.

JL: What is a heroic dose of psilocybin?

TM: Five dried grams. Five dried grams will flatten the most resistant ego.

JL: And mescaline?

TM: Eight hundred milligrams. I'm less fond of mescaline because it's an amphetamine. And it's rough on you.

JL: And peyote?

TM: Well, I can give it to you in a nutshell. There are three questions that you should ask yourself about a drug you're considering taking. Number one, does it occur naturally in a plant or an animal?

Because nature has use-tested these compounds over millions and millions of years. Something that came out of the laboratory four or five years ago—who knows? So it should be a product of the natural world. Number two, does it have a history of human usage? Mushrooms do. Mescaline does. LSD doesn't. Ecstasy doesn't. And number three, and most important, it should have some affinity to brain chemistry. It shouldn't be just like landing on the moon; it should be related to what is driving ordinary consciousness. This last criteria is the most narrow, because mescaline won't get through that. LSD won't get through that. I think that drugs should be as noninvasive as possible, and I know I'm on the right track because the strongest psychedelic drugs there are are the ones that last the shortest amount of time. Now, what does that mean? It means that your brain recognizes the compound and within a few minutes can completely neutralize it. DMT is the strongest psychedelic there is, yet it lasts only five minutes. Twenty minutes after you do it, it's like you never did it at all.

Nature is the great guide in all of this. The natural chemistry of the brain. The natural history of the planet. The naturally evolved shamanic institutions of small groups of human beings that are still in touch with reasonable social values.

JL: Let's talk about schematic definitions of your various experiences. I've heard you speak about something that brought you closest to what Gnostics and Kabbalists call the Logos, the ultimate source of all knowledge. If you made a chart of the levels of the unconscious you've experienced, how would you schematize it?

TM: I guess this is how I'd schematize it: Psilocybin "speaks." The speaking voice of psilocybin is absolutely extraordinary. DMT combines the speaking voice and the seeing eye—the most extraordinary thing about the DMT experience is that you see *entities*. You encounter beings whom I've described as self-transforming machine elves. They are the denizens of this other dimension. They are trying to teach something. Well, if I'm not completely mad, then it's big news. Straight people—skeptical people—if given DMT will be conveyed to what is essentially the hall of the Mountain King with gnome revelry in progress. We're not prepared for this. We expect everything to fall into the rational maps that science has given us, and science doesn't describe a hyperdimensional universe teeming with alien intelligences that can be contacted within a moment if you have recourse to a certain chemical compound. Science is hard-pressed to admit that light-years away, there might be beings living on planets in orbit around another star.

JL: What already existing metaphysical map would describe this? Would the Sufi experience be close to it?

TM: I think of Mahayana Buddhism, the multileveled, many-inhabited, demon-haunted, Buddha-haunted realms of peace and joy. The insistence of Mahayana Buddhism that there is really no center, that everything is a construct of time and space, is the most sophisticated psychology. But I'm not willing to climb aboard the Buddhist ethic because Buddhism says suffering is inevitable. That's not a psychedelic point of view. I think that the psychology of Buddhism is the older strata, and that arises out of shamanism. Shamanism worldwide insists that the universe is multileveled, populated by beings that can do you great good, do you great harm. And beings who don't give a hoot about you, one way or the other.

JL: While we are on the track of exploring existing cosmologies, how do you see the Christ mind? I'm talking about the Christ mind as the Heart mind.

TM: This is sort of a problematic area for me. I would think that if you wanted to talk about the heart opening, the rebirth of the Goddess is a more viable metaphor. The problem with Christianity is it's the single most reactionary force in human history. I don't even know what is in second place, it's so far in front. And I believe that the destruction of paganism was probably the greatest disservice to the evolution of the human psyche that has ever been done. The repression of witchcraft is really the repression of botanical knowledge, of shamanism. So I see Christianity as part of this paternalistic shell game.

JL: You seem to infer that the highest shamanism is plant shamanism, and that paganism represents a higher form of consciousness because it is in touch with beings of another level. But in Jewish spiritual practice, through combined study of the Kabbalah and the Torah, there's demonstrable evidence of the ability to attain high degrees of shamanistic power without the use of drugs. Kabbalists also recognize the pagan level as one level of higher consciousness that, while achievable and while real, is not the highest or most transcendent or closest to God. The promise is that combined Kabbalah-Torah study can take you to a much greater dimension than drugs—or any form of Buddhism.

TM: I am not familiar with Jewish mysticism, but I do know it is powerful. My feeling is that abstractions of the kind represented by

Kabbalistic theory suck immediacy from experience and are part of the
historical movement that has brought us down the track of modern science, Aristotelian theory, dualism, materialism, and so forth.

JL: You think you've gotten from your visions some sense of the
nature of where we are going, but is there, in fact, a "choice point," a
moment when the individual—or the species collectively—has to make
a choice about this direction rather than that? Or is it simply that there is
a direction of history in which we are naturally going?

TM: The thing is, reality itself is not static. This is one of the
things that the psychedelic is trying to put across, that the reality we're
embedded in is itself some kind of an organism and is evolving toward a
conclusion. Twentieth-century history is not simply a fluke or an anoma-
ly—it is the culmination of a process that has been in motion for as long
as the planet has been in existence. We are not alienated and outside of
nature; we are somehow the cutting edge of it. And this vast output of
buildings and highways and all the things that characterize the modern
world is actually a feature of the natural world. Similarly, the evolution
of technical intelligence on the surface of the planet, while new, is not
unnatural.

Human beings are therefore the natural agents for a compression
that is building up in the temporal world toward transition into some
higher dimension of existence. History is going to end. This is the astonishing conclusion that I draw out of the psychedelic experience. And all
the scenarios of history's ending that haunt human thinking on the matter, ranging from the Apocalypse of John down to the latest prophecies
of the flying saucer cults, are attempts to grasp or come to grips with an
intuition of transcendental departure from business as usual.

Looking at present cultural trends and extrapolating them, it's
reasonable to suggest that by the end of the Mayan calendar—which is
in 2012 A.D.—we *will* be unrecognizable to ourselves, that what we take
to be our creations, computers and technology, are actually another *level*
of ourselves. And that when we have worked out this peregrination
through the profane labyrinth of history, we will recover what we knew
in the beginning: the archaic union with nature that was seamless, unmediated by language, unmediated by notions of self and other, of life
and death, of civilization and nature. These are all dualisms that are
temporary and provisional within the labyrinth of history. This Archaic
Revival means that all our religions were pale imitations of the Mystery
itself. Then people will say, "Now I understand! Now I understand why
the pyramids, why the fall of Rome, why Auschwitz, why the H-bomb."
All these things are signposts on the way to the transcendental object.
And once we reach it, meaning will flood the entire human experience.

JL: But to see people so transformed, so back in tune with nature on a mass level, would mean we were collectively prepared to put such low-consciousness matters as planetary pollution or the Arab-Israeli struggle behind us virtually overnight. For that to happen, wouldn't there have to be some kind of transcendent event? A visit from a flying saucer? Nuclear warfare? I don't know, I'm trying to remain a rationalist.

TM: It seems highly improbable that such a thing would occur. However, look at something like the phenomenon of language in our species. How probable was that before it existed? It represents some kind of intersection of the monkey species with a transcendental force of some sort. And yet, once it came into existence, it is seen to be inherent in our biological organization.

JL: Nothing in your drug experiences has shown you what that single shamanic event might be?

TM: I think that it could be something like this: The transcendental object, which has been well described since the sixteenth century, is the union of spirit and matter. The transcendental object is matter that behaves like thought, and it is a doorway into the imagination. This is where we're all going to live. This is why the psychedelic experience is so important, because it anticipates a life lived entirely in the imagination.

Now you ask, "How could such a thing be?" Well, as just one hypothesis: Suppose a way were found to integrate human and machine intelligence to create a culture in which humans and machines were psychologically indistinguishable. This would allow us to influence the dimensions of that interaction. If we're creating another dimension, it might as well be paradise. So what today we contemplate as a transcendental object may be a salable technology by 2012.

JL: In other words, you're saying that the transcendent event might conceivably be the creation by 2012 of a computer program that we would interact with to bring us to a heightened state of existence? Maybe one created by a genius computer programmer and metaphysician while tripping on psilocybin?

TM: Yes, a computer program. The two concepts, drugs and computers, are migrating toward each other. If you add in the concept "person" and say these three concepts—drugs, computer, and person—are migrating toward each other, then you realize that the monkey body is still holding a lot of our linguistic structure in place. But if the monkey body were to be dissolved, then we would be much more likely to define ourselves as pure information. I think this is what is happening—that beyond 2012, everybody becomes everything. All possibilities are realized, even possibilities that are mutually exclusive. Because the resolution and the realization of these possibilities occurs in a different kind of space—"nanotechnological" space or psychological space, or a true hyperdimension. It's very hard to imagine what it will be like, because we simply do not have the metaphors and the experience to cognize what we are moving toward.

JL: I assume you don't mean a literal end to the monkey body but a transcendence of the way we see and use the body. I assume you don't think we won't have sex and procreation?

TM: Of course. We will have everything that we have now.

JL: Can you conceptualize—or visualize—the nature of a computer program that would facilitate this higher-consciousness process?

TM: Well, I have actually developed a piece of software that I call Timewave Zero. It's a fractal wave, a mechanical description of time that shows that all times are actually interference patterns created by other times interacting with each other and that all of these times originate from a single end state. Advanced versions of this kind of program could be created in the twenty-four years we have left until 2012.

This isn't something human beings have to decide to do—this is something that is happening! The trick is to figure out what's going to happen that allows you to relate. The psychedelics help to do this because they anticipate the transcendental object. All religions anticipate the transcendental object. All great spiritual personalities, somehow, anticipate and embody the transcendental object. This is no longer centuries or millennia away. It is right here, right now. It is what explains the precipitous drop into novelty that the twentieth century represents. The twentieth century does not make any sense whatsoever unless it ends in a complete transformation of the species. And the nuclear death and the life-affirming factors are so inextricably intertwined that it will remain a horse race right up until the last moment.

In one of my lectures, I asked, "What mushroom is it that blooms at the end of human history? Is it the mushroom of Teller and Fermi and Oppenheimer, or is it the mushroom of Albert Hofmann and Gordon Wasson and Richard Evans Schultes and Timothy Leary?" I believe that it will be very hard for people who are not insiders to figure out where to place their bets. But the very fact that you and I can have this conversation is proof of the nearness of this event. People couldn't say these things even thirty years ago—no one would understand. You know, in testing high-performance aircraft there's an expression "stretching the envelope," meaning pushing the performance capabilities to the absolute outer limits. This is what the twentieth century is doing to the planet and the human organism. We are stretching the envelope as we approach, not the sound barrier but the . . . call it the "mind barrier," the "social barrier." We will not disintegrate when we reach it and fall out of the sky. Instead, if we have designed our social spaceship correctly, we will slip right on through into an infinite realm of potential human becoming.

JL: Certainly urban culture isn't going to disappear.

TM: No, but a new design process of that culture will arise out of the clear perception of human needs rather than the present unclear and politically arguable perception of human beings. We're basically bumping along not in a Model-T Ford but in a Roman chariot. And we have twenty-four years to turn that into a starship. That's why it is so important to communicate, for all of us to put our best foot forward, to put our best metaphors on the table. Because we can move no faster than the evolution of our language. And this is certainly part of what the psychedelics are about: they *force* the evolution of language. And no culture, so far as I am aware, has ever consciously tried to evolve its language with the awareness that evolving language was evolving reality. And yet, we are on the brink of that. Madison Avenue understands that, but in a perverse way. If we can get away from the idea of making a buck, get into the idea of using this idea to save our skins, then the transcendental object moves that much nearer.

The strange thing about psilocybin, my career, and this conversation is that it has to do with the empowerment of language. That's what gives me my cachet, why people say, "You say things that nobody else ever says," "You speak clearly." The social consequence of the psychedelic experience is clear thinking—which trickles down as clear speech. Empowered speech.

JL: What if you're wrong and the world still has so much sickness in 2012?

TM: Well, at least I had the courage to make a specific prophecy. I'll be sixty-five in 2012, time to cash it in anyway.

JL: Speaking of empowered speech, one of your raps that I found particularly perspicacious was about the octopus as the symbol of the dawning age. Want to explain?

TM: What is not well known is the communication model that is happening in the octopus. Octopi change their color not for camouflage purposes, as might be supposed, but as a mode of communication. The blushes, spots, and traveling bands of color that an ordinary octopus can manifest are reflective of its linguistic intent. Its language appears on the surface of its skin.

Ordinarily, telepathy is imagined to be you hearing me think, then me hearing you think. But a richer notion of telepathy would be if you could see my words, rather than hear them—if they were actually sculptural objects. I would make an utterance, then you and I would stand and regard this utterance from all angles. There would be no ambiguity. And this is exactly what is going on with the octopi. Shamans do the same thing. These shamanistic songs that are sung are not intended to be heard, they are intended to be seen by other people who are intoxicated. This crossing from the heard to the seen is a very important part of the revelation of the transcendental object.

We are going to go from a linguistic mode that is heard to a linguistic mode that is beheld. When this transition is complete, the ambiguity, the uncertainty, and the subterfuge that haunt our efforts at communication will be obsolete. And it will be in this environment of beheld communication that the new world of the Logos will be realized.

JL: And MTV and the computers are just rushing us there?

TM: Yes, they're pushing us right there.

JL: The metaphysical experiences always promise that once the ego is dropped, and true knowledge is arrived at, that in fact you begin to experience reality through the embodiment of God—which is supposedly yourself. And that that embodiment is joy and love, a profundity of pleasure, experiential awareness, consciousness, and radiance beyond what most people have ever experienced on the most profound levels. How does that integrate with your sensibility?

TM: My notion of the posttransition felt experience is that it is a domain where appropriate activity is the path of least resistance. In other words, in this current realm Tao and ego seem impossibly opposed. Things are either one or the other. In the posttransition world, it's possible that there will appear to be only ego, and there will actually be only Tao. And that's a good working definition of what a telepathic society would be like: appropriate activity. It's nothing more than that.

Imagine if every problem were solved appropriately, if every relationship evolved appropriately, if every act were an appropriate one.

That alone would be the kingdom of heaven. And that is, I think, what we're pushing toward. Not cosmic fireworks or the descent of alien beings in flying saucers, but simply appropriate activity—empowered, felt experience—and the abandonment of the illusion of separateness.

High Frontiers Interview

W

N: I WONDER if you could share with us the experience that shaped your life and work, your journey to the Amazon Basin.

TM: Certainly. There have actually been a number of journeys to the Amazon that I have participated in—the earliest in 1971, the most recent in 1981. In 1981, a joint ethnobotanical expedition composed of people from Harvard and the University of British Columbia went to Iquitos in the far east of Peru. My brother was also part of that expedition. He is an ethnochemist at the University of British Columbia. We were looking at *ayahuasca*, which is a hallucinogenic beverage taken over a very wide area in the lowland jungles of Ecuador, Colombia, and Peru. We were also looking at a very little-studied hallucinogen called *oo-koo-hey* or *kuri-coo*, which is used by the Witoto, Boro, and Muinane people. In both cases these hallucinogenic drugs are based on DMT or DMT in combination with some other chemical that potentiates the experience. These are probably the two least studied of the hallucinogens, although *ayahuasca* is a major folk religion over a very large area. It is involved in shamanic curing and is very familiar to the poor classes of the lowland jungles of Peru and well known to the mestizo populations. *Kuri-coo* is a much less-known substance. We were studying it because the orthodox pharmacological theories say that it should not be orally active, yet it is. So there was a scientific problem there to deal with.

■■■

Will Noffke's interview with me appeared in *High Frontiers*, no. 1, 1984. The magazine has gone through two name changes since then and is now called *Mondo 2000*.

WN: Something of discovering a new reality for science?

TM: Well, you have to have a scientific problem to center these expeditions. Then what you actually brush up against is the phenomenology of the drug—the drug as it is experienced—and this is far removed from the pharmacological issues that are being sorted out now in the laboratory. But the experience of taking these drugs in the Amazon, up small tributaries that run into the main body of the river, among preliterate people who are definitely not middle-class, and in the ambiance of the equatorial continental jungles, was very interesting, very enlightening.

WN: How did you respond to that? I assume that you'd experimented with other hallucinogens in the recent past before you made that journey, and that indeed you were looking for the effect, the psychophysical response in yourself. Yet apparently you came upon something quite unexpected.

TM: Yes. Since the mid-sixties we had been interested in dimethyltryptamine, DMT, because of both the experience and its rapid onset. When DMT is smoked, it comes on in about fifteen to thirty seconds. The content of the experience seemed to go beyond the orthodox model of what the psychedelic experience should constitute. In other words, the psychedelic experience has been discussed in terms of consciousness expansion, or exploring the contents of the personal or collective unconscious, or achieving great empathy with works of art, and things of that sort. What we found with the tryptamines was that there seemed to be an unanticipated dimension that involved contact with an alien intelligence. I call it this for want of a better description. Organized entelechies presented themselves in the psychedelic experience with information that seemed not to be drawn from the personal history of the individual or even from the collective human experience. Later, we came to feel that this effect was unique to the tryptamine hallucinogens. In other words, not only DMT and *ayahuasca* and the more exotic Amazonian substances, but also psilocybin, which is probably the most widely experienced of these drugs. To me it was astonishing that a voice could address you in that state and impart information in a dialogue. Gordon Wasson, who discovered the psilocybin mushroom and brought it formally to the attention of Western science, also wrote about this phenomenon. So did Plato in discussing the importance of the Logos for Hellenistic religion.

This experience of an interior guiding voice with a higher level of knowledge is not alien in Western history; however, the intellectual adventure of the last thousand years has made an idea like that seem preposterous if not psychopathological. So as moderns and as pharmacologists exploring these states, my brother and I came upon this phenomenon. In the ensuing years we've worked with it and directed others' attention to it; I would say a consensus has emerged that this is real. But a consensus has yet to emerge about exactly what it is. Are we dealing with an aspect, an autonomous psychic entity, as the Jungians would style it—a subself that has slipped away from the control of the ego? Or are we dealing with something like a species Overmind—a kind of collective entelechy? Or are we in fact dealing with an alien intelligence with all that this implies? It's not an easy question to answer. It's not even an easy question to grapple with, because the phenomenon does not manifest itself except at heroic doses.

WN: There are certain parallels that are quite obvious, and one of them that comes to mind is Saint Joan hearing voices and gaining direction. Granted, she was a farm girl, and perhaps she was growing mushrooms in the backyard. Throughout history there seems to be the hearing of voices within the realms of religious experience and it is always attributed to "god," whatever that image is for the individual who is experiencing it. That experience does not, well, necessarily come from the ingestion of any drug. It can come through some other aspect of altering human consciousness.

TM: Right. It always arises through a shift in the interior chemistry of the body and the brain. But this can be induced by plants or stress, or a person or family line can simply have a predilection for these states. You're quite right, religion as understood in premodern terms is essentially humans' response to the problem of interior prompting, but enough people have it that it is a culture-shaping phenomenon, if not, in fact, a culture-steering phenomenon.

Unfortunately, religion for the past five hundred years has been a hierarchical pyramid at whose top were theologians interpreting dogma. This interpretation was handed down through a hierarchy to the faithful. I think religious hierarchies are very unsettled by the idea of direct revelation. Nevertheless, this phenomenon is certainly thriving in preliterate cultures all over the world. We discovered in dealing with this that the only people you could talk to about it or who seemed to have familiarity with it were shamans.

And they say, "Yes. Of course. This is how information is obtained: from helping spirits or hindering spirits in that dimension." The idea of autonomous alien intelligences contacted in the mental dimension seems to them commonplace. I think it probably is. I think that Western culture has taken a long, idiosyncratic detour away from the spirit, and we are just now beginning to realize that we may have lost something. In fact, we do not represent the pinnacle of understanding of the nature of reality. We have very interesting maps of, say, the heart of the atom or the far reaches of the universe, but in the areas closest to home—our own minds, our own experiences of ourselves and each other—I believe these primitive cultures, by being phenomenological and by not being encumbered by technical apparatus or abstract theories of what's going on, come closer to the mark. In other words, they are folk psychiatrists, folk psychoanalysts who leave us far behind. Anthropologists have commented on the absence of serious mental disease in many preliterate cultures. I believe that the mediation of the shaman and through him the contact to the centering Logos, this source of information or gnosis, is probably the cause of this ability to heal or minimize psychological disorders.

WN: You mentioned something in relation to organized religion. I think Western Christianity has been very successful at establishing its turf by instilling fear, doubt, and suspicion of anything that comes from inner sources. It's established a criteria that says, "If it isn't in the scriptures, it is to be ignored and suspected as being from a dark force." There is a distinct denial of the validity of personal experience. I find that a great many people look at the psychedelic experience as highly suspect, highly dangerous, and uncontrollable. How have you found people deal with this?

TM: It's uncontrollable to the degree that it is not well understood. These preliterate cultures have an unbroken tradition of shamanic understanding and ethnomedicine that reaches back to Paleolithic times and beyond. We have nothing comparable. So people in our culture who get into deep water with these plants, whom do they turn to? Whom do they ask with certain knowledge? In Peru, we saw people who were naive about *ayahuasca*. People who had come from Lima for the experience got to the place where they were definitely having a bad trip. But the shaman is able to come over to them and blow tobacco smoke over them and chant—things that appear to us to be symbolic but that nevertheless act with the same efficacy as if the person had received a shot of Demerol. So one man's symbolism is another man's technology. This should be kept in mind when dealing with these cultures. How things appear to us may not be how they appear to the people who are enmeshed in them. Unless you shed your language and enter into these cultures entirely, you will always have the point of view of a stranger and an outsider.

WN: Even in that aspect of society that might be categorized as New Age, for want of a better term, where there's a great deal of break-

ing away from dogmatic upbringing and movement into direct experience, the psychedelic experience is suspect. So such things as working
with the kundalini, hypnosis, mantras, and physical activities—psychophysical manipulations of consciousness—seem to be safe ground and
acceptable as areas for investigation. But I see this incredible bias against
using chemical means, even the organic ones you speak of.

TM: I think there's a very strong Calvinistic bias against a free
lunch. The idea that you could achieve a spiritual insight without suffering, soul-searching, flagellation, and that sort of thing, is abhorrent to
people because they believe that the vision of these higher dimensions
should be vouchsafed to the good, and probably to them only after
death. It is alarming to people to think that they could take a substance
like psilocybin or DMT and have these kinds of experiences.
Nevertheless, it is a fact of reality that we are only now beginning to
come to terms with. I don't believe that these things are a substitute for
spiritual practice. On the other hand, I don't believe that spiritual practice could ever be a substitute for these experiences. I scoured India and
Indonesia and a number of other places and found these traditions you
mentioned, including the Tantra of kundalini, the trance dancing in Bali,
under the control of priests and embedded in traditions in which you
have to accept the mind-set to have the experience. They are very elusive. The drug experience, on the other hand, is not. It is overpowering.
Certainly with the tryptamines there is nothing elusive. It is the great
convincer. These things are going to have to be integrated into the culture without a sense of guilt and with a sense that they point the way toward something. I think Aldous Huxley called them "gratuitous
graces," explaining that they were neither necessary nor sufficient for
salvation, but they were, nevertheless, a miracle.

WN: You make a strong point for set and setting as part of the
experience—that they are not to be taken lightly or used recreationally
and that they need to be dealt with in respect. And that it is preferable to
have someone available to serve as a guide. I'll also be interviewing
Timothy Leary. I'm not quite sure of his attitude, whether it's one of fun
and games at any cost, or whether it is intensely serious.

TM: I think he is a man who probably has had ample opportunity
to change his mind. The euphoria of the sixties, the assumption of the intellectuals around Huxley and Humphrey Osmond that all that needed
to be done was to lay this before the people and humanity would transform itself, was terribly naive. Nevertheless, people had never stood at a
cultural crossroads quite like that. I hear people saying there may be an-

other pass at the psychedelic experience as a social phenomenon. I certainly hope if there is that those of us who went through the 1960s will have processed that experience and learned the lessons from it. I think these things should not be done in large groups.

The most fruitful way to approach the psychedelic experience is in the environment almost, though not formally, of sensory deprivation. Lie down in complete darkness and silence and watch the back of your eyelids. I'm amazed how exotic this advice seems to be to other people. It is common sense that would lead you to do that. After all, you're trying to observe a mental phenomenon. To see the mental phenomenon uncontaminated by outside sources of information, you must put yourself in a situation where it can fully manifest itself. At the effective doses of these substances, I guarantee anyone that it is not going to be a boring experience. Perhaps too many people have meditated and so they imagine that it is like meditation. It is the exact antithesis of meditation. It is, in fact, to leave your body and to journey into mental space—which is an area at least as large as outer space. The distinction between these two may be cultural convention. You journey into a deployed field of information that appears to be light-years in extent. This can only be done if the exterior input has been brought to a minimum. Then you see what Blake saw and what Meister Eckhart saw, what St. John of the Cross saw. You may not be able to bring to bear on these things the kind of insight they did, but on the other hand no one can measure the ocean, not Meister Eckhart or anybody else. It is not easy to measure the ocean, but we can be measured by it, confront it, and be in it.

I think these substances have had, are having, and will have a great impact on human history. They may in fact be the *cause* of human history. We're so familiar with the doctrine of evolution—the idea that we descended from the apes—that we tend to overlook how odd a creature man really is. Man is a very odd creature. And to have arisen in a million years from the chipping of flint to the launching of the space shuttle and the hurling of instruments out of the solar system, it seems preposterous to maintain that the forces and facts of nature as we know them could have allowed us to do what we are doing. Instead, I take a very premodern view: we are in league with the demiurge. We are the children of a force that we can barely imagine. It is calling us out of the trees and across the plains of history toward itself. This process is taking ten, twenty, one hundred thousand years—an instant. The lifetimes of many individuals come and go, but nature acts from the point of view of the species, and, on that scale, hardly a moment has passed since there was nothing happening on this planet except the chipping of flint and pharmacology. Pharmacology preceded agriculture because the properties of plants were understood long before the husbandry of plants was understood. The visions conveyed on psilocybin—visions of enormous machines in orbit and distant planets and strange creatures and vast biomechanistic landscapes—can hardly be processed. You don't know whether you are walking around inside an enormous instrument or organism. We are barely able to assimilate these things. Yet these visions are the current guiding image, being released into historical time. As it released the differential calculus a couple of hundred years ago; as it released all the great advances in human history. The history of scientific or technical advances has the character of revelation. The people who have the real breakthroughs always say, "It was just handed to me one morning; it was there." Descartes invented the calculus while lying in bed one morning. Newton was doing the same thing a few hundred miles away, and they didn't even know each other. Over the millennia there has been a dialogue between the individual self and the Other, between the collective self and the Other. We have called this God. Priests have gotten control of it and freighted it down with all kinds of thou-shalts and thou-shalt-nots, but the real religious experience is not about that. It is about the dialogue with the Logos and where it can lead you and what it can show you. So now, when we as a species are about to leave or destroy the planet, the Logos reemerges with great intensity. We are not going to leave this planet with our minds untransformed. What is happening is an overall transformation of humanity into an entirely different kind of creature. The monkey is being shed. And the thing that is made of language and of image and imagination, that has resided in the monkeys for so long, is now superseding biological evolution and, through culture, taking over the reins of its own form and destiny. And the chaos of our age, which is so troubling to us all, is nothing unusual at all. It is the normal situation when a species prepares to leave the planet. This is the chaos at the end of history.

There is no question about it. The signs are all around us. The signs that are not all around us, but that are known to the aficionados of psychedelic substances, are the transformations of consciousness that are simultaneous with the transformation of technical culture. These two are, in fact, expressions of each other. These times are the birth pangs of a new humanity.

Tryptamine Hallucinogens and Consciousness

THERE is a very circumscribed place in organic nature that has, I think, important implications for students of human nature. I refer to the tryptophan-derived hallucinogens dimethyltryptamine (DMT), psilocybin, and a hybrid drug that is in aboriginal use in the rain forests of South America, *ayahuasca*. This latter is a combination of dimethyltryptamine and a monoamine oxidase inhibitor that is taken orally. It seems appropriate to talk about these drugs when we discuss the nature of consciousness; it is also appropriate when we discuss quantum physics.

It is my interpretation that the major quantum mechanical phenomena that we all experience, aside from waking consciousness itself, are dreams and hallucinations. These states, at least in the restricted sense that I am concerned with, occur when the large amounts of various sorts of radiation conveyed into the body by the senses are restricted. Then we see interior images and interior processes that are psychophysical. These processes definitely arise at the quantum mechanical level. It's been shown by John Smythies, Alexander Shulgin, and others that there are quantum mechanical correlates to hallucinogenesis. In other words, if one atom on the molecular ring of an inactive compound is moved, the compound becomes highly active. To me this is a perfect proof of the dynamic linkage at the formative level between quantum mechanically described matter and mind.

■■■

A talk given at the Lilly/Goswami Conference on Consciousness and Quantum Physics at Esalen, December 1983. It was to be the first of many lectures at Esalen Institute on the Big Sur Coast of California.

Hallucinatory states can be induced by a variety of hallucinogens and disassociative anesthetics, and by experiences like fasting and other ordeals. But what makes the tryptamine family of compounds specifically interesting is the intensity of the hallucinations and the concentration of activity in the visual cortex. There is an immense vividness to these interior landscapes, as if information were being presented three-dimensionally and deployed fourth-dimensionally, coded as light and as evolving surfaces. When one confronts these dimensions, one becomes part of a dynamic relationship relating to the experience while trying to decode what it is saying. This phenomenon is not new—people have been talking to gods and demons for far more of human history than they have not.

It is only the conceit of the scientific and technological postindustrial societies that allows us to even propound some of the questions that we take to be so important. For instance, the question of contact with extraterrestrials is a kind of red herring premised upon a number of assumptions that a moment's reflection will show are completely false. To search expectantly for a radio signal from an extraterrestrial source is probably as culture-bound a presumption as to search the galaxy for a good Italian restaurant. And yet, this has been chosen as the avenue by which it is assumed contact is likely to occur. Meanwhile, there are people all over the world—psychics, shamans, mystics, schizophrenics—whose heads are filled with information, but it has been ruled a priori irrelevant, incoherent, or mad. Only that which is validated through consensus via certain sanctioned instrumentalities will be accepted as a signal. The problem is that we are actually so inundated by these signals—these other dimensions—that there is a great deal of noise in the circuit.

It is no great accomplishment to hear a voice in the head. The accomplishment is to make sure that it is telling you the truth, because the demons are of many kinds: "Some are made of ions, some of mind; the ones of ketamine, you'll find, stutter often and are blind." The reaction to these voices is not to kneel in genuflection before a god, because then one will be like Dorothy in her first encounter with Oz. There is no dignity in the universe unless we meet these things on our feet, and that means having an I/Thou relationship. One says to the Other: "You say you are omniscient, omnipresent, or you say you are from Zeta Reticuli. You're long on talk, but what can you show me?" Magicians, people who invoke these things, have always understood that one must go into such encounters with one's wits about oneself.

What does extraterrestrial communication have to do with this family of hallucinogenic compounds I wish to discuss? Simply this: that the unique presentational phenomenology of this family of compounds has been overlooked. Psilocybin, though rare, is the best known of these neglected substances. Psilocybin, in the minds of the uninformed public and in the eyes of the law, is lumped together with LSD and mescaline, when in fact each of these compounds is a phenomenologically defined universe unto itself. Psilocybin and DMT invoke the Logos, although DMT is more intense and more brief in its action. This means that they work directly on the language centers, so that an important aspect of the experience is the interior dialogue. As soon as one discovers this about psilocybin and about tryptamines in general, one must decide whether or not to enter into the dialogue and to try and make sense of the incoming signal. This is what I have attempted.

I call myself an explorer rather than a scientist, because the area that I'm looking at contains insufficient data to support even the dream of being a science. We are in a position comparable to that of explorers who map one river and only indicate other rivers flowing into it; we must leave many rivers unascended and thus can say nothing about them. This Baconian collecting of data, with no assumptions about what it might eventually yield, has pushed me to a number of conclusions that I did not anticipate. Perhaps through reminiscence I can explain what I mean, for in this case describing past experiences raises all of the issues.

I first experimented with DMT in 1965; it was even then a compound rarely met with. It is surprising how few people are familiar with it, for we live in a society that is absolutely obsessed with every kind of sensation imaginable and that adores every therapy, every intoxication, every sexual configuration, and all forms of media overload. Yet, however much we may be hedonists or pursuers of the bizarre, we find DMT to be too much. It is, as they say in Spanish, *bastante*, it's enough—so much enough that it's too much. Once smoked, the onset of the experience begins in about fifteen seconds. One falls immediately into a trance. One's eyes are closed and one hears a sound like ripping cellophane, like someone crumpling up plastic film and throwing it away. A friend of mine suggests this is our radio entelechy ripping out of the organic matrix. An ascending tone is heard. Also present is the normal hallucinogenic modality, a shifting geometric surface of migrating and changing colored forms. At the synaptic site of activity, all available bond sites are being occupied, and one experiences the mode shift occurring over a period of about thirty seconds. At that point one arrives in a place that defies description, a space that has a feeling of being underground, or somehow insulated and domed. In *Finnegans Wake* such a space is called the "merry go raum," from the German word *raum*, for "space." The room is actually going around, and in that space one feels like a child, though one has come out somewhere in eternity.

The experience always reminds me of the twenty-fourth fragment of Heraclitus: "The Aeon is a child at play with colored balls." One not only becomes the Aeon at play with colored balls but meets entities as well. In the book by my brother and myself, *The Invisible Landscape*, I describe them as self-transforming machine elves, for that is how they appear. These entities are dynamically contorting topological modules that are somehow distinct from the surrounding background, which is itself undergoing a continuous transformation. These entities remind me of the scene in the film version of *The Wizard of Oz* after the Munchkins come with a death certificate for the Witch of the East. They all have very squeaky voices and they sing a little song about being "absolutely and completely dead." The tryptamine Munchkins come, these hyper-dimensional machine-elf entities, and they bathe one in love. It's not erotic but it is open-hearted. It certainly feels good. These beings are like fractal reflections of some previously hidden and suddenly autonomous part of one's own psyche.

And they are speaking, saying, "Don't be alarmed. Remember, and do what we are doing." One of the interesting characteristics of DMT is that it sometimes inspires fear—this marks the experience as existentially authentic. One of the interesting approaches to evaluating a compound is to see how eager people are to do it a second time. A touch of terror gives the stamp of validity to the experience because it means, "This is real." We are in the balance. We read the literature, we know the maximum doses, the LD-50, and so on. But nevertheless, so great is one's faith in the mind that when one is out in it one comes to feel that the rules of pharmacology do not really apply and that control of existence on that plane is really a matter of focus of will and good luck.

I'm not saying that there's something intrinsically good about terror. I'm saying that, granted the situation, if one is not terrified then one must be somewhat out of contact with the full dynamics of what is happening. To not be terrified means either that one is a fool or that one has taken a compound that paralyzes the ability to be terrified. I have nothing against hedonism, and I certainly bring something out of it. But the experience must move one's heart, and it will not move the heart unless it deals with the issues of life and death. If it deals with life and death it will move one to fear, it will move one to tears, it will move one to laughter. These places are profoundly strange and alien.

The fractal elves seem to be reassuring, saying, "Don't worry, don't worry; do this, look at this." Meanwhile, one is completely "over there." One's ego is intact. One's fear reflexes are intact. One is not "fuzzed out" at all. Consequently, the natural reaction is amazement; profound astonishment that persists and persists. One breathes and it persists. The elves are saying, "Don't get a loop of wonder going that quenches your ability to understand. Try not to be so amazed. Try to focus and look at what we're doing." What they're doing is emitting sounds like music, like language. These sounds pass without any quan-

tized moment of distinction—as Philo Judaeus said that the Logos
would when it became perfect—from things heard into things beheld.
One hears and beholds a language of alien meaning that is conveying
alien information that cannot be Englished.

Being monkeys, when we encounter a translinguistic object, a
kind of cognitive dissonance is set up in our hindbrain. We try to pour
language over it and it sheds it like water off a duck's back. We try again
and fail again, and this cognitive dissonance, this "wow" or "flutter"
that is building off this object causes wonder, astonishment, and awe at
the brink of terror. One must control that. And the way to control it is to
do what the entities are telling one to do, to do what they are doing.

I mention these "effects" to invite the attention of experimental-
ists, whether they be shamans or scientists. There is something going on
with these compounds that is not part of the normal presentational spectrum of hallucinogenic drug experience. When one begins to experiment
with one's voice, unanticipated phenomena become possible. One experiences glossolalia, although unlike classical glossolalia, which has been
studied. Students of classical glossolalia have measured pools of saliva
eighteen inches across on the floors of South American churches where
people have been kneeling. After classical glossolalia has occurred, the
glossolaliasts often turn to ask the people nearby, "Did I do it? Did I
speak in tongues?" This hallucinogen-induced phenomenon isn't like
that; it's simply a brain state that allows the expression of the assembly
language that lies behind language, or a primal language of the sort that
Robert Graves discussed in *The White Goddess,* or a Kabbalistic language
of the sort that is described in the *Zohar,* a primal *ur sprach* that comes
out of oneself. One discovers one can make the extradimensional objects—the feeling-toned, meaning-toned, three-dimensional rotating
complexes of transforming light and color. To know this is to feel like a
child. One is playing with colored balls; one has become the Aeon.

This happened to me twenty seconds after I smoked DMT on a
particular day in 1966. I was appalled. Until then I had thought that I
had my ontological categories intact. I had taken LSD before, yet this
thing came upon me like a bolt from the blue. I came down and said
(and I said it many times), "I cannot believe this; this is impossible, this
is completely impossible." There was a declension of gnosis that proved
to me in a moment that right here and now, one quanta away, there is
raging a universe of active intelligence that is transhuman, hyperdimensional, and extremely alien. I call it the Logos, and I make no judgments
about it. I constantly engage it in dialogue, saying, "Well, what are you?
Are you some kind of diffuse consciousness that is in the ecosystem of
the earth? Are you a god or an extraterrestrial? Show me what you
know."

The psilocybin mushrooms also convey one into the world of the tryptamine hypercontinuum. Indeed, psilocybin is a psychoactive tryptamine. The mushroom is full of answers to the questions raised by its own presence. The true history of the galaxy over the last four and a half billion years is trivial to it. One can access images of cosmological history. Such experiences naturally raise the question of independent validation—at least for a time this was my question. But as I became more familiar with the epistemological assumptions of modern science, I slowly realized that the structure of the Western intellectual enterprise is so flimsy at the center that apparently no one knows anything with certitude. It was then that I became less reluctant to talk about these experiences. They are experiences, and as such they are primary data for being. This dimension is not remote, and yet it is so unspeakably bizarre that it casts into doubt all of humanity's historical assumptions.

The psilocybin mushrooms do the same things that DMT does, although the experience builds up over an hour and is sustained for a couple of hours. There is the same confrontation with an alien intelligence and extremely bizarre translinguistic information complexes. These experiences strongly suggest that there is some latent ability of the human brain/body that has yet to be discovered; yet, once discovered, it will be so obvious that it will fall right into the mainstream of cultural evolution. It seems to me that either language is the shadow of this ability or that this ability will be a further extension of language. Perhaps a human language is possible in which the intent of meaning is actually beheld in three-dimensional space. If this can happen on DMT, it means it is at least, under some circumstances, accessible to human beings. Given ten thousand years and high cultural involvement in such a talent, does anyone doubt that it could become a cultural convenience in the same way that mathematics or language has become a cultural convenience?

Naturally, as a result of the confrontation of alien intelligence with organized intellect on the other side, many theories have been elaborated. The theory that I put forth in *Psilocybin: The Magic Mushroom Grower's Guide*, held that the mushroom was in fact an extraterrestrial. I suggested that the *Stropharia cubensis* mushroom was a species that did not evolve on earth. Within the mushroom trance, I was informed that once a culture has complete understanding of its genetic information, it reengineers itself for survival. The *Stropharia cubensis* mushroom's version of reengineering is a mycelial network strategy when in contact with planetary surfaces and a spore-dispersion strategy as a means of radiating throughout the galaxy. And, though I am troubled by how freely Bell's nonlocality theorem is tossed around, nevertheless the alien intellect on the other side does seem to be in possession of a huge body of information drawn from the history of the galaxy. It/they say that there is

nothing unusual about this, that humanity's conceptions of organized
intelligence and the dispersion of life in the galaxy are hopelessly culture-bound, that the galaxy has been an organized society for billions of
years. Life evolves under so many different regimens of chemistry, tem-
perature, and pressure, that searching for an extraterrestrial who will sit
down and have a conversation with you is doomed to failure. The main
problem with searching for extraterrestrials is to recognize them. Time is
so vast and evolutionary strategies and environments so varied that the
trick is to know that contact is being made at all. The *Stropharia cubensis*
mushroom, if one can believe what it says in one of its moods, is a symbiote, and it desires ever deeper symbiosis with the human species. It
achieved symbiosis with human society early by associating itself with
domesticated cattle and through them human nomads. Like the plants
men and women grew and the animals they husbanded, the mushroom
was able to inculcate itself into the human family, so that where human
genes went these other genes would be carried.

But the classic mushroom cults of Mexico were destroyed by the
coming of the Spanish conquest. The Franciscans assumed they had an
absolute monopoly on theophagy, the eating of God; yet in the New
World they came upon people calling a mushroom *teonanacatl,* the flesh
of the gods. They set to work, and the Inquisition was able to push the
old religion into the mountains of Oaxaca so that it only survived in a
few villages when Valentina and Gordon Wasson found it there in the
1950s.

There is another metaphor. One must balance these explanations.
Now I shall sound as if I didn't think the mushroom is an extraterrestrial. It may instead be what I've recently come to suspect—that the human
soul is so alienated from us in our present culture that we treat it as an
extraterrestrial. To us the most alien thing in the cosmos is the human
soul. Aliens Hollywood-style could arrive on earth tomorrow and the
DMT trance would remain more weird and continue to hold more
promise for useful information for the human future. It is that intense.
Ignorance forced the mushroom cult into hiding. Ignorance burned the
libraries of the Hellenistic world at an earlier period and dispersed the
ancient knowledge, shattering the stellar and astrological machinery that
had been the work of centuries. By ignorance I mean the Hellenistic-
Christian-Judaic tradition. The inheritors of this tradition built a triumph
of mechanism. It was they who later realized the alchemical dreams of
the fifteenth and sixteenth centuries—and the twentieth century—with
the transformation of elements and the discovery of gene transplants.
But then, having conquered the New World and driven its people into
cultural fragmentation and diaspora, they came unexpectedly upon the
body of Osiris—the condensed body of Eros—in the mountains of

Mexico where Eros had retreated at the coming of the Christos. And by finding the mushroom, they unleashed it.

Phillip K. Dick, in one of his last novels, *Valis*, discusses the long hibernation of the Logos. A creature of pure information, it was buried in the ground at Nag Hammadi, along with the burying of the Chenoboskion Library circa 370 A.D. As static information, it existed there until 1947, when the texts were translated and read. As soon as people had the information in their minds, the symbiote came alive, for, like the mushroom consciousness, Dick imagined it to be a thing of pure information. The mushroom consciousness is the consciousness of the Other in hyperspace, which means in dream and in the psilocybin trance, at the quantum foundation of being, in the human future, and after death. All of these places that were thought to be discrete and separate are seen to be part of a single continuum. History is the dash over ten to fifteen thousand years from nomadism to flying saucer, hopefully without ripping the envelope of the planet so badly that the birth is aborted and fails, and we remain brutish prisoners of matter.

History is the shock wave of eschatology. Something is at the end of time and it is casting an enormous shadow over human history, drawing all human becoming toward it. All the wars, the philosophies, the rapes, the pillaging, the migrations, the cities, the civilizations—all of this is occupying a microsecond of geological, planetary, and galactic time as the monkeys react to the symbiote, which is in the environment and which is feeding information to humanity about the larger picture. I do not belong to the school that wants to attribute all of our accomplishments to knowledge given to us as a gift from friendly aliens—I'm describing something I hope is more profound than that. As nervous systems evolve to higher and higher levels, they come more and more to understand the true situation in which they are embedded. And the true situation in which we are embedded is an organism, an organization of active intelligence on a galactic scale. Science and mathematics may be culture-bound. We cannot know for sure, because we have never dealt with an alien mathematics or an alien culture except in the occult realm, and that evidence is inadmissible by the guardians of scientific truth. This means that the contents of shamanic experience and of plant-induced ecstasies are inadmissible even though they are the source of novelty and the cutting edge of the ingression of the novel into the plenum of being.

Think about this for a moment: If the human mind does not loom large in the coming history of the human race, then what is to become of us? The future is bound to be psychedelic, because the future belongs to the mind. We are just beginning to push the buttons on the mind. Once we take a serious engineering approach to this, we are going to discover the plasticity, the mutability, the eternal nature of the mind and, I believe,

release it from the monkey. My vision of the final human future is an effort to exteriorize the soul and internalize the body, so that the exterior
soul will exist as a superconducting lens of translinguistic matter generated out of the body of each of us at a critical juncture at our psychedelic
bar mitzvah. From that point on, we will be eternal somewhere in the
solid-state matrix of the translinguistic lens we have become. One's
body image will exist as a holographic wave transform while one is at
play in the fields of the Lord and living in Elysium.

Other intelligent monkeys have walked this planet. We exterminated them and so now we are unique, but what is loose on this planet is
language, self-replicating information systems that reflect functions of
DNA: learning, coding, templating, recording, testing, retesting, recod-
ing against DNA functions. Then again, language may be a quality of an
entirely different order. Whatever language is, it is in us monkeys now
and moving through us and moving out of our hands and into the noo-
sphere with which we have surrounded ourselves.

The tryptamine state seems to be in one sense transtemporal; it is
an anticipation of the future. It is as though Plato's metaphor were
true—that time *is* the moving image of eternity. The tryptamine ecstasy
is a stepping out of the moving image and into eternity, the eternity of
the standing now, the *nunc stans* of Thomas Aquinas. In that state, all of
human history is seen to lead toward this culminating moment.
Acceleration is visible in all the processes around us: the fact that fire
was discovered several million years ago; language came perhaps thirty-
five thousand years ago; measurement, five thousand; Galileo, four hundred; then Watson-Crick and DNA. What is obviously happening is that
everything is being drawn together. On the other hand, the description
our physicists are giving us of the universe—that it has lasted billions of
years and will last billions of years into the future—is a dualistic conception, an inductive projection that is very unsophisticated when applied
to the nature of consciousness and language. Consciousness is somehow
able to collapse the state vector and thereby cause the stuff of being to
undergo what Alfred North Whitehead called "the formality of actually
occurring." Here is the beginning of an understanding of the centrality
of human beings. Western societies have been on a decentralizing ben-
der for five hundred years, concluding that the earth is not the center of
the universe and man is not the beloved of God. We have moved ourselves out toward the edge of the galaxy, when the fact is that the most
richly organized material in the universe is the human cerebral cortex,
and the densest and richest experience in the universe is the experience
you are having right now. Everything should be constellated outward
from the perceiving self. That is the primary datum.

The perceiving self under the influence of these hallucinogenic
plants gives information that is totally at variance with the models that

we inherit from our past, yet these dimensions exist. On one level, this information is a matter of no great consequence, for many cultures have understood this for millennia. But we moderns are so grotesquely alienated and taken out of what life is about that to us it comes as a revelation. Without psychedelics the closest we can get to the Mystery is to try to feel in some abstract mode the power of myth or ritual. This grasping is a very overintellectualized and unsatisfying sort of process.

As I said, I am an explorer, not a scientist. If I were unique, then none of my conclusions would have any meaning outside the context of myself. My experiences, like yours, have to be more or less a part of the human condition. Some may have more facility for such exploration than others, and these states may be difficult to achieve, but they are part of the human condition. There are few clues that these extradimensional places exist. If art carries images out of the Other from the Logos to the world—drawing ideas down into matter—why is human art history so devoid of what psychedelic voyagers have experienced so totally? Perhaps the flying saucer or UFO is the central motif to be understood in order to get a handle on reality here and now. We are alienated, so alienated that the self must disguise itself as an extraterrestrial in order not to alarm us with the truly bizarre dimensions that it encompasses. When we can love the alien, then we will have begun to heal the psychic discontinuity that has plagued us since at least the sixteenth century, possibly earlier.

My testimony is that magic is alive in hyperspace. It is not necessary to believe me, only to form a relationship with these hallucinogenic plants. The fact is that the gnosis comes from plants. There is some certainty that one is dealing with a creature of integrity if one deals with a plant, but the creatures born in the demonic artifice of laboratories have to be dealt with very, very carefully. DMT is an endogenous hallucinogen. It is present in small amounts in the human brain. Also it is important that psilocybin is 4-phosphoraloxy-N, N-dimethyltryptamine and that serotonin, the major neurotransmitter in the human brain, found in all life and most concentrated in humans, is 5-hydroxytryptamine. The very fact that the onset of DMT is so rapid, lasting five minutes and coming on in forty-five seconds, means that the brain is absolutely at home with this compound. On the other hand, a hallucinogen like LSD is retained in the body for some time.

I will add a cautionary note. I always feel odd telling people to verify my observations since the sine qua non is the hallucinogenic plant. Experimenters should be very careful. One must build up to the experience. These are bizarre dimensions of extraordinary power and beauty. There is no set rule to avoid being overwhelmed, but move carefully, reflect a great deal, and always try to map experiences back onto the history of the race and the philosophical and religious accomplishments of the species. All compounds are potentially dangerous, and all compounds, at sufficient doses or repeated over time, involve risks. The library is the first place to go when looking into taking a new compound.

We need all the information available to navigate dimensions that are profoundly strange and alien. I have been to Konarak and visited Bubaneshwar. I'm familiar with Hindu iconography and have collected thankas. I saw similarities between my LSD experiences and the iconography of Mahayana Buddhism. In fact, it was LSD experiences that drove me to collect Mahayana art. But what amazed me was the total absence of the motifs of DMT. It is not there; it is not there in any tradition familiar to me.

There is a very interesting story by Jorge Luis Borges called "The Sect of the Phoenix." Allow me to recapitulate. Borges starts out by writing: "There is no human group in which members of the sect do not appear. It is also true that there is no persecution or rigor they have not suffered and perpetrated." He continues,

> The rite is the only religious practice observed by the sectarians. The rite constitutes the Secret. This Secret . . . is transmitted from generation to generation. The act in itself is trivial, momentary, and requires no description. The Secret is sacred, but is always somewhat ridiculous; its performance is furtive and the adept do not speak of it. There are no decent words to name it, but it is understood that all words name it or rather inevitably allude to it.

Borges never explicitly says what the Secret is, but if one knows his other story, "The Aleph," one can put these two together and realize that the Aleph is the experience of the Secret of the Cult of the Phoenix.

In the Amazon, when the mushroom was revealing its information and deputizing us to do various things, we asked, "Why us? Why should we be the ambassadors of an alien species into human culture?" And it answered, "Because you did not believe in anything. Because you have never given over your belief to anyone." The sect of the phoenix, the cult of this experience, is perhaps millennia old, but it has not yet been brought to light where the historical threads may run. The prehistoric use of ecstatic plants on this planet is not well understood. Until recently, psilocybin mushroom taking was confined to the central isthmus of Mexico. The psilocybin-containing species *Stropharia cubensis* is not known to be in archaic use in a shamanic rite anywhere in the world. DMT is used in the Amazon and has been for millennia, but by cultures quite primitive—usually nomadic hunter-gatherers.

I am baffled by what I call "the black hole effect" that seems to surround DMT. A black hole causes a curvature of space such that no light can leave it, and, since no signal can leave it, no information can leave it. Let us leave aside the issue of whether this is true in practice of spinning black holes. Think of it as a metaphor. Metaphorically, DMT is like an intellectual black hole in that once one knows about it, it is very hard for others to understand what one is talking about. One cannot be heard. The more one is able to articulate what it is, the less others are able to understand. This is why I think people who attain enlightenment, if we may for a moment comap these two things, are silent. They are silent because we cannot understand them. Why the phenomenon of tryptamine ecstasy has not been looked at by scientists, thrill seekers, or anyone else, I am not sure, but I recommend it to your attention.

The tragedy of our cultural situation is that we have no shamanic tradition. Shamanism is primarily techniques, not ritual. It is a set of techniques that have been worked out over millennia that make it possible, though perhaps not for everyone, to explore these areas. People of predilection are noticed and encouraged.

In archaic societies where shamanism is a thriving institution, the signs are fairly easy to recognize: oddness or uniqueness in an individual. Epilepsy is often a signature in preliterate societies, or survival of an unusual ordeal in an unexpected way. For instance, people who are struck by lightning and live are thought to make excellent shamans. People who nearly die of a disease and fight their way back to health after weeks and weeks in an indeterminate zone are thought to have strength of soul. Among aspiring shamans there must be some sign of inner strength or a hypersensitivity to trance states. In traveling around the world and dealing with shamans, I find the distinguishing characteristic is an extraordinary centeredness. Usually the shaman is an intellectual and is alienated from society. A good shaman sees exactly who you are and says, "Ah, here's somebody to have a conversation with." The anthropological literature always presents shamans as embedded in a tradition, but once one gets to know them they are always very sophisticated about what they are doing. They are the true phenomenologists of this world; they know plant chemistry, yet they call these energy fields "spirits." We hear the word "spirits" through a series of narrowing declensions of meaning that are worse almost than not understanding. Shamans speak of "spirit" the way a quantum physicist might speak of "charm"; it is a technical gloss for a very complicated concept.

It is possible that there are shamanic family lines, at least in the case of hallucinogen-using shamans, because shamanic ability is to some degree determined by how many active receptor sites occur in the brain, thus facilitating these experiences. Some claim to have these experiences naturally, but I am underwhelmed by the evidence that this is so. What it comes down to for me is "What can you show me?"

I always ask that question; finally, in the Amazon, informants said, "Let's take our machetes and hike out here half a mile and get some vine and boil it up and we will show you what we can show you."

Let us be clear. People die in these societies that I'm talking about all the time and for all kinds of reasons. Death is really much more among them than it is in our society. Those who have epilepsy who don't die are brought to the attention of the shaman and trained in breathing and plant usage and other things—the fact is that we don't really know all of what goes on. These secret information systems have not been well studied. Shamanism is not, in these traditional societies, a terribly pleasant office. Shamans are not normally allowed to have any political power, because they are sacred. The shaman is to be found sitting at the headman's side in the council meetings, but after the council meeting he returns to his hut at the edge of the village. Shamans are peripheral to society's goings on in ordinary social life in every sense of the word. They are called on in crisis, and the crisis can be someone dying or ill, a psychological difficulty, a marital quarrel, a theft, or weather that must be predicted.

We do not live in that kind of society, so when I explore these plants' effects and try to call your attention to them, it is as a phenomenon. I don't know what we can do with this phenomenon, but I have a feeling that the potential is great. The mind-set that I always bring to it is simply exploratory and Baconian—the mapping and gathering of facts.

Herbert Guenther talks about human uniqueness and says one must come to terms with one's uniqueness. We are naive about the role of language and being as the primary facts of experience. What good is a theory of how the universe works if it's a series of tensor equations that, even when understood, come nowhere tangential to experience? The only intellectual or noetic or spiritual path worth following is one that builds on personal experience.

What the mushroom says about itself is this: that it is an extraterrestrial organism, that spores can survive the conditions of interstellar space. They are deep, deep purple—the color that they would have to be to absorb the deep ultraviolet end of the spectrum. The casing of a spore is one of the hardest organic substances known. The electron density approaches that of a metal.

Is it possible that these mushrooms never evolved on earth? That is what *Stropharia cubensis* itself suggests. Global currents may form on the outside of the spore. The spores are very light and by Brownian motion are capable of percolation to the edge of a planet's atmosphere. Then, through interaction with energetic particles, some small number could actually escape into space. Understand that this is an evolutionary strategy where only one in many billions of spores actually makes the transition between the stars—a biological strategy for radiating throughout the galaxy without a technology. Of course this happens over very long periods of time. But if you think that the galaxy is roughly a hundred thousand light-years from edge to edge, if something were moving only one one-hundredth the speed of light—now that's not a tremendous speed that presents problems to any advanced technology—it could cross the galaxy in one hundred million years. There's life on this planet 1.8 billion years old; that's eighteen times longer than one hundred million years. So, looking at the galaxy on those time scales, one sees that the percolation of spores between the stars is a perfectly viable strategy for biology. It might take millions of years, but it's the same principle by which plants migrate into a desert or across an ocean.

There are no fungi in the fossil record older than forty million years. The orthodox explanation is that fungi are soft-bodied and do not fossilize well, but on the other hand we have fossilized soft-bodied worms and other benthic marine invertebrates from South African gunflint chert that is dated to over a billion years old.

I don't necessarily believe what the mushroom tells me; rather we have a dialogue. It is a very strange person and has many bizarre opinions. I entertain it the way I would any eccentric friend. I say, "Well, so that's what you think." When the mushroom began saying it was an extraterrestrial, I felt that I was placed in the dilemma of a child who wishes to destroy a radio to see if there are little people inside. I couldn't figure out whether the mushroom is the alien or the mushroom is some kind of technological artifact allowing me to hear the alien when the alien is actually light-years away, using some kind of Bell nonlocality principle to communicate.

The mushroom states its own position very clearly. It says, "I require the nervous system of a mammal. Do you have one handy?"

4

Remarks to ARUPA, 1984

WAS STRUCK by something that Arthur Young said. Someone brought him a machine and asked him to improve the machine. Arthur asked what the machine was supposed to do. The person who brought the machine said he didn't know what it was supposed to do. Arthur asked how, then, he could be expected to improve it. I feel that we are in that situation with psychedelics. I would not leave my book-lined study to participate in a conference on a breakthrough in the orthomolecular treatment of neurosis, so I don't choose to view any of this, at its core, as having to do with that. I am much more radical and millenarian and perhaps "teched" than that point of view. What I think is going on with psychedelics, especially the tryptamine family (and I will return to that), is some kind of intimation of an objective reality.

When I am asked, "What is your fantasy?" or "What is your vision?" I answer that I would like to bring back a chunk of the other dimension. Sometimes I see it not as a bringing back of a chunk but as a punching of a hole so that it pours through. Marilyn Ferguson and I were talking earlier and she said, "Psychedelics are windows." I said, "My hope is that they are doors and we could open them and walk through and move from room to room in some kind of hyperdimensional world where the reality of these things is confirmed."

Plato said, "If God didn't exist, man would invent him." If this psychedelic, hyperdimensional world didn't exist, we would invent it

■■

This talk was given at Esalen Institute in Big Sur California in the fall of 1984 at a gathering of the Association for the Responsible Use of Psychedelics, an informal group of psychologists, chemists, and therapists who regularly met at Esalen from 1983 to 1986 under the sponsorship of the late and much beloved Richard Price.

through computers and human-machine interphasing. Fortunately, it does exist in the worldwide tradition of the use of psychedelic substances. I appreciate the efforts of people like Fritjof Capra to give an account of consciousness in terms of quantum physics, but my own conviction is that the first premise should be that we actually know absolutely nothing about the nature of reality. This is why we are unable to give an adequate definition of "mind" or "being" or "self."

We are probably as far from any godlike notion of objective truth as any society in the past. I find the notion that we are descended from ant-people who came out of the urine of the sky god when he got out of his canoe at the seventh waterfall to relieve himself more palpable than that we are derivatives of the Big Bang—a moment when the whole universe sprang from nothing and for no reason at all. It is a matter of relativism of mythologies. We are actually at square one in trying to figure out the nature of being in the world. That is why I wish there were more excitement, or conviction, or some way that we could break down the barriers between ourselves so that we could cease to be the blind men with the elephant and have some kind of consensus about what this dimension is and what it portends.

Yesterday, Stan Grof brought up the notion of the "psychoid." This word occurs in Jung's thought when he hedges slightly on the nature of the dynamics of the unconscious. He suggests that it is both in the world and within and that there is some congruence. This is the dimension that the psychedelics are adapted to explore: these intermediate states between mind and matter. Migration of coincidence, synchronistic meshing of the exterior and interior flow of events, are phenomena that can be repeatedly triggered with these compounds. This is very important.

We need to admit that there is something toxic about the historical process—that we cannot really fine-tune it and save ourselves. The notion was very strong in Fritjof Capra's talk that science needs a new suit of clothes and then it will be adequate for conveying the unfolding nature of reality. I wonder if that is true. One of the things that psychedelics bring to the fore that would run any physicist wild is the curious literary quality that is visible on the surface of existence. We discover ourselves to be characters in a novel, being both propelled by and victimized by various kinds of coincidental forces that shape our lives. This is what recognition of the synchronistic factor is. It is as though you trapped the mind in the act of making reality.

Frank Barr and I were talking about Finnegans Wake and relating it to a fractal by saying a fractal is a curve that, by virtue of its complexity, attains a partial dimension more of self-expression in the universe. Finnegans Wake is a book that, in some sense, tries to climb into the world and be instead an autonomous event system. I think psychedelics show that the interphasing between an ordinary world of three-dimensional experience and these higher-dimensional spaces can be attained. The psychedelic allows, by raising us a fraction of a dimension, some kind of contemplative access to hyperspace.

What my brother Dennis McKenna was saying in his talk was that humanness was formed out of the interphase between the plants and primates. I can see that as an ongoing process, only interrupted on the face of the planet in Europe about fifteen hundred years ago. These various substances act as a mediating force in human history. You have only to think of the impact of sugar, tobacco, coffee, alcohol, opium, or psychedelics.

I was surprised at the discussion suggesting that psychedelics can make you a good citizen. My assumption about psychedelics has always been that the reason they are not legal is not because it troubles anyone that you have visions, but that there is something about them that casts doubts on the validity of reality. They are inevitably deconditioning agents simply by demonstrating the existence of a nearby reality running on a different dynamic. I think they are inherently catalysts of intellectual dissent. This makes it very hard for societies, even a democratic society, to come to terms with them.

The thing I am brought here to say is that these botanical tryptamines are different. There is a problem with the history of psychedelics: LSD emerged at a certain point and became a social problem. A huge amount of research was poured into that. The other hallucinogens—psilocybin, DMT, etc.—were considered to be similar compounds that only required more physical material to elicit their effects. They were lumped together in the standard texts. Actually the tryptamines have a quality very different from LSD, almost to the point where the word "psychedelic" needs to be split in two to accommodate the ontological difference between tryptamines and these other substances.

Albert Hofmann: Do you count psilocybin with the tryptamines?

TM: Yes, absolutely.

Albert Hofmann: Then you see big differences between LSD and psilocybin?

TM: Surely. It seems LSD is only reluctantly a visionary hallucinogen. In terms of activity in the visual cortex, psilocybin is a fantastically prolific generator of visual hallucinations. Visual hallucinations are, I think, much more accessible to most people on psilocybin. However, the truly distinguishing quality between them, and you discussed this briefly in Santa Barbara, is that the tryptamines have a quality of animation. There seems to be a Logos-like Other—an alien presence—not easily referenced to the components of the psyche. And it is animate, strange, and imbued with an alienness and a personality that is not present in LSD. Do you think that is true?

Albert Hofmann: Yes, but I believe there is a difference between psilocybin and the tryptamines. Psilocybin works orally; the other tryptamines must be smoked.

TM: *Ayahuasca* is an orally active tryptamine. On a good strong hit of *ayahuasca* at about the hour-and-twenty-minute mark you will very slowly come into a place indistinguishable from having smoked DMT. The same thing happens on psilocybin, at the thirty-milligram level, at about the hour and twenty-minute point. It is known that psilocybin does not degrade into DMT, but DMT is present in *ayahuasca* as a pure compound. It is strange: tryptamines are the most common hallucinogens in organic nature, but they are the least explored by science. I believe this is a reluctance to face this alien and peculiar dimension. Sasha Shulgin describes DMT as "dark"; that is his gloss on it. "Demonic" is a word frequently used. I am not entirely certain what that means. Jung always talked about "demons," and he associated "demons" with the earth. I recall he speaks of the Mexican demons of the earth.

It is true that people are very reticent with the mushroom, approaching very carefully. The tryptamines are the compounds least subject to abuse because even enthusiasts move very gingerly.

This is because the experience is so weird. It involves ingression into an extrahuman dimension that is autonomous from the ego, a dimension whose measure cannot be taken. It is not about working out our personal introspective processes. All psychedelics appear to be the same psychedelic at low doses, doses just over threshold. But as larger doses that are still pharmacologically safe are taken, differences appear. Exotic synesthesias occur, including the generation of three-dimensional languages; a situation where, using voice, one can create three-dimensional colored modalities that have linguistic content. This visible language can be displayed to a partner who is in the same state. It is as though language has a potential that is only rarely expressed. Robert Graves has written about an *ur sprach*—a primal language of poetry that had its power in the beholding of it. And Hans Jonas has talked about the notion of a more perfect Logos—a Logos not of the ears, but of the eyes.

I believe that psychedelic research is not a peripheral historical backwater. Psychedelics are not a breakthrough primarily directed at the neurotic or the mentally ill. They are literally "the new world." Land has been sighted in hyperspace. We now have four or five hundred years of exploration ahead of us. In the psychedelic human–machine interphase, there can be castles in the imagination. We can decide that this was what human history was for—this marriage of imagination and ability—so that a civilization can be created that is truly civilized through being rooted in the psychedelic experience.

There is concern, perhaps even anxiety, that we as a group, we as a people who share this knowledge, need to create a political climate where more research can be done and where these matters can be more freely talked about. In principle I agree with all of that, but I am not interested in putting much energy into it. In the past there has been a lot of clinical experimentation with LSD; one speaker referred to data from eight thousand LSD administrations. Surely what could be learned in that mode was learned, or at least the surface was scratched.

Instead of the horizontal broadening of the faith, I would be much more interested in a vertical strengthening of the faith by having the people who have taken these compounds take more of them, take different ones, and take larger doses. The real crucible of this research is the Self. We should be keeping journals and recording experiences into a data bank so that common themes can be tracked through large groups of filed reports. In other words, strengthen the community rather than broaden it.

I believe that the psychedelic experience was the light at the beginning of history. That this is actually *the* thing; that we have now reached a sufficient level of analytical sophistication to discern the force that pushed the animal mind onto the human stage. It is a process that, once it is set into motion, will not end. It is as though these botanical hallucinogens were exohormones, message-bearing chemicals shed by Gaia to control the development of the historical process in the catalytic trigger species that is introducing change on the planet. It isn't merely a matter of noetic archaeology that we have now learned something about the past. This is also true of Albert Hofmann's discovery about Eleusis; this may ultimately have a greater impact than the discovery of LSD itself. It is a discovery of a skeleton in the closet. There are skeletons in the closet of human origins and of the origin of religion. I would wager that these skeletons are all plant psychedelics. If we can come to terms with them, we can begin to understand the shape of the human future.

The psychedelic experience is not easy to measure. It appears to be a world nearly as large as the previous domain of nature. It is not simply the Jungian collective unconscious—the repository of all human species' experience—still less is it the Freudian notion of the repository of memories of individual experience. It seems that what Freud and Jung thought of as a place in the organization of the psyche is cognized in the shamanic model as a place, a nearby, adjacent dimension into which the mind can project itself and, by self-scaling itself to these interior dimensions, experience them as realities.

The goal of William Blake, to release the human spirit into the imagination, is a reasonable cultural goal, probably within reach through the judicious application of cybernetics and psychedelic substances. I see it coming fast, and, since this group is at the cutting edge by some definition, I am surprised we are as low-key as we are. How we line up on these various issues, how we understand and interpret these experiences, will set the tone for how the issue flowers out over the world.

One question is how we can make bridges into the future. There are about five or six very hot hallucinogen-related botanical questions hanging fire in various places in the world, drugs or shamanic preparations where the literature is very suggestive and the plant families involved have hallucinogens already identified in them. Five years of work by physicians, anthropologists, ethnobotanists, and adventurers could probably double the amount of information known about botanical hallucinogens.

In the past the stress has been on the laboratory elaboration of structural relatives of known compounds. But even compounds like 2CB, which is related to DOM, would never have been discovered if someone had not noticed that the natural product myristicin had some form of psychoactivity. The whole MDMA family can be seen as an elaboration of the myristicin molecule. We need to know if there are hallucinogens, in unknown chemical families, that hold the secret to the elaboration of new compounds in the laboratory.

The original approach of pharmaceutical botany was to send people to the forest and jungle to make collections, then extractions, then characterizations, and then, as the art of synthesis advanced, there was less and less of this and more and more synthesis from theory based on structure-activity relationships. Now a lot of that work has been done and no new hallucinogenic family of importance has been discovered. There is important botanical survey work to be done in the world to nail down hallucinogens whose usage may be fading, restricted, or very endemic. All of these things are ways of expanding our hold on what hallucinogens are. What is their place in nature? That could be done. It is not in the mental health care delivery context.

The Italian Renaissance ran on spices; they had to get spices from somewhere, so they bought them. "Spices" is a very ambiguous term. If we could get psychedelics reclassified as spices they would come under the control not of psychotherapists and mental health care people but of chefs and maître d's. Then we would have an entirely different approach to the administration of psychedelic substances, set, setting, goals.

It seems we are in the stone age in every phase of these explorations. There is so much to be done. It is amazing—and it is an amazing privilege for all of us to be in on the ground floor. It is hard to believe that twenty-five years after Leary waged the LSD wars we could still be in on the ground floor; but that is what it seems, by default; no one else wants this.

Ralph Metzner: May I make a couple of comments about that? Your ideas, as well as Albert Hofmann's idea about the role of ergotlike plants in Eleusis, tie into the notion of the reawakening of the old gods. These are sacred plants that were treated as sacred beings, divine beings, basically deities. If we are in fact able to identify what soma was, we will be able to identify and re-create the original source-energy behind the Indo-European civilization. Similarly, if we rediscover and are able to incorporate whatever was used at Eleusis, we will have the original impetus behind Greek-European civilization that carried it for two thousand years as the primary vehicle of religious experience.

TM: Soma is the light at the beginning and end of history. This is the notion. It infuses history. History is a process that it created for its own purposes. We are involved in a symbiotic relationship with a biological creature that is like a god because it is so advanced, different, and in possession of such a peculiar body of information compared with ourselves.

Ralph Metzner: Another brief point about soma: Whatever soma was, why did it disappear? There are not any *Stropharia cubensis* or *Amanita* or any of these other hallucinogens in India now. If it is there, it is fairly remote and not a widespread thing like alcohol or wine, which became a widespread religious-social drug in all of Western culture. My theory about what happened then is the same as what happens now, that the use of soma, which was a genuine religious intoxicant in the sense that it produced a religious experience and direct knowledge of God, was stamped out systematically by the priesthoods, who were primarily intent upon maintaining their own power structure. If people could have a direct experience of God by taking mushrooms or any other plant they would not be interested in priestly power structures—they couldn't care less. Why should they talk to a priest if they could talk directly to God?

TM: This is the deconditioning factor.

Ralph Metzner: We saw in the sixties and we see now that the power holders in society do not want large numbers of people taking substances or plants that expand their consciousness. A few here or there do not bother them. But if it grows into large numbers that make a lot of noise, they don't want it.

TM: That is why the vertical approach is better. Deeper experiences for a harder core.

5

A Conversation Over Saucers

N: IN THE two books that you have written you mention UFO influences. Would you explain just what you think a UFO is?

TM: In our first book, *The Invisible Landscape*, the UFO reference is scant indeed, touched on only once. I deliberately suppressed it because I thought the book was already lit up like a Christmas tree with bizarre ideas. I saved that particular ornament for its own treatment later, in the talking book *True Hallucinations*. It seems to me that with the tryptamine hallucinogens in general and with psilocybin in particular we actually experience a state of mind that is very similar to the state of mind reported to accompany the UFO contact. Shamanic states of mind and UFO contact can, somehow, be mapped onto each other. At active levels, psilocybin induces visionary ideation of spacecraft, alien creatures, and alien information. There is a general futuristic, science fiction quality to the psilocybin experience that seems to originate from the same place as the modern myth of the UFO.

My brother and I discovered during our expedition to the Amazon in 1971 that accumulation of the tryptamines in one's system seems to confer the ability to inhabit more than one world at once, as though another world were superimposed over reality. This is a super-reality, a hyperdimensional world where information is accessible in magical ways. In the wake of our Amazonian discoveries, I surveyed the

■■■

This interview appeared in the winter 1989 issue of *Revision*. Will Noffke conducted the interview.

literature of mystical experience, UFO experiences, and occult systems such as alchemy. Eventually I saw that these different bodies of thought were all talking about the same thing. For modern people, the experience that is gaining ascendancy is called "contact with the UFO," but it is not reducible to any of the explanations suggested by UFO experts and enthusiasts. It is not, strictly speaking, a contact from a space-faring race that has come from the stars, nor is it mass hysteria or delusion. There is, in fact, something very odd going on, something that is as challenging to modern epistemological notions as a U.S. Air Force jet transport landing in a nearby field would be to uncontacted villagers in New Guinea. A very large percentage of people claim to have seen UFOs, yet science cannot explain them. It seems as though reality is haunted by a spinning vortex that renders science helpless. The spinning vortex is the UFO, and it comes and goes on a mass scale, haunting history like a ghost.

I'm speaking specifically of the post–World War II spinning silver disc in the sky, and the accompanying myth of the pointed-eared, cat-eyed aliens. This myth has numerous variations, but it's clearly an idea complex emerging in the collective psyche. The question is, what is it? Is it prophecy? Is it a vision of the human future? What is it? The postmodern phase of UFO speculation recognizes that the UFO is no mere light seen in the sky, but that it is somehow mixed up with human psychology. Researchers have determined that people who have seen UFOs were in many cases thinking about something very odd and unusual immediately prior to the sighting. The UFO seemed to act as a kind of ideological catalyst for some purpose. Jacques Vallee was the first person to suggest what I would call the "cultural thermostat theory" of UFOs, in a book called *The Invisible College*. He proposed that the flying saucer is an object from the collective unconscious of the human race that appears in order to break the control of any set of ideas that are gaining dominance in their explanatory power at the expense of ethics. It is a confounding that enters history again and again whenever history builds to a certain kind of boil.

Colin Wilson suggests a similar idea in his novel *The Mind Parasites*, stating that the career of Christ was an earlier confounding in which Roman science and Roman militarism were unseated by a peculiar religion that no educated Roman could take seriously. Educated Romans were well versed in Democritean atomism, Epicureanism, and Sophism; yet their servants were telling stories about a rabbi who had risen from the dead and opened a gate that had been closed since creation, permitting the soul of man to be reunited with God. Though these stories made no sense to the Roman authorities, their adherents quickly overwhelmed the empire. Today science has replaced Roman Imperial aspirations as the dominant mythos of control and thought; it offers neat and tidy explanations of the world. Yet the folk persist in telling stories of lights in the sky, strange beings, and bizarre encounters that cannot quite be laid to rest.

My own personal encounter with a UFO has led me to view them as real, whatever "real" means. They are phenomenologically real. In fact, my contention is that psilocybin reveals an event at the end of history of such magnitude that it casts miniature reflections of itself back into time. These are the apocalyptic concrescences that haunt the historical continuum, igniting religions and various hysterias, and seeping ideas into highly tuned nervous systems.

For the Eschaton, positioned in eternity, all things are somehow coexistent in time or outside of time. All events have already happened. Shamanism is a formal technique for viewing this hyperdimensional object outside of time in a three-dimensional way, by transecting it many, many times until an entire picture of it emerges. The mushroom evokes a profound planetary consciousness that shows one that history is a froth of artifact production that has appeared in the last ten to fifteen thousand years and spread across the planet very quickly. But mind in human beings precedes the history of technology and goes back into the archaic darkness.

One of the things we were saying in *The Invisible Landscape* is that there are avenues of understanding in the human body that have not been followed because of epistemological bias; for instance, using voice to effect physiological change in one's own nervous system. This sounds on one level preposterous, but on the other hand, it is simply a formalized way of noting the fact that sound is energy, that energy can be transduced in a number of ways, and that when it is directed toward the body it obviously does make changes. Chanting and singing are worldwide shamanic practices. The shamanic singers navigate through a space with which we have lost touch as a society.

When the shaman's song fails, his world erupts into a situation of weakened psychic constitution that contains an element of "panic" in the mythological sense that evokes Pan bursting through from the underworld. The equivalent panic in our society is the emergence of the UFO as an autonomous psychic entity that has slipped from the control of the ego and approaches laden with the "Otherness" of the unconscious. As one looks into it one beholds oneself, one's world information field, all deployed in a strange, distant, almost transhumanly cool way, which links it to the myth of the extraterrestrial. The extraterrestrial is the human Oversoul in its general and particular expression on the planet. Though this doesn't rule out the faint possibility that the mushroom also places one in contact with extraterrestrials on planets circling other suns somewhere in the galaxy, it probably means that this communication is mediated through the Oversoul. The Oversoul is some kind of field that is generated by human beings but that is not under the control of any institution, any government, or any religion. It is actually the most intelligent life form on the planet, and it regulates human culture through the release of ideas out of eternity and into the continuum of history.

The UFO is an idea intended to confound science, because science has begun to threaten the existence of the human species as well as the ecosystem of the planet. At this point, a shock is necessary for the culture, a shock equivalent to the shock of the Resurrection on Roman imperialism. The myths that are building now are like the messianic myths that preceded the appearance of Christ. They are myths of intervention by a hyperintelligent entity that comes from the stars to reveal the right way to live. The UFO would wreck science by a series of demonstrations designed to convince the majority of humanity that the purpose of history is nothing less than total immersion in the teachings of the UFO. Once this message is slammed home via worldwide TV broadcasts, the UFO might simply disappear. Following in the wake of such a departure would be a hysteria of abandonment similar to the hysteria of abandonment that swept the Christian communities after the Resurrection. The development of science would cease. The UFO-oriented religion would embody an archetype of enormous power, able to hold sway in the same way that Christianity halted the development of science for a thousand years.

WN: Scientists are not going to like your opinion.

TM: I think that to some degree science has betrayed human destiny. We have been led to the brink of star flight, but we've also been led to the brink of thermonuclear holocaust. The result of this betrayal is that science may well be swept away by the revelation of the UFO. Scientists have always been like the apostle Thomas, wanting to put their hands into the wound of the incorporeal body. If the wound is offered, if the saucer comes and is seen by millions of people, scientists will be the first to be converted. We should be forewarned and act now to preserve our freedom of thought by deconditioning ourselves to the flying saucer revelation before it happens. A religion operates by the law of large numbers, and, as long as 80 percent of the people believe, it can transform a civilization. But it *is* possible to be one of the 20 percent who don't believe, to stand where the high water never reaches.

A voice that gave guidance and revelation to Western civilization has been silent for about seventeen hundred years. This is the Logos and all ancient philosophers strove to invoke it. For Hellenistic philosophy it was a voice that told self-evident truth. With the passing of the Aeon and the death of the pagan gods, awareness of this phenomenon faded. However, it is still available through the mediation of the plant teachers. If we could intelligently examine dimensions that the psychedelic plants make available, we could contact the Oversoul and leave behind this era where dominance hierarchies must be disciplined by UFOs and messiahs, and where progress is halted for millennia because culture cannot advance ethics at the same rate as technology. If we could have a dialogue with the Other, we would understand all these things and begin to contact the Tao of the ancestors. Perhaps we would develop a shamanic alternative in which trained people mediate the group experience that is available from psychedelic plant use.

We have ascertained by questionnaire that UFO contact is perhaps the motif most frequently mentioned by people who take psilocybin recreationally, using fifteen-milligram-range doses sufficient to elicit the full spectrum of psychedelic effects. They encounter another space with UFOs and aliens—classic little green men. DMT is similar. It also conveys one into wild, zany, elf-infested spaces. It's as though there were an alternative reality, linguistically as well as dimensionally. One tunes to a different language channel and then, with this language pouring through one's head, one can observe the other place. This alternative reality is surprisingly different from most cultural traditions that describe what such realities are like. Nothing prepares one for its crackling, electronic, hyperdimensional, interstellar, extraterrestrial, science fiction quality; it is a complex space filled with highly polished curved surfaces, machines undergoing geometric transformations into beings, and thoughts that condense as visible objects.

One recurring motif that is very interesting to me is the hyperdimensional language. On DMT one hears a language that is very faint and far away, and, as it gets louder and louder, without ever going over a quantifiable distinct transition, it becomes a phenomenon not of the audible field but of the visual field. It is, in fact, a fully evolving hallucination of extremely realistic and utterly bizarre proportions. It is an Arabian maelstrom of color and form, and one senses somehow the Sistine Chapel, the Kaaba, and Konarak. A hyperdimensional infundibulum, if you will. There is alien information deployed everywhere in that other space. The really astonishing thing is that human history and art reflect so little of it.

WN: But they do—you do see it?

TM: Oh, you see it, but very faintly. When you see the real thing you wonder, "My God, how do they keep the lid on this stuff?" It is rag-

ing right next door. Modern epistemological methods are just not prepared for dealing with chattering, elf-infested spaces. We have a word
for those spaces—we call them "schizophrenia" and slam the door. But
these dimensions have been with us ten thousand times longer than
Freud. Other societies have come to terms with them. Because of accidents of botany and history, European culture has been away from the
psychedelic dimensions awhile. We have forgotten the dimension of the
tryptamines and psilocybin since at least the burning of Eleusis. We've
accomplished marvelous things with science and technology while other
cultures around the world have kept the archaic flame burning. The
disks that haunt the skies of earth indicate that the unconscious cannot
be kept waiting forever. When we discover that the imagination really is
the ground of being, then it will be as if man had discovered fire for the
second time. The imagination is to be the golden pathway to a new cultural hyperspace.

WN: What, then, are we to do?

TM: I think that the task of history is what I call turning ourselves inside out. The body is to be internalized and the soul exteriorized
as a living golden disc. Yeats put it this way in "Sailing to Byzantium":

> O sages standing in God's holy fire
> As in the gold mosaic of a wall,
> Come from the holy fire, perne in a gyre,
> And be the singing-masters of my soul.
> Consume my heart away; sick with desire
> And fastened to a dying animal
> It knows not what it is; and gather me
> Into the artifice of eternity.

The phrase "the artifice of eternity" evokes a strangely mechanistic yet
spiritualistic future into which the archetype of the UFO is calling humanity. Over the course of ten thousand years, from the earliest machines to the present, humanity is becoming a transplanetary creature. It
is, as H. G. Wells said of history, "a race between education and catastrophe." Increasingly destructive chemical and atomic processes are being released, forcing the species to realize that its aspirations are alien to
the ecology of the planet and that it and the planet must part. The transformation of humanity into a space-faring, perhaps time-faring, race is
on a biological scale, the great goal of history. The coming of agriculture
and urbanization are minor compared to what is going to happen to this

species, to these monkeys, as they leave the planet with their computers and their dreams.

Information is loose on planet three. Something unusual is going on here. The world is not made of quarks, electromagnetic wave packets, or the thoughts of God. The world is made of language. Language is replicating itself in DNA, which, at the evolutionary apex, is creating societies of civilized beings that possess languages and machines that use languages. Earth is a place where language has literally become alive. Language has infested matter; it is replicating and defining and building itself. And it is in us. My voice speaking is a monkey's mouth making little mouth noises that are carrying agreed-upon meaning, and it is meaning that matters. Without the meaning one has only little mouth noises. Meaning is a crude form of telepathy—as you listen to my voice, my thoughts become your thoughts and we compare them. This is communication, understanding. Reality is a domain of codes, and that is why the UFO problem is like a grammatical problem—like a dangling participle in the fourth-dimensional language that makes reality. It eludes simple approaches because its nature is somehow embedded in the machinery of epistemic knowing itself.

WN: So we won't be able to find it if we go into space?

TM: No, it is within; it is the soul of us. We won't be able to find it until we somehow come to terms with the hidden part, the collective unconscious, the Overmind. We need to face the fact that there is a level of hierarchical control being exerted on the human species as a whole and that our destiny is not ours to decide. It is in the hands of a weirdly democratic, amoeboid, hyperintelligent superorganism that is called Everybody. As we come to terms with this, as we take our place embedded in the body of Everybody, information flows more freely and the reality of this informational creature is seen more clearly. The fact is that we are in a symbiotic relationship with an organism made of information, and this is the situation classic shamanic plant hallucinogens reinforce very strongly.

It's in the psychedelic dimension that one finally can key into the voice of the organism and undertake a dialogue. Then it explains that things are not as you took them to be at all, and that there is in fact layer upon layer of interlocking meaning and very little else. The imagination is the true ground of being. There is a dimension parallel to time, outside of time, that is accessible only to the degree that one can decondition oneself from the history-bound cognitive systems that have carried one to this point. This is why it's always been said that the psychedelic experience acts as a sociological catalyst.

WN: What are shamans? How does the shaman bring the message to the tribe?

TM: The tribe is a system set up to receive the message. Our society has a different way of doing it: power elites in political control pass down state-approved philosophies that are then applied.

WN: The state as shaman?

TM: The state as shaman, the state as mediator of God's holy will, rather than a personal relationship—a Protestant approach, if you will—to the Overmind. The UFO represents an instance of crisis between the individual and the Overmind, where the Overmind breaks through the oppressive screen thrown around it and comes to meet the individual. It is like an interview with an angel—or a demon. It is laden with intense psychological resonances for the person experiencing it; it is a profoundly numinous experience.

WN: Every moment of recognizable creation, then, falls into the category of seepage from the Overmind, where you get a synthesis of information that becomes your creative thought, your discovery of the Other?

TM: My theory of time mathematically formalizes the notion that novelty is the standing wave of eternity. Novelty seeps into time at a variable rate that can actually be mathematically described using the transforms inherent in the I Ching.[*] The UFOs seem to come from eternity. They don't come from the stars unless they can move instantly to and from the stars. The UFOs come from another dimension; one could almost say they come from beyond death. They come from a dimension somehow totally different from our own, but tied up with the human psyche in a way that is puzzling, alarming, and reassuring—and shamanic. It is difficult to know to what degree nonparticipants in twentieth-century civilization perceive this. What is the experience of people who take mushrooms but have nothing to do with twentieth-century society? Have they always accepted, since Paleolithic times, the presence of a superfuturistic dimension? Perhaps in any century people have had this commerce with the end of time, with the far future. Yet now we have bootstrapped ourselves to the point that we can leave the planet, leave the monkey shell, leave all earthbound conceptions of ourselves behind, and push off into the pure imagination.

[*]See chapter 8, "Temporal Resonance."

WN: Scary.

TM: Scary. Gnostic. Perhaps, as someone said, "It sounds like megalomania to me, Martha." But we must ask how mad would the twentieth century have sounded recited to anyone in the nineteenth or the fifteenth? What it comes down to is trying to have faith that human beings are capable of doing good, because, whatever we are, human beings are taking control of the definition of being human. Through genetic engineering, through drug design, through probing of the psychedelic dimension, through mind/machine interphasing, we are beginning to become a mirror of our deepest aspirations. The question then becomes, "What are our deepest aspirations? What will the future be?" Will it be some kind of Mephistophelian nightmare, the Nietzschean superman come back to haunt us in a way that could make the Third Reich look like a picnic? Or will we choose the element of care and control, the aesthetic element, the wish to escape into a universe that is, in fact, art? This is what is possible—that we could become inhabitants of our own imaginations. With the technology for building large habitats in space, it is possible to imagine the complete social galaxy of science fiction created in a region less than twelve light-hours in diameter with the sun at the center. One can imagine fifty or sixty thousand independent habitats pursuing social experiments of every sort, spatially independent, but electronically linked, in very long-term slow orbits from the near sun to the outer planets.

Using current technology, we could, right now, produce the Hawaiian environment at distances up to fourteen light-hours away from the sun, which is several light-hours farther out than Pluto. That means the entire solar system has become habitable real estate, but only if we can transform the human imagination to realize that getting high is not a metaphor, getting high is what the whole human enterprise is about. It's true that the earth is the cradle of mankind, but one cannot remain in the cradle forever. The universe beckons. It has been only a geological moment since our shamanic ancestors began to munch the mushrooms and glimpse the vision of human beings radiating out through the galaxy as a perfected, superintelligent force for life. Postindustrial historical time is a fifteen-round slug-out that will decide whether or not that happens.

WN: Is it not so that the muse is a sort of a catalyst of the imagination, in a way, the source of inspiration?

TM: Precisely, it's an ecstasy. The claim is made that these states can be attained in various ways. There are many different kinds of ecstasy, but the peculiar, extraterrestrial dimension that these tryptamines convey one into is not the standard ecstasy of the mystics, or we would have more of a reflection of that in the mystical literature. In fact, one of the things most puzzling to me is why the bizarre motifs of the DMT flash have not made their way into any culture anywhere, as far as I'm aware.

WN: Does that imply that people were fearful of these visions when they had them and so kept them undercover, thinking that they might be going insane?

TM: I think the change is so radical and the implication so hard to digest that—you're right—people either feel their own sanity is being threatened, or they recognize it as a challenge to the reality myth of their society and so they repress it. It's very hard to assimilate these contradictory realities that throw into doubt everything one assumes about the reality one inhabits. What a strange, strange world it must be if there are alternative continua operating all around us filled with strange alien information that is the product of its own history and has an appetite for its own future.

WN: These are science fiction theories. I mean, one comes across a smattering of these ideas here and there in fiction; yet you are saying that they're real and that this is your mission—basically, your "rap."

TM: I'm not saying mine is the only interpretation possible, but I am certainly saying that the shamanically sanctioned tryptamine compounds elicit an experience that is extremely peculiar and that has more relationship with the UFO experience than with classical, mystical experience, or with other hallucinogenic compounds, and that social attitudes and other factors have conspired to keep this under wraps. The UFO connection has not been closely studied, because the people who are interested in flying saucers are not interested in psychedelics. The great majority of people interested in flying saucers are hardware nuts convinced that UFOs are ships from Zeta Reticuli. The shamanic and psychological explanation is not particularly welcome anywhere.

Meanwhile, the community of psychedelic researchers feel themselves to be laboring under enough of a stigma already, without allying themselves with flying saucer people, which would be like adding an albatross to an anchor. Since I'm outside all of that, I can read and appreciate the work of researchers like Mircea Eliade but still feel critical that orthodox anthropological reporting on shamanism has not really come to grips with how strange the shamanic psychedelic experience really is.

The psychedelic experience poses problems not only for the so-called
primitive people who use these plants, it poses fundamental, equally
deep problems for *our* society. We can no better assimilate the content of
the psychedelic experience than can a villager in the New Guinea highlands or a Witoto Indian in the Amazon. In fact, we have less of a basis
for coming to terms with it; hence, our culture is in a very desperate crisis—a birth crisis and a terminal crisis. If we are not fully informed as to
the nature of reality, we should correct that oversight. My motivation is
to help make that correction.

WN: Have you ever gone to these places with another human
and actually been able to have a parallel, combined experience?

TM: I think that happens. Certainly in taking *ayahuasca* with
groups of people in the Amazon, when the shaman is singing, you definitely have the feeling that you're all being carried through the same
experiential topology and being shown the same things. Also when you
take psilocybin with just one other person and you're lying together
bemushroomed, you have the feeling that you're flowing together
into a single act of perception. Sometimes one person can describe the
vision and then trail off, and the other one can continue to describe
the vision, and it all flows together. I am totally convinced that telepathy occurs on these compounds, though I'm not sure how to go about
making it a repeatable phenomenon.

Unfortunately for research into such phenomena, psilocybin was
made illegal as an afterthought in a Luddite panic that saw most research psychedelics made illegal. It never had any independent hearing
or examination—it was a hallucinogenic agent, therefore illegal. This has
deprived it of the attention it deserves as a tool for throwing light on the
psyche and for catalyzing the imagination.

WN: How do you propose to reeducate people concerning these
substances?

TM: What's always been lacking in psychedelic research is an examination of the content of the experience, so we need to give these
compounds to very intelligent people who are willing to work with
them in situations other than a clinical setting.

We must instead answer the question: How does this experience
change people's lives when they are in an open, nonstressed environment? In the Amazon, which is not exactly a nonstressed environment,
we found that as we traveled up jungle rivers and contacted small villages where plant hallucinogens were known and used, reality was

transformed. Reality is truly a creature made of language and of linguistic structures that you carry, unbeknown to yourself, in your mind, and that under the influence of psilocybin these begin to dissolve and allow you to perceive beyond the speakable. The contours of the unspeakable begin to emerge into your perception, and though you can't say much about the unspeakable, it has power to color everything you do. You live with it; it is the invoking of the Other. The Other can become the Self, and many forms of estrangement can be healed. This is why the term *alien* has these many connotations.

WN: What's the next step?

TM: The next step is to confirm some of what I've said in order to form a consensus among groups of researchers and to then try to figure out a strategy, chemical, clinical, or otherwise.

WN: How would you set up such a research program?

TM: It is important to give these compounds to volunteers, but also to give them to the researchers who are actually going to grapple with the problem. So much therapeutic talk orbits around the psychedelic experience, but how many therapists have had a psychedelic experience? The early approach with psychedelics was the correct one. This is the notion that intelligent, thoughtful people should take psychedelics and try and understand what's going on. Not groups of prisoners, not graduate students, but mature, intelligent people need to share their experiences. It's too early for a science. What we need now are the diaries of explorers. We need many dairies of many explorers so we can begin to get a feeling for the territory.

It is no coincidence that a rebirth of psychedelic use is occurring as we acquire the technological capability to leave the planet. The mushroom visions and the transformation of the human image precipitated by space exploration are spun together. Nothing less is happening than the emergence of a new human order. A telepathic, humane, universalist kind of human culture is emerging that will make everything that preceded it appear like the Stone Age.

WN: Does the Overmind, Oversoul, whatever, assimilate the personal knowledge that's gained within one lifetime?

TM: When consciousness is finally understood, it will mean that the absence of consciousness will be understood. The study of consciousness leads, inevitably, to the study of death. Death is both a historical and

an individual phenomenon about which we, as monkeys, have great anxiety. But what the psychedelic experience seems to be pointing out is that
actually the reductionist view of death has missed the point and that
there is something more. Death isn't simple extinction. The universe does
not build up such complex forms as ourselves without conserving them
in some astonishing and surprising way that relates to the intuitions that
we have from the psychedelic experience. The UFO comes from this
murky region, beyond the end of history, beyond the end of life. It is both
suprahistorical and supraorganic. It is uncanny, alien; it raises the hair on
the back of one's neck. It is both the apotheosis and the antithesis of the
monkey's journey toward mind. It is the mind revealing itself. This is
what all religion is about: shock waves given off by an event at the end of
history. We are now very close to that event, and psilocybin can help us
to understand it because psilocybin conveys one into the place where it is
happening constantly. The Aeon, eternity, and the millennium are accomplished facts, not an anticipation. Hence the mushroom stands at the
end of history. It stands for an object that pulls all history toward itself.
It's a causal force that operates upon us backward through time. It is why
things happen the way they do; because everything is being pulled forward toward a nexus of transformation.

6

Alien Love

THE IDEA of sexual relationships between human and nonhuman beings is a persistent subtheme through much of mythology. Ralph Metzner reminded me that in the Old Testament it says, "And the gods found the daughters of men fair." The Persephone myth is a good example of this. Another example that should be mentioned are the incubi and succubi of medieval mythology. These were male and female spirits that were thought to come to people in the night and have intercourse with them. This was thought to be very bad for one's health, and general wasting diseases were often explained by invoking this phenomenon.

Recently the flying saucer phenomenon has begun to take on a new character—an erotic dimension. There is no hint of this kind of thing in the early literature, meaning from 1947 through 1960. But now it seems to be a rising theme. Though this idea is the darling of a screwball fringe, it represents an interesting developing folkway that we can learn from.

It's only in the last sixty years, since the discovery of DNA and the Hertzsprung-Russell equation, that we have begun to get an idea of the true size of the universe. Until then, the notion of extraterrestrial life and extraterrestrial intelligence could not even be coherently framed. Before that time, humanity's relationships with transhuman intelligence tended to be demonic or angelic and fall into those categories of beings that occupied levels above and below us in the hierarchy of being. These beings were all terrestrial in some sense. But science, by clarifying the

■■

More about UFOs, this from a talk at Shared Visions in Berkeley. An edited and revised transcript was later printed in *Magical Blend,* no. 17, 1987.

nonuniqueness of biology and giving us an idea of what's going on in the galaxy and beyond, has validated the notion that life is ubiquitous and that intelligence is a property that accompanies life and is probably common in the universe. This legitimates fantasy about the existence of extraterrestrial intelligence. In the last half of the twentieth century, the mythological outlines of what the alien must be are being cast. The expectations of a public who has been given the rudimentary knowledge of biology and astronomy allows the thing to be conceived. Public expectations are casting the extraterrestrial archetype into a mold that it will hold until it is confirmed or denied by true extraterrestrial contact, whatever that means.

We now know enough to fantasize realistically about what an alien might be like, and this sets up polarities in the collective psyche that previously we have seen only at the level of the individual. What the developing archetype of the extraterrestrial "Other" means, and the source of our fascination with it, is that, collectively, for the first time we are beginning to yearn. This new collective yearning is happening in religion on a very broad scale. The previous concerns of salvation and redemption are shifting into the background for the great majority of people, and what is driving religious feeling is a wish for contact—a relationship to the Other. The alien then falls into place in that role; the alien fulfills it. I believe that if religion survives into the long centuries of the future, this will be its compelling concern—an attempt to define a collective relationship with the Other that assuages our yearning and our feeling of being cast out or, as Heidegger says, "cast into matter, alone in the Universe."

It's as though by passing into the psychedelic phase—the space-faring phase—the entire species were passing into adolescence and becoming aware of the possibility of something like a sexual completion with an Other, with an intelligent, nonhuman species. This is an idea that had previously been masked for us in our collective pre-pubescence or polymorphically perverse phase, during which we were self-absorbed. One dimension of the culture crisis is a collective erotic drive for a connection with the Other.

To sum up what I've said about religion, it is as though the Father-God notion were being replaced by the alien-partner notion. The alien-partner is like the angelic tetramorph. It is androgynous, hermaphroditic, transhuman; it is all these things that the unconscious chooses to project upon it until we have enough information to define what it might actually be for itself.

Eventually this contact will occur. We are now in the pubescent stage of yearning, of forming an image of the thing desired. This image of the thing desired will eventually cause that thing to come into being. In other words, our cultural direction is being touched by the notion of

alien love, and it comes to us through the rebirth of the use of plant hallucinogens. The shamanic vision plants seem to be the carriers of this
pervasive entelechy that speaks and that can present itself to us in this
particular way.

The appetite for this fusion is what is propelling global culture toward an apocalyptic transformation. It isn't recognized as that in the culture yet, but nevertheless it is this fascination with the Other that
propels us forward. Culturally we are growing toward the potential for
falling in love, but then if there is no one to love this potential can turn
to rancor and disillusionment. We have embarked on the exploration of
a unique historical opportunity in which for the first time the issue of
the Other is being fully constellated and dealt with by the species. The
question is being asked, "Are we alone?," and though we now focus on
that question, we need to think beyond that to what if we are not alone.
Then what becomes the next imperative question? It is obviously the exploration of the relationship to the Other, part of which has an erotic
character.

We will discover, as soon as communication is even remotely
possible, that we are obsessed with it. It becomes very important to
know whether or not we are alone. It becomes very important to open a
dialogue if any dialogue is possible. I think that at this stage the facts are
secondary to the description of what is going on. In other words, this option could slip away from us. It is a potential that has drifted near the
historical continuum, and if it is invoked by enough people, it will become a fact. But it could also slip away. We could harden; there are
dominator, hypertechnological futures that we could sail toward and realize. That would eliminate this possibility of opening to the Other.

I always try to define for myself what the historical importance of
psychedelics is, because we know that shamans have used these plants
for millennia and have plumbed these depths as individuals. Still, I always have the intuition that there is a historical impact of some sort, and
I think this is it: that we are actually positioned to attempt something
that has never been attempted before, to open a dialogue as a collectivity
with the Other and to use that synergy to bootstrap ourselves to a new
cultural level. There isn't a great deal of talk about it; this intuition exists
at the folk level. None of the managerial or analytical elements in society
are looking at this at the moment. But it is forming and crystallizing in
the background.

Contact with extraterrestrials and voices in the head and Logos-
like phenomena are not a part of the general mythology of LSD. Certain
exceedingly intense individuals may have achieved this intermittently,
but it is not something that is attached to the notion of what LSD does to
you. With psilocybin, on the other hand, it definitely is. Our survey
showed that as people's doses increased, their susceptibility to this phe-

nomenon increased markedly. The issue of contact with the extraterrestrial for large numbers of people has been broached by mushrooms. It's
very puzzling to people, because our expectations are always that we
are cells in a vast societal animal and that the news of anything truly important will be conveyed electronically to us. That if flying saucers land,
the president and the secretary-general of the United Nations will convey the word to us. But the challenge of the psychedelics is to realize
that the potential for an alchemical wedding with the alien exists now. It
is a tribal phenomenon that is happening as an experience at the individual level. People in the confines of their own apartments are becoming
Magellans of the interior world, reaching out to this alien thing, beginning to map invisible landscapes and to bring back stories that can only
be compared to the kind of stories that the chroniclers of the New World
brought back to Spain at the close of the fifteenth century. Stories of in-
sect gods, starships, unfathomable wisdom, endless realities.

Many times I've spoken of the psychedelic experience as a landscape and as a confidant—a kind of girl Friday who tells you things. But
another facet of it is the erotic element. There is no other word for it, because it inspires a feeling of opening and merging that is, in our cultural
conditioning, what we associate with Eros. To distinguish it from ordinary love I always think of it as LUV. It's the kind of love that you get
with the alien. What it means is that the relationship to the alien can be
thought of as modeled on the relationships to the Other that each of us
forms through relating to other people. This is similar to the Jungian notion of the Conunctio, a situation in which two people get together and
try to function as alchemical mirrors for each other. Tantra and Taoist
sexual practices also have to do with fusing into dyads. In that situation
each party to the fact is taking on the quality of the other. In a nonerotic
context that's called becoming what you behold.

We are uniquely susceptible to becoming what we behold. This is
why we have always been led into the future by our imaginations; because we dream and then we realize the dreams. This fact about our
monkeyhood, when put in combination with a relationship with an alien
mind, means that we will become the Other we behold. This is, in fact,
what I think is happening. The curious intimations of the deepening
contact with the Other make it seem probable to me that we are in love,
but we're only slowly realizing this because we've never been in love before. So articulating this kind of idea, one person saying it to another
and discussing it, is actually an attempt to conjure this into being—to
call it forth and make this supposition become fact. Because all facts are
the suppositions of very large numbers of people, the fate of this
archetype now hangs in the balance.

There is tension around the flying saucer, aside from the erotic
connotation, because the flying saucer represents a tremendous chal-

lenge to science, perhaps the ultimate challenge. It may be as confounding to science as the resurrection of Christ was to Greek empiricism and Roman imperialism. The flying saucer is essentially an agent of cultural change. On the level of the machine, it bids distress for our most cherished explanatory schema, but on the level of the alien as flesh, it presents a much more basic and fundamental challenge, because the erotic complex is being redefined by this phenomenon.

Many people take LSD, and yet it's very difficult to get precise numbers on this matter because people don't talk about it. Yet in the last fifteen years, sexual researchers have had a field day because people are very, very willing to discuss their bizarre sexual peculiarities and to pour out their hearts to people with clipboards. So we now know a great deal about human sexuality. I suggest that our taboos are on the move. They are moving so that as we become more sexually polymorphic and open with each other and our ego is less identified with our sexuality, we become very private and constrained, secretive and religious about our psychic experiences, particularly the psychedelic experiences. We are much more open with each other sexually and in our examination of our libidinal drives, but the taboo has now moved to this interior world where we have an adolescent sensitivity about our developing relationship to the Other.

These attitudes are elements in the emerging human future, a human future that is accelerating exponentially. It is not a mere linear propagation of the present; peculiar factors are impinging on it: psychedelic substances, the ability to erect large structures in deep space, the presence of the alien Logos in the mind of the collectivity, the presence of the cybernetic network that is developing, the politics of feminism—all these things are going toward release of humanity into the imagination. To date, the cultural engineers have not stressed enough that the erotic element be included in the design of the human future.

Let me sum up by saying that there is an emerging zeitgeist of hyperspace. I call it a zeitgeist of hyperspace because electronic culture will add another dimension whose effects will reverberate at every level. We are now living in a hyperdimensional collectivity, not only of earth and space but of information of past and future, of conscious and unconscious. The technological culmination of this is the projection of human consciousness into whatever form it seeks to take. The zeitgeist of hyperspace that is emerging, initially freighted with technology and cybernetics, requires that it be consciously tuned to an erotic ideal. It is important to articulate the presence of this erotic ideal of the Other early. This is an opportunity to fall in love with the Other, get married, and go off to the stars; but it's only an opportunity and not evolutionarily necessary.

If we only live with the ideal of the Other and never find and fuse with the Other, we can still evolve along whatever pathways lie ahead of us. But if the opportunity is seized, if we take seriously the experience of the last ten millennia and complete the modern program of realizing the ideals of the Archaic Revival, recognizing that what the twentieth century really is about is an effort to establish and perfect the ideals of late Paleolithic shamanism, then we will have acted with integrity in relating to this opportunity and we guarantee ourselves a grand and peculiar historical adventure—which I cheer for.

Q: Could you say a bit more about the role of the psychedelic experience?

TM: Once we set ourselves the task of describing the psychedelic experience, it will become more accessible, because if we each gave our best metaphor and then all used those metaphors to produce a better metaphor, we eventually would retool our language so that we would be able to handle these modalities. And this will happen. Historically, the psychedelic experience is a new object for the Western languages. It will be very interesting to see what English, the language of Milton, Chaucer, and Shakespeare, will be able to do with the psychedelic experience. In William Blake you get the feeling that English can do staggering things with it. Passages in Andrew Marvell imply the same.

The relationship of the psychedelic experience to literature is a whole field unto itself; there are certain moments where great literature has passed near it. Flaubert's *Temptation of Saint Anthony* got it, very succinctly. Huysman's *Against the Grain* is an amazing novel about a man who is so sensitized to perception that he can't leave his apartments. He has his walls covered in felt and keeps the lights very low. He collects Redon when nobody had ever heard of Redon. He buys turtles and has jewels affixed to their backs. Then he sits in a half-lit room and smokes hashish and watches the turtles crawl around on his Persian rugs. Let's all go home and do this.

Q: I'm curious about whether the chemical induction is necessary. I've been exploring vision through dream work and it seems promising. In sleep we see a lot of things.

TM: Yes, I think dreaming and states of psychedelic intoxication, possibly the after-death state, possibly the postapocalypse state for the collectivity, all these are related to each other. Certainly dreaming is the natural access point, because it's a part of everyday experience. But these places are what's called state-bounded. It's very hard to bring back information—you have to have a natural inclination or a technique. It doesn't matter whether you are using psychedelics or yoga or dream-manipulation; it's just a matter of exploring the mind by whatever means works. I've seen studies that show that the deepest part of sleep is the high point of production of endogenous hallucinogens, such as DMT and beta-carbolines, in the human brain. Nevertheless, it's only in the wildest dreams, which are necessarily the most difficult to recover, that one passes into places that are like DMT and psilocybin ecstasy. Yoga makes the claim that it can deliver you into these spaces, but people have different proclivities for these altered states of consciousness. It's very hard to move me off the baseline of consciousness. I am very stolid and set in the here and now. So plants work better than anything else for me. I scoured India and could not convince myself that it wasn't a shell game of some sort or was any more real than the states manipulated by the various schools of New Age psychotherapy.

But in the Amazon and other places where plant hallucinogens are understood and used, you are conveyed into worlds that are appallingly different from ordinary reality. Their vividness cannot be stressed enough. They are more real than real. And that's something that you sense intuitively. They establish an ontological priority. They are more real than real, and once you get that under your belt and let it rattle around in your mind, then the compass of your life begins to spin and you realize that you are not looking in on the Other; the Other is looking in on you. This is a tremendous challenge to the intellectual structures that have carried us so far during the last thousand years. We can do tricks with atoms; there's no question about that. But these tricks immolate us. The higher-order structure of molecules, let alone organelles and that kind of thing, is intellectual terra incognita to us; we have no notion of how these things work or what is going on. Yet it is from those levels that the constituent modalities of reality are being laid down. What do I mean by that? I mean that you can understand all this fine nuclear chemistry about the atom, but where does it put you if you are an intellectual? The story you tell yourself about how the world works can't explain to you how forming the wish to close your open hand into a fist makes it happen. This is the true status of present science. It cannot offer so much as a clue about how that happens. Scientists know how muscles contract—all *that* they know. It's the initiating phenomenon, that which decides "I will close my hand." They know as much about that as—and perhaps less than—Western or Eastern philosophy knew in the twelfth century.

And it is at that level, at the level of the body experience and the mind experience, that we operate. You can live in the social and religious system of Hellenistic Greece and offer sacrifice to Demeter, or you can live in twentieth-century America and watch the evening news, but you should have no faith that you are getting the true story on reality. These are just historical contexts that can be transcended only by the acquisition of gnosis, knowledge that is experienced as self-evidently true.

It's hard for people to even realize what I might be talking about because they believe that something like logical consistency or ability to be reduced to mathematical formalism is how you judge the efficacy of an idea. Ideas such as that are what led us into this extremely alienated state. We haven't demanded that the stories we tell ourselves about how the world works confirm our direct experience of how it works. The psychedelic substances, by focusing attention on the mind-body-brain interactions, are reframing these questions. And not a moment too soon, because the cybernetic and technical capabilities of this society demand that this all be looked at very clearly or we're just going to sail right off the moral edge of things and into the abyss.

Q: Could you comment further on the interaction between various sexual yogas and the psychedelic experience or intoxication as tools—as in effect potential tools for approaching the kind of extraterrestrial eroticism you're talking about?

TM: Certainly. You have all kinds of things going on when people are having sexual intercourse. The physiological state is one of activation, there's production of pheromones. I've noticed on psilocybin that there is a disappearance of normal resistance across a membrane, especially if there is perspiration, so that two people with large amounts of skin in contact become one entity. I'm convinced enough of this that I would suggest to Masters and Johnson, or whoever has license to do these kinds of things, to check it out if they are serious about validating telepathy. This is a very simple experiment.

Taoist sexual practices lay a lot of stress on the generation of unusual substances in the genitals or in the perspiration, which is a theme that is absent from Indian yoga but that is picked up in Amazonian shamanism, where there is a lot of discussion of magical forms of perspiration, magical objects that are generated out of the body or put into the bodies of other people.

In the matter of Taoist alchemy, it appears that there was an erotic control language, so that much of what appear to be prescriptions for sexual practices are actually recipes for plant combinations, because words that were used with sexual connotations were also code words for plants and fungi. The association in the Taoist mind between the fungi and the feminine genitalia was very close. The words and the concepts are the same. This is a prevailing motif of the so-called esoteric schools of Chinese eroticism, meaning the schools where actually nothing appears to be going on, but the presence of certain plants and certain objects in a composition indicate that it actually is an erotic cryptogram of some sort.

Q: Could it be that the natural psychedelics that exist on the planet are a kind of love offering from the Other to us with which, when we accept them, we can develop that bond sought by the Other?

TM: I have spoken about extraterrestrial contact and the relationship to the psilocybin mushrooms. I've mentioned that psilocin, which is what psilocybin quickly becomes as it enters your metabolism, is 4 hydroxy dimethyltryptamine. It is the only 4-substituted indole in all of organic nature. Let this rattle around in your mind for a moment. It is the only 4-substituted indole known to exist on earth. It happens to be this psychedelic substance that occurs in about eighty species of fungi, most of which are native to the New World. Psilocybin has a unique chemical signature that says, "I am artificial; I come from outside." I was suggesting that it was a gene—an artificial gene—carried perhaps by a space-borne virus or something brought artificially to this planet, and that this gene has insinuated itself into the genome of these mushrooms.

It is an unresolved problem in botany why there is such a tremendous concentration of plant hallucinogens in the New World—in North and South America. Africa, which is where man is generally thought to have arisen and gone through his formative cultural development, is the poorest of all continents in hallucinogens. The New World is very, very rich, and this is why hallucinogenic shamanism is so highly developed in the New World. So, yes: the fact that the psilocybin compound is chemically unique, the fact that it induces this Logos-like experience, causes me at least to entertain the possibility that this is an extraterrestrial contact and that the notion of extraterrestrials, as we have previously conceived them, as someone from far away who would come in ships and get in touch with us, is an obsolete notion.

As human history goes forward, we develop the linguistic discrimination to be able to recognize the extraterrestrials that are already insinuated into the planetary environment around us, some of which may have been here millions and millions of years. In other words, space is not an impermeable barrier to life; there is slow drift. There is genetic material that is transferred through space and time over vast distances.

Operationally, I deal with the mushroom that way. It may well be an adumbration or some slice of the human collectivity, but since it presents itself as the Other, I treat it as the Other. Sometimes, as I have said, it is my colleague, and sometimes it is my Jewish godfather, and sometimes it is what Jung called the soror mystica, and what my brother, Dennis, called the sore mistress. It all has to do with changing our preconceptions of things so that the idea that a mushroom could be an intelligent extraterrestrial, which is preposterous from one point of view, can be seen to move from possible to highly probable. This change of mind occurs by simply shifting language around; the evidence has been left untouched.

The evidence is equally friendly to either point of view because the evidence is so impersonal—science is totally impersonal. The empirical evidence that the mushroom is an extraterrestrial is thin and circumstantial. But the subjective experience of those who have formed a relationship with it overwhelmingly supports that view. This, then, is where we have ideas in competition. The evolution of points of view through time. That's why I say the opportunity should not be missed to open a cultural dialogue concerning this phenomenon among ourselves, and with the thing itself. It's a unique opportunity.

Q: I'm going to ask you to speculate just for a minute.

TM: I never speculate.

Q: Just try. Given that we are led by our imaginations into the future, and that facts are indeed suppositions that are agreed upon by a large group of people, how many people do you suppose it would take to agree on these facts and what sort of rituals or ceremonies would be required to align everybody's thinking to agree on specific elements of the invisible landscape to the point where it would be possible to retool the language to accommodate the new visions and take advantage of this opportunity to perfect the Paleolithic ideals of shamanism?

TM: I don't know. Maybe there's a critical 5 percent, or something like that. Political revolutions are made by 10 percent. Psilocybin mushrooms have emanated throughout society. In the last eight years we have undergone something like a second neolithic revolution. The first neolithic revolution was the invention of agriculture; the second neolithic revolution was the invention of home fungus cultivation. Suddenly, twenty or thirty species of psilocybin-containing mushrooms, which were previously rarely met forest endemics or the coprophilic kinds of mushrooms—the ones that grew on the dung of cattle—all of which had restricted endemic zones of occupation, these all have become available. *Stropharia cubensis*, the most ubiquitous in the natural state, was before the invention of human cultivation a rare tropical mushroom. Now it grows from Nome to Tierra del Fuego in every attic, basement, and garage around. The strategy by which the mushroom conquers society is exactly the same strategy by which the mycelium spreads across a petri dish; it simply moves out in all directions. My brother and I wrote the book *Psilocybin: Magic Mushroom Grower's Guide* in 1975. It sold a hundred thousand copies. We had competition from Bob Harris, who also wrote a cultivation book. Jonathan

Ott wrote a book. So did Gary Menser and Stephen Pollock. Spore companies sprang up; it's very hard to imagine how many people are doing this.

I'm very bullish on psilocybin. I think that the word "drug" is inappropriate and that the model of hallucinogenic substances that we have inherited from our experience with LSD is completely inadequate—that the fact that LSD is our model hallucinogen for doctors and researchers is only a historical accident. It was discovered first, or characterized first, in the laboratory, and then millions and millions of people took it. It's active in the one hundred–gamma range, whereas psilocybin is active at fifteen milligrams. Millions and millions of people were able to be touched by LSD. I don't think that mass drug taking is a good idea. But I think that we must have a deputized minority—a shamanic professional class, if you will—whose job is to bring ideas out of the deep, black water and show them off to the rest of us. Such people would perform for our culture some of the cultural functions that shamans performed in preliterate cultures.

I like the plant hallucinogens. I think that a true symbiosis is happening there. LSD was a *thing* of the laboratory. Psilocybin is a creature of the forests and fields. When we propagate it, when we spread it, when it stones us, there is a reciprocal relationship and transfer of energy and information. This is a true symbiosis. Both parties are gaining; nobody is giving up anything. We have domesticated many plants and animals; that's not big news. But this is not a walnut or an apple; it isn't even a cat or a dog; it may be smarter than we are. So the implications of this relationship have to be couched in at least human terms, and that's why the erotic metaphor is not inappropriate.

Q: If psychedelic substances were legal and this were a class in introductory psychedelic appreciation, what do you suppose our first assignment would be?

TM: From me? I guess I would have you plant some seeds and read some history; when you had read the history and grown the seeds (and I don't know what they would be—morning glory seeds or the spores of mushrooms), when you had assimilated and cared for the plant and brought it to its fullest self-expression of fruitful production of alkaloids, then you would be at the threshold of your career and I would adjourn the class.

Appreciation of history is very important to doing well in the psychedelic experience. Psilocybin shows you movies of history; it sees us as historical creatures. It has this above-everything point of view where it isn't dealing in the slice of the moment. It's dealing with the phenomenon of the monkeys over the last million years; that is how it sees us. You can assimilate some of its viewpoints by having a real feeling for the ancestors, all the people who are dead and the people who went before. What a long, strange trip it's been, you know—from the cave paintings at Altamira to the doorway of the starship. And now we stand on that threshold, hand in hand with this strange new partner; out of historical change comes the unexpected. The problem of the Other, the need for the Other, the presence of the Other, the nature of the Other—these are the questions and the concerns that will drive the next order of human knowing.

Q: You don't preclude at all the possibility that the yearning for the Other is just a yearning for the Self—that the Other really is an undisclosed Self.

TM: No, I don't. In fact, I said at the beginning that the nature of the archetype is being set now in the light of scientific knowledge concerning other intelligence in the universe. It's a combination of our need for connection and science giving its blessing to this form of expression of that need that is creating the potential phenomenon of alien love. We don't know what the Self is; Buddhism says that everything is bodhi-mind; that means that there could be extraterrestrials, and if it's true that everything is bodhi-mind, they too are an aspect of the Self. This word "Self" is as great a mystery as the word "Other." It's just a polarity between two mysteries and then the thin, thin myths that are spun to hold you suspended there without freaking out. The myths of science and religion and shamanism all represent a polarity between the mystery of the Self and the mystery of the Other—and remember a mystery is not to be confused with an unsolved problem; a mystery is by its nature mysterious and will not collapse into solution. We are unfamiliar with that kind of thing. We think that if there's a mystery, then experts of whatever kind can get it straightened out and issue a report. But this approach only works for trivia. And what's important—our hearts, our souls, our hopes, our expectations—is completely mysterious to us. So how must they appear, then, to the Other, if it truly is Other?

We need to cultivate a sense of mystery. The mystery is not only in the Other; it is in us. This reverberates again with the idea that we become what we behold. The nature of history is suddenly transforming in the postquantum physics, postmodern phase; this was not expected. The nineteenth century, the early twentieth century—they didn't realize this was what they were pointed into. Although some few people, the 'Pataphysicians, the surrealists, saw what was coming. But now here we are.

Q: The discussion earlier of how the mushroom was likely seeded from afar reminded me of the pan-spermia theory—of the idea that life itself was sent and that we were all sent down here together.

TM: Yes, I should have mentioned that theory because it is the best support I have for the idea I was putting forth. The pan-spermia theory was formulated by Cyril Ponnamperuma, who was the discoverer, along with James Watson and Francis Crick, of DNA. Ponnamperuma and Crick are proposing a much more radical theory than what I put forth, at least in terms relative to biology. They are saying that prebiotic molecules arise in the greatest numbers in deep space, not on the surfaces of planets. That planets are only biologically important at a late stage in the development of complex polymers and prebiotic compounds. I'm sure you know the old adage that we each are made of stars, that the atoms in your bodies were once cooked in the hearts of stars. This is true, but an unremarked accompanying necessity of that fact would be that there must, therefore, be some atoms in your body that were not cooked in the heart of stars but were part of the planets that circled around those stars before they exploded.

My point being that not all of this material that is circulated in the galaxy has been through something as violent as nuclear burning at the heart of a star. When stars go nova, their planets are blown to pieces, and if biotic material has evolved on those planets it is injected into the general cosmic soup of circulating material. That is more my idea of what the spore strategy may have originally been about. The spore evolved in very harsh environments where seeds could not survive. Mushroom spores survive best in an environment as much like that of deep space as possible. Ideal is a total vacuum at minus sixty degrees centigrade. There they last virtually forever. The logic of the case is well founded. What is on much shakier ground, of course, is the idea that the mushroom is an intelligent life form. That's my special obsession and province. Most people say I'm welcome to it.

It's very interesting that in a book called *Scientific Perspectives on Extraterrestrial Communication* by Cyril Ponnamperuma, there is an article by R. N. Bracewell, an astrophysicist, who talks about the logic of searches for intelligent life. He concludes that no matter what kind of life form you are, no matter what kind of technology you have, if you are seriously going to search space by physically sending probes from one star to another, then the only strategy that would work would be what is called a von Neumann machine, meaning a machine that can reproduce itself. Four of these machines are sent out in four opposed directions from a parent star. At a certain distance from the parent star, each machine replicates, giving eight machines. At double that distance, they replicate again, giving sixteen machines, and so on. The notion is that only by this process of replication can all bets be covered. And then what you do is send an initial contact message that says, "We are searching the galaxy for intelligence by an exhaustive means. If you read this message, please call the following, toll-free number and we will initiate contact." Only in this way could you hope to have contact with all the habitable worlds in the galaxy. This scenario makes clear that it may be very important to understand what the message is that the mushroom conveys.

The Mandaeans, an obscure religious cult of Gnostics in the Middle East of very long survivability, believe that at the end of time what they call the Secret Adam will come to earth. The Secret Adam is a messiahlike figure, but he builds a machine that then transmits all the souls back to their hidden source in the All-Father outside of the machinery of cosmic fate. This notion of the messiah building a machine is very interesting. It's conceivable that if there is an extraterrestrial message in our environment, it is a message to build some kind of device so that a less tenuous form of communication can be opened up. Bracewell makes this point; to him this is inherent in the logic of the situation.

It would be an interesting branch of logic—the logic of protocols of extraterrestrial contact. What can we define about contact that is so basic that whatever form of life and intelligence you were, you would have to flow along those creodes? This is probably an undeveloped field at this point, but it certainly could be done. It's like alternative physics. We need alternative theories of social contact and social contract-making in the event that we meet an extraterrestrial. This is a fertile theme in science fiction, the logic of contact, how to make it without giving away too much and yet still get something out of it. It's poker, but the stakes are very high. We're talking survivability, viability, and evolutionary fates of species, if not entire planets.

Q: I would like to ask whether you see a difference with what you're doing with your life and what a shaman would do? The last time I heard you speak, you said you didn't consider yourself a shaman.

TM: The primary characteristic of shamans are that they cure. In other words, they perform a medical function. If I'm performing a medical function, it is a fairly curious one. That's how I differentiate, because I respect that and it is often lost sight of. People think of the psychedelic plants and the magic and the magical feats, but they forget the curing. In Carlos Castaneda's work I don't think anybody cures anybody in about twelve hundred pages of material; nevertheless, classically and statistically, shamans are healers. I think there is something called "lived

shamanic ideals," which is what I'm trying to do—to try to explore reality with a shamanic spirit and by shamanic means. But the curing is the
sine qua non of shamanism.

Q: Could you give me your best understanding of what space is
from the psychedelic perspective and the differentiation between inner
mental space and outer physical space, and the validity of that differentiation? Just the relationship between space in general and consciousness?

TM: The world is reconstructed in the mind through the input of
sensation. The sensation is canalized through the preceptors so that
we're getting at least three or four lines of unrelated input, or it's generally thought of as unrelated. But the body is the interface between the
mind and the world, and language seems to be the through-put from the
mind to the world and then from the world back into the mind. As for
space—there is this curious thing in biology: The earliest forms of
life had no perception of the world at all. If food was in their way, they
took it in. Then later, with the development of eyespots and pigment-
sensitive chemicals concentrated in certain cells, you get the differentiation between light and darkness. Then later still you get mobile animals
and the evolution of complicated eyes and so forth. You see, what is
happening is that biology is a conquest of dimensions and that if you
view culture as the extension of biological evolution, it too is a conquest
of a dimension. It is the conquest of a dimension of time where, through
the invention of alphabets and coding systems and oral traditions, experience is able to be coded. Now we seem to be coming into a place where
we are coding space and time, but the evolution of the conquest of space
through motion allows our whole mapping of the world. Culture is
turning into a hyperdimensional entity fulfilling the biological program
of life. Whatever it is, it is transforming itself through a series of dimensions, bootstrapping itself from one dimension to another. You'll notice
that currently human culture is very two-dimensional or it's very flat.
What is the highest building in the world, a thousand feet high? And
generally most buildings are twenty feet high; but now we are proposing to build space colonies where the notion of how high the building is
doesn't exist because the world is the building and the building is fifty
or a hundred miles long.

We can record essentially anything we want about any event and
recall it later. There is a synthesis of all this, which leads to the discovery
of the inner dimension, which may be thought of as a higher or lower dimension. The human imagination is the dimension beyond space and
time, or it precedes all dimensions. At some level it has pointlike characteristics; that's why all this talk about the hologram, because it has the

pointlike characteristics of new consciousness. It has all-at-onceness. Its everywhere-at-the-same-timeness has fascinated commentators.

Q: You talked about the collapse of the distinction of inner and outer space. Would you go into that more?

TM: The distinction of inner and outer space is rooted in association of the Self with the body. I think as the Self moves out into the ocean of electronic consciousness and, as we explored, into the erotic dimensions with the Other that I've indicated tonight, this identification between Self and body will become secondary, in the same way that the identification between king and Self has become rather secondary over the last five thousand years. We don't even have a king. We seem to manage without one. It's conceivable we could manage without a body as well. These are just ways that loyalty is transferred toward forms of cultural concrescence validated by local languages.

Q: It seems that the talk is of humanity being on the threshold of a New Age, and that maybe contact with aliens will help us cross this threshold.

TM: I definitely think that there is a process that has been long under way that has been gaining momentum since its very beginning. It is the process that formed the planet, that called life out of the ocean, that called higher animals out of the lower animals, that called humanity out of the primates, and that called history out of tribal, sacral, timeless existence. What it is leading toward is some kind of transcendental transformative flowing together of everything that is beyond our language system. It is the umbilicus of being; it is where it's all tied together, and, therefore, it's very hard to describe. I think that all of our science and religion and history are patterns thrown across a limited set of dimensions by the hyperdimensional presence of a certain object at the end of history toward which we are moving and toward which we are being drawn. I think that most things about human beings are mysterious and that what is happening to us is mysterious. The sudden explosive development of the neocortex is entirely out of context with what we know about the rates of evolution that occur in other species and previously went on in the primates.

It's been very fashionable in the past fifty years to think that it's all very humdrum; yet every ideological system that has been granted the status of being the official view of reality has always proclaimed that it had everything nailed down but the last 5 percent. Their best people were working on that. But I think that we know practically nothing. Though I am not in most senses religious, I think that religious thinking about the transformation of the world is more on the right track than the notion that the laws of physics will always be what they are, the laws of biology will always be what they are, and we're all just going to go along and things are going to get worse and worse, or better and better, but that there are no surprises. I think that we do not see what's going on.

One of the reasons I like to make this argument about the mushroom and the extraterrestrial is to show people how one can see things differently. If things can be seen that differently, how many ways can they be seen differently? Try to get people to stop waiting for the president to enlighten them. Stop waiting for history and the stream of historical events to make itself clear to you. You have to take seriously the notion that understanding the universe is your responsibility, because the only understanding of the universe that will be useful to you is your own understanding. It doesn't do you any good to know that somewhere in some computer there are equations that perfectly model or perfectly don't model something that is going on. We have all tended to give ourselves away to official ideologies and to say, "Well I may not understand, but someone understands." The fact of the matter is that only your own understanding is any good to you. Because it's *you* that you're going to live with and it's *you* that you're going to die with. As the song says, the last dance you dance, you dance alone.

7

New Maps of Hyperspace

N JAMES JOYCE's *Ulysses*, Stephen Dedalus tells us, "History is the nightmare from which I am trying to awaken." I would turn this around and say that history is what we are trying to escape from into dream. The dream is eschatological. The dream is zero time and outside of history. We wish to escape into the dream. Escape is a key thing charged against those who would experiment with plant hallucinogens. The people who make this charge hardly dare face the degree to which hallucinogens are escapist. Escape. Escape from the planet, from death, from habit, and from the problem, if possible, of the Unspeakable.

If one leaves aside the last three hundred years of historical experience as it unfolded in Europe and America, and examines the phenomenon of death and the doctrine of the soul in all its ramifications—Neoplatonic, Christian, dynastic-Egyptian, and so on, one finds repeatedly the idea that there is a light body, an entelechy that is somehow mixed up in the body during life and at death is involved in a crisis in which these two portions separate. One part loses its *raison d'être* and falls into dissolution; metabolism stops. The other part goes we know not where. Perhaps nowhere if one believes it does not exist; but then one has the problem of trying to explain life. And, though science makes great claims and has done well at explaining simple atomic systems, the idea that science can make *any* statement about what life is or where it comes from is currently preposterous.

Science has nothing to say about how one can decide to close one's hand into a fist, and yet it happens. This is utterly outside the

■■

A talk given at the invitation of Ruth and Arthur Young of the Berkeley Institute for the Study of Consciousness, 1984.

realm of scientific explanation because what we see in that phenomenon is mind as a first cause. It is an example of telekinesis: matter is caused by mind to move. So we need not fear the sneers of science in the matter of the fate or origin of the soul. My probe into this area has always been the psychedelic experience, but recently I have been investigating dreams, because dreams are a much more generalized form of experience of the hyperdimension in which life and mind seem to be embedded.

Looking at what people with shamanic traditions say about dreams, one comes to the realization that for those people dream reality is experientially a parallel continuum. The shaman accesses this continuum with hallucinogens as well as with other techniques, but most effectively with hallucinogens. Everyone else accesses it through dreams. Freud's idea about dreams was that they were what he called "day-residues," and that one could trace the content of the dream down to a distortion of something that happened during waking time.

I suggest that it is much more useful to try to make a kind of geometric model of consciousness, to take seriously the idea of a parallel continuum, and to say that the mind and the body are embedded in the dream and the dream is a higher-order spatial dimension. In sleep, one is released into the real world, of which the world of waking is only the surface in a very literal geometric sense. There is a plenum—recent experiments in quantum physics tend to back this up—a holographic plenum of information. All information is everywhere. Information that is not here is nowhere. Information stands outside of historical time in a kind of eternity—an eternity that does not have a temporal existence, not even the kind of temporal existence about which one may say, "It always existed." It does not have temporal duration of any sort. It is eternity. We are not primarily biological, with mind emerging as a kind of iridescence, a kind of epiphenomenon at the higher levels of organization of biology. We are hyperspatial objects of some sort that cast a shadow into matter. The shadow in matter is our physical organism.

At death, the thing that casts the shadow withdraws, and metabolism ceases. Material form breaks down; it ceases to be a dissipative structure in a very localized area, sustained against entropy by cycling material in, extracting energy, and expelling waste. But the form that ordered it is not affected. These declarative statements are made from the point of view of the shamanic tradition, which touches all higher religions. Both the psychedelic dream state and the waking psychedelic state acquire great import because they reveal to life a task: to become familiar with this dimension that is causing being, in order to be familiar with it at the moment of passing from life.

The metaphor of a vehicle—an after-death vehicle, an astral body—is used by several traditions. Shamanism and certain yogas, including Taoist yoga, claim very clearly that the purpose of life is to familiarize oneself with this after-death body so that the act of dying will not create confusion in the psyche. One will recognize what is happening. One will know what to do and one will make a clean break. Yet there does seem to be the possibility of a problem in dying. It is not the case that one is condemned to eternal life. One can muff it through ignorance.

Apparently at the moment of death there is a kind of separation, like birth—the metaphor is trivial, but perfect. There is a possibility of damage or of incorrect activity. The English poet-mystic William Blake said that as one starts into the spiral there is the possibility of falling from the golden track into eternal death. Yet it is only a crisis of a moment—a crisis of passage—and the whole purpose of shamanism and of life correctly lived is to strengthen the soul and to strengthen the ego's relationship to the soul so that this passage can be cleanly made. This is the traditional position.

I want to include an abyss in this model—one less familiar to rationalists, but familiar to us all one level deeper in the psyche as inheritors of the Judeo-Christian culture. That is the idea that the world will end, that there will be a final time, that there is not only the crisis of death of the individual but also the crisis of death in the history of the species.

What this seems to be about is that from the time of the awareness of existence of the soul until the resolution of the apocalyptic potential, there are roughly one hundred thousand years. In biological time, this is only a moment, yet it is ten times the entire span of history. In that period, everything hangs in the balance, because it is a mad rush from hominid to starflight. In the leap across those one hundred thousand years, energies are released, religions are shot off like sparks, philosophies evolve and die, science arises, magic arises, all of these concerns that control power with greater and lesser degrees of ethical constancy appear. Ever present is the possibility of aborting the species' transformation into a hyperspatial entelechy.

We are now, there can be no doubt, in the final historical seconds of that crisis—a crisis that involves the end of history, our departure from the planet, the triumph over death, and the release of the individual from the body. We are, in fact, closing distance with the most profound event a planetary ecology can encounter—the freeing of life from the dark chrysalis of matter. The old metaphor of psyche as the caterpillar transformed by metamorphosis is a specieswide analogy. We must undergo a metamorphosis in order to survive the momentum of the historical forces already in motion.

Evolutionary biologists consider humans to be an unevolving species. Some time in the last fifty thousand years, with the invention of culture, the biological evolution of humans ceased and evolution became an epigenetic, cultural phenomenon. Tools, languages, and philosophies began to evolve, but the human somatotype remained the same. Hence, physically, we are very much like people of a long time ago. But technology is the real skin of our species. Humanity, correctly seen in the context of the last five hundred years, is an extruder of technological material. We take in matter that has a low degree of organization; we put it through mental filters, and we extrude jewelry, gospels, space shuttles. This is what we do. We are like coral animals embedded in a technological reef of extruded psychic objects. All our tool making implies our belief in an ultimate tool. That tool is the flying saucer, or the soul, exteriorized in three-dimensional space. The body can become an internalized holographic object embedded in a solid-state, hyperdimensional matrix that is eternal, so that we each wander through a true Elysium.

This is a kind of Islamic paradise in which one is free to experience all the pleasures of the flesh provided one realizes that one is a holographic projection of a solid-state matrix that is microminiaturized, superconducting, and nowhere to be found: it is part of the plenum. All technological history is about producing prototypes of this situation with greater and greater closure toward the ideal, so that airplanes, automobiles, space shuttles, space colonies, starships of the nuts-and-bolts, speed-of-light type are, as Mircea Eliade said, "self-transforming images of flight that speak volumes about man's aspiration to self-transcendence."

Our wish, our salvation, and our only hope is to end the historical crisis by becoming the alien, by ending alienation, by recognizing the alien as the Self, in fact—recognizing the alien as an Overmind that holds all the physical laws of the planet intact in the same way that one holds an idea intact in one's thoughts. The givens that are thought to be writ in adamantine are actually merely the moods of the Goddess, whose reflection we happen to be. The whole meaning of human history lies in recovering this piece of lost information so that man may be dirigible or, to paraphrase James Joyce's *Finnegans Wake* on Moicane, the red light district of Dublin: "Here in Moicane we flop on the seamy side, but up ne'nt, prospector, you sprout all your worth and you woof your wings, so if you want to be Phoenixed, come and be parked." It is that simple, you see, but it takes courage to be parked when the Grim Reaper draws near. "A blessing in disguise," Joyce calls him.

What psychedelics encourage, and where I hope attention will focus once hallucinogens are culturally integrated to the point where large groups of people can plan research programs without fear of persecution, is the modeling of the after-death state. Psychedelics may do more than model this state; they may reveal the nature of it. Psychedelics will show us that the modalities of appearance and understanding can be shifted so that we can know mind within the context of the One Mind. The One Mind contains all experiences of the Other. There is no dichotomy between the Newtonian universe, deployed throughout light-years of three-dimensional space, and the interior mental universe. They are adumbrations of the same thing.

We perceive them as unresolvable dualisms because of the low quality of the code we customarily use. The language we use to discuss this problem has built-in dualisms. This is a problem of language. All codes have relative code qualities, except the Logos. The Logos is perfect and, therefore, partakes of no quality other than itself. I am here using the word *Logos* in the sense in which Philo Judaeus uses it—that of the Divine Reason that embraces the archetypal complex of Platonic ideas that serve as the models of creation. As long as one maps with something other than the Logos, there will be problems of code quality. The dualism built into our language makes the death of the species and the death of the individual appear to be opposed things.

Likewise, the scenarios that biology has created through examining the physical universe versus the angel- and demon-haunted worlds that depth psychology is reporting is also a dichotomy. The psychedelic experience acts to resolve this dichotomy. All that is needed to go beyond an academic understanding of the plant hallucinogens is the experience of the tryptamine-induced ecstasy. The dimethyltryptamine (DMT) molecule has the unique property of releasing the structured ego into the Overself. Each person who has that experience undergoes a mini-apocalypse, a mini-entry and mapping into hyperspace. For society to focus in this direction, nothing is necessary except for this experience to become an object of general concern.

This is not to suggest that everyone should experiment with mushrooms or other naturally occurring sources of psychoactive tryptamines. We should try to assimilate and integrate the psychedelic experience since it is a plane of experience that is directly accessible to each of us. The role that we play in relationship to it determines how we will present ourselves in that final, intimated transformation. In other words, in this notion there is a kind of teleological bias; there is a belief that there is a hyperobject called the Overmind, or God, that casts a shadow into time. History is our group experience of this shadow. As one draws closer and closer to the source of the shadow, the paradoxes intensify, the rate of change intensifies. What is happening is that the hyperobject is beginning to ingress into three-dimensional space.

One way of thinking of this is to suppose that the waking world and the world of the dream have begun to merge so that in a certain sense the school of UFO criticism that has said flying saucers are hallucinations was correct in that the laws that operate in the dream, the laws that operate in hyperspace, can at times operate in three-dimensional space when the barrier between the two modes becomes weak. Then one gets these curious experiences, sometimes called psychotic breaks, that always have a tremendous impact on the experient because there seems to be an exterior component that could not possibly be subjective. At such times coincidences begin to build and build until one must finally admit that one does not know what is going on. Nevertheless, it is preposterous to claim that this is a psychological phenomenon, because there are accompanying changes in the external world. Jung called this "synchronicity" and made a psychological model of it, but it is really an alternative physics beginning to impinge on local reality.

This alternative physics is a physics of light. Light is composed of photons, which have no antiparticle. This means that there is no dualism in the world of light. The conventions of relativity say that time slows down as one approaches the speed of light, but if one tries to imagine the point of view of a thing made of light, one must realize that what is never mentioned is that if one moves at the speed of light there is no time whatsoever. There is an experience of time zero. So if one imagines for a moment oneself to be made of light, or in possession of a vehicle that can move at the speed of light, one can traverse from any point in the universe to any other with a subjective experience of time zero. This means that one crosses to Alpha Centauri in time zero, but the amount of time that has passed in the relativistic universe is four and a half years. But if one moves very great distances, if one crosses two hundred and fifty thousand light-years to Andromeda, one would still have a subjective experience of time zero.

The only experience of time that one can have is of a subjective time that is created by one's own mental processes, but in relationship to the Newtonian universe there is no time whatsoever. One exists in eternity, one has become eternal, the universe is aging at a staggering rate all around one in this situation, but that is perceived as a fact of the universe—the way we perceive Newtonian physics as a fact of this universe. One has transited into the eternal mode. One is then apart from the moving image; one exists in the completion of eternity.

I believe that this is what technology pushes toward. There is no contradiction between ecological balance and space migration, between hypertechnology and radical ecology. These issues are red herrings; the real historical entity that is becoming imminent is the human soul. The monkey body has served to carry us to this moment of release, and it will always serve as a focus of self-image, but we are coming more and more to exist in a world made by the human imagination. This is what is meant by the return to the Father, the transcendence of *physis*, the rising out of the Gnostic universal prison of iron that traps the light: nothing less than the transformation of our species.

Very shortly an acceleration of this phenomenon will take place in the form of space exploration and space colonies. The coral-reef-like animal called Man that has extruded technology over the surface of the earth will be freed from the constraints of anything but the imagination and the limitations of materials. It has been suggested that the earliest space colonies include efforts to duplicate the idyllic ecosystem of Hawaii as an ideal. These exercises in ecological understanding will prove we know what we are doing. However, as soon as this understanding is under control we will be released into the realm of art. This is what we have always striven for. We will make our world—all of our worlds—and the world we came from will be maintained as a garden. What Eliade discussed as metaphors of self-transforming flight will be realized shortly in the technology of space colonization.

The transition from earth to space will be a staggeringly tight genetic filter, a much tighter filter than any previous frontier has ever been, including the genetic and demographic filter represented by the colonization of the New World. It has been said that the vitality of the Americas is due to the fact that only the dreamers and the pioneers and the fanatics made the trip across. This will be even more true of the transition to space. The technological conquest of space will set the stage; then, for the internalization of that metaphor, it will bring the conquest of inner space and the collapse of the state vectors associated with this technology deployed in Newtonian space. Then the human species will have become more than dirigible.

A technology that would internalize the body and exteriorize the soul will develop parallel to the move into space. *The Invisible Landscape*, a book by my brother and myself, made an effort to short-circuit that chronology and, in a certain sense, to force the issue. It is the story, or rather it is the intellectual underpinnings of the story, of an expedition to the Amazon by my brother and myself and several other people in 1971. During that expedition, my brother formulated an idea that involved using harmine and harmaline, compounds that occur in *Banisteriopsis caapi*, the woody vine that is the basis for *ayahuasca*. We undertook an effort to use harmine in conjunction with the human voice in what we called "the experiment at La Chorrera." It was an effort to use sound to charge the molecular structure of harmine molecules metabolizing in the body in such a way that they would bind preferentially and permanently with endogenous molecular structures.

Our candidate at the time was neural DNA, though Frank Barr, a researcher into the properties of brain melanin, has made a convincing case that there is as great a likelihood that harmine acts by binding with melanin bodies. In either case, the pharmacology involves binding with a molecular site where information is stored, and this information is then broadcast in such a way that one begins to get a mental readout on the structure of the soul. Our experiment was an effort to use a kind of shamanic technology to bell the cat, if you will, to hang a superconducting, telemetric device on the Overmind so that there would be a continuous readout of information from that dimension. The success or failure of this attempt may be judged for oneself.

The first half of the book describes the theoretical underpinnings of the experiment. The second half describes the theory of the structure of time that derived from the bizarre mental states that followed the experiment. I do not claim that we succeeded, only that our theory of what happened is better than any theory proposed by critics. Whether we succeeded or not, this style of thinking points the way. For example, when I speak of the technology of building a starship, I imagine it will be done with voltages far below the voltage of a common flashlight battery. This is, after all, where the most interesting phenomena go on in nature. Thought is that kind of phenomenon; metabolism is that kind of phenomenon.

A new science that places the psychedelic experience at the center of its program of investigation should move toward a practical realization of this goal—the goal of eliminating the barrier between the ego and the Overself so that the ego can perceive itself as an expression of the Overself. Then the anxiety of facing a tremendous biological crisis in the form of the ecocrises, and the crisis of limitation in physical space forced upon us by our planet-bound situation, can be obviated by cultivating the soul and by practicing a new shamanism using tryptamine-containing plants.

Psilocybin is the most commonly available and experientially accessible of these compounds. Therefore my plea to scientists, administrators, and politicians who may read my words is this: look again at psilocybin, do not confuse it with the other psychedelics, and realize that it is a phenomenon unto itself with an enormous potential for transforming human beings—not simply transforming the people who take it, but transforming society in the way that an art movement, a mathematical understanding, or a scientific breakthrough transforms society. It holds the possibility of transforming the entire species simply by virtue of the information that comes through it. Psilocybin is a source of gnosis, and the voice of gnosis has been silenced in the Western mind for at least a thousand years.

When the Franciscans and the Dominicans arrived in Mexico in the sixteenth century, they immediately set about stamping out the mushroom religion. The Indians called it *teonanacatl*, "the flesh of the gods." The Catholic church had a monopoly on theophagia and was not pleased by this particular approach to what was going on. Now, four hundred years after that initial contact, I suggest that Eros, which retreated from Europe with the rise of Christianity, retreated to the mountains of the Sierra Mazateca. Finally, pushed into seclusion there, it now reemerges in Western consciousness.

Our institutions, our epistemologies are bankrupt and exhausted; we must start anew and hope that with the help of shamanically inspired personalities, we can cultivate this ancient mystery once again. The Logos can be unleashed, and the voice that spoke to Plato and Parmenides and Heraclitus can speak again in the minds of modern people. When it does, the alienation will be ended because we will have become the alien. This is the promise that is held out; it may seem to some a nightmare vision, but all historical changes of immense magnitude have a charged emotional quality. They propel people into a completely new world.

I believe that this work must be done using hallucinogens. Traditionally it has been thought that there were many paths to spiritual advancement. In this matter I must fall back on personal experience. I have not had good results with any other techniques. I spent time in India, practiced yoga, visited among the various rishis, roshis, geysheys, and gurus that Asia had to offer, and I believe they must be talking about something so pale and so far removed from closure with the full tryptamine ecstasy that I don't really know what to make of them and their wan hierophanies.

Tantra claims to be another approach. Tantra means "the shortcut path," and certainly it might be on the right track. Sexuality, orgasm, these things do have tryptaminelike qualities to them, but the difference between psilocybin and all other hallucinogens is information—immense amounts of information.

LSD seemed somehow to be largely related to the structure of the personality. Often it seemed to me the visions were merely geometric patterns unless synergized by another compound. The classic psychedelic experience that was written about by Aldous Huxley was two hundred micrograms of LSD and thirty milligrams of mescaline. That combination delivers a visionary experience rather than an experience of hallucinations. In my opinion the unique quality of psilocybin is that it reveals not colored lights and moving grids, but places—jungles, cities, machines, books, architectonic forms of incredible complexity. There is no possibility that this could be construed as neurological noise of any sort. It is, in fact, the most highly ordered visual information that one can experience, much more highly ordered than the normal waking vision.

This is why it's very hard with psychedelic compounds to bring back information. These things are hard to English because it is like try-

ing to make a three-dimensional rendering of a fourth-dimensional object. Only through the medium of sight can the true modality of this
Logos be perceived. That is why it is so interesting that psilocybin and
ayahuasca—the aboriginal tryptamine-containing brew—both produce a
telepathic experience and a shared state of mind. The unfolding group
hallucination is shared in complete silence. It's hard to prove this to a
scientist, but if several people share such an experience, one person can
describe it and then cease the monologue and another person may then
take it up. Everyone is seeing the same thing! It is the quality of being
complex visual information that makes the Logos a vision of a truth that
cannot be told.

The information thus imparted is not, however, merely restricted
to the mode of seeing. The Logos is capable of going from a thing heard
to a thing seen, without ever crossing through a discernible transition
point. This seems a logical impossibility; yet when one actually has the
experience, one sees—aha!—it is as though thought that is heard does
become something seen. The thought that is heard becomes more and
more intense until, finally, its intensity is such that, with no transition,
one is now beholding it in three-dimensional, visual space. One commands it. This is very typical of psilocybin.

Naturally, whenever a compound is introduced into the body,
one must exercise caution and be well informed with regard to possible
side effects. Professional psychedelic investigators are aware of these
factors and freely acknowledge that the obligation to be well informed is
of primary importance.

Speaking for myself, let me say that I am not an abuser. It takes
me a long time to assimilate each visionary experience. I have never lost
my respect for these dimensions. Dread is one of the emotions that I feel
as I approach the experience. Psychedelic work is like sailing out onto a
dark ocean in a little skiff. One may view the moon rising serenely over
the calm black water, or something the size of a freight train may roar
right through the scene and leave one clinging to an oar.

The dialogue with the Other is what makes repetition of these experiences seem worthwhile. The mushroom speaks to you when you
speak to it. In the introduction to the book that my brother and I wrote
(under pseudonyms) called *Psilocybin: Magic Mushroom Grower's Guide*,
there is a mushroom monologue that begins: "I am old, fifty times older
than thought in your species, and I came from the stars." That's verba-
tim. I was writing it furiously. Sometimes it's very human. My approach
to it is Hasidic. I rave at it; it raves at me. We argue about what it is going to cough up and what it isn't. I say, "Well, look, I'm the propagator,
you can't hold back on me," and it says, "But if I showed you the flying
saucer for five minutes, you would figure out how it works," and I say,
"Well, come through." It has many manifestations. Sometimes it's like

Dorothy of Oz; sometimes it's like a very Talmudic sort of pawnbroker. I asked it once, "What are you doing on earth?" It said, "Listen, if you're a mushroom, you live cheap; besides, I'm telling you, this was a very nice neighborhood until the monkeys got out of control."

"Monkeys out of control": that is the mushroom voice's view of history. To us, history is something very different. History is the shock wave of eschatology. In other words, we are living in a very unique moment, ten or twenty thousand years long, where an immense transition is happening. The object at the end of and beyond history is the human species fused into eternal tantric union with the superconducting Overmind/UFO. It is that mystery that casts its shadow back through time. All religion, all philosophy, all wars, pogroms, and persecutions happen because people do not get the message right. There is both the forward-flowing casuistry of being, causal determinism, and the interference pattern that is formed against that by the backward-flowing fact of this eschatological hyperobject throwing its shadow across the temporal landscape. We exist, yet there is a great deal of noise. This situation called history is totally unique; it will last only for a moment, it began a moment ago. In that moment there is a tremendous burst of static as the monkey goes to godhood, as the final eschatological object mitigates and transforms the forward flow of entropic circumstance.

Life is central to the career of organization in matter. I reject the idea that we have been shunted onto a siding called organic existence and that our actual place is in eternity. This mode of existence is an important part of the cycle. It is a filter. There is the possibility of extinction, the possibility of falling into *physis* forever, and so in that sense the metaphor of the fall is valid. There is a spiritual obligation, there is a task to be done. It is not, however, something as simple as following a set of somebody else's rules. The noetic enterprise is a primary obligation toward being. Our salvation is linked to it. Not everyone has to read alchemical texts or study superconducting biomolecules to make the transition. Most people make it naively by thinking clearly about the present at hand, but we intellectuals are trapped in a world of too much information. Innocence is gone for us. We cannot expect to cross the rainbow bridge through a good act of contrition; that will not be sufficient.

We have to understand. Whitehead said, "Understanding is the apperception of pattern as such"; to fear death is to misunderstand life. Cognitive activity is the defining fact of humanness. Language, thought, analysis, art, dance, poetry, mythmaking: these are the things that point the way toward the realm of the eschaton. We humans may be released into a realm of pure self-engineering. The imagination is everything. This was Blake's perception. This is where we come from.

This is where we are going. And it is only to be approached through cognitive activity.

Time is the notion that gives ideas such as these their power, for they imply a new conception of time. During the experiment at La Chorrera, the Logos demonstrated that time is not simply a homogeneous medium where things occur, but a fluctuating density of probability. Though science can sometimes tell us what can happen and what cannot happen, we have no theory that explains why, out of everything that could happen, certain things undergo what Whitehead called "the formality of actually occurring." This was what the Logos sought to explain, why out of all the myriad things that could happen, certain things undergo the formality of occurring. It is because there is a modular hierarchy of waves of temporal conditioning, or temporal density. A certain event, rated highly improbable, is more probable at some moments than at others.

Taking that simple perception and being led by the Logos, I was able to construct a fractal model of time that can be programmed on a computer and that gives a map of the ingression of what I call "novelty"—the ingression of novelty into time. As a general rule, novelty is obviously increasing. It has been since the very beginning of the universe. Immediately following the Big Bang there was only the possibility of nuclear interaction, and then, as temperatures fell below the bond strength of the nucleus, atomic systems could be formed. Still later, as temperatures fell further, molecular systems appeared. Then much later, life became possible; then very complex life forms evolved, thought became possible, culture was invented. The invention of printing and electronic information transfer occurred.

What is happening to our world is ingression of novelty toward what Whitehead called "concrescence," a tightening gyre. Everything is flowing together. The "autopoetic lapis," the alchemical stone at the end of time, coalesces when everything flows together. When the laws of physics are obviated, the universe disappears, and what is left is the tightly bound plenum, the monad, able to express itself for itself, rather than only able to cast a shadow into *physis* as its reflection. I come very close here to classical millenarian and apocalyptic thought in my view of the rate at which change is accelerating. From the way the gyre is tightening, I predict that concrescence will occur soon—around 2012 A.D. It will be the entry of our species into hyperspace, but it will appear to be the end of physical laws accompanied by the release of the mind into the imagination.

All these images—the starship, the space colony, the lapis—are precursory images. They follow naturally from the idea that history is the shock wave of eschatology. As one closes distance with the eschatological object, the reflections it is throwing off resemble more and more the thing itself. In the final moment the Unspeakable stands revealed. There are no more reflections of the Mystery. The Mystery in all its nakedness is seen, and nothing else exists. But what it is, decency can safely scarcely hint; nevertheless, it is the crowning joy of futurism to seek anticipation of it.

8

Temporal Resonance

THE NEWTONIAN-EINSTEINIAN description of nature is the Ur-myth of our civilization, yet in an important area it is at variance with perceived experience. I refer to its description of the temporal dimension. Time for Newton was represented by a flat plane; it was pure duration, a domain necessary for the description of events. Einstein added the possibility of slight and smooth curvature of the space–time continuum. Both points of view overlook a property of reality that my model building has taken very seriously: the phenomenon of the conservation of connectedness. We find this principle active at the very beginning of the universe, and connectedness continues to be conserved and concentrated throughout the entire subsequent history of space/time.

An interesting thing about this concatenation of connectedness is that each stage of its condensation took place more rapidly than the stages that preceded it. At its birth the universe was as a pure plasma; there were no atomic systems; there was so much energy within the system that electrons either did not yet exist or were unable to settle into stable orbits. Then, as the universe cooled, atomic systems began to form; stars condensed and through nuclear chemistry cooked up heavier elements, from which eventually developed a carbon-based chemistry. This opened the possibility of molecular chemistry—new realms of connectedness—a new proliferation of opportunity for novelty. This opportunity led to life, to higher animals, to culture, and eventually and

■ ■

Appeared in *Revision*, vol. 10, no. 1, summer 1987. This is an attempt to make a succinct statement concerning my ideas about time and the timewave.

comparatively recently to culture and epigenetic coding systems such as language and, even more recently, writing. The legacy of the conservation of connectedness is the metaconnected chaostrophy of twentieth-century planetary culture. My model building has sought to unify all of these diverse phenomena and to treat them as manifestations of a single set of laws: laws that describe the ingression of novelty into time and its conservation and concentration in ordinary space/time and ordinary immediate experience.

This idea differs from orthodox cosmology in that orthodox physics is very concerned with the very early history of the universe, which is imagined as a succession of very brief epochs each with its own special boundary constraints and species of physics, declensions from a singularity that precedes any physics. My notion reverses this procedure and places the compressed epochs of ultraconnectedness leading to singularity at the end of the cosmological event, precisely where the standard model has the universe running down into an entropic heat-death. The standard model treats biology as so epiphenomenal as to be unworthy of even being mentioned.

In seeking the basis for a new model of time outside the "pure-duration" model of Western science, I naturally examined Eastern approaches that seem more in tune with subjective intuitions and immediate felt experience. The experience we have of time is much more closely related to the description that we inherit from a tradition such as Taoism than it is to science. Indeed, the *Tao Te Ching* opens with the observation that "The Way that can be told of is not an unvarying way."

The idea that time is experienced as a series of identifiable elements in flux is highly developed in the *I Ching*. In fact, the temporal modeling of the *I Ching* offers the only well-developed alternative to the "flat-duration" point of view. The *I Ching* views time as a finite number of distinct and irreducible elements, in the same way that the chemical elements compose the world of matter. For the Taoist sages of pre-Han China, time was composed of sixty-four irreducible elements. It is upon relations among these sixty-four elements that I have sought to erect a new model of time that incorporates the idea of the conservation of novelty and recognizes time as a process of becoming.

The earliest arrangement of the hexagrams of the *I Ching* is the King Wen sequence. It was this sequence that I chose to study as a possible basis for a new model of the relationship of time to the ingression and conservation of novelty. In studying the kinds of order in the King Wen sequence of the *I Ching*, I made a number of remarkable discoveries. It is well known that hexagrams in the King Wen sequence occur in pairs. The second member of each pair is obtained by inverting the first.

In any sequence of the sixty-four hexagrams there are eight hexagrams that remain unchanged when inverted. In the King Wen sequence these eight hexagrams are paired with hexagrams in which each line of the first hexagram has become its opposite (yang changed to yin and vice versa).

The question remains of what rule or principle governs the arrangement of the thirty-two pairs of hexagrams comprising the King Wen sequence. My intuition was to look at the first order of difference—that is, how many lines change as one moves through the King Wen sequence from one hexagram to the next. The first order of difference will always be an integer between one and six. When the first order of difference within pairs is examined it is always found to be an even number. Thus, all instances of first order of difference that are odd occur at transitions from one pair of hexagrams to the next pair. When the complete set of first order of difference integers generated by the King Wen sequence is examined, the integers are found to fall into a perfect ratio of three to one, three even integers to each odd integer. The ratio of 3:1 is not a formal property of the complete sequence but was a carefully constructed artifact achieved by arranging hexagram transitions between pairs to generate fourteen instances of three and two instances of one. Fives were deliberately excluded. The fourteen threes and two ones constitute sixteen instances of an odd integer occurring out of a possible sixty-four. This is a 3:1 ratio exactly.

In addition, when the first order of difference of the King Wen sequence is graphed, it appears random or unpredictable. However when an image of the graph is rotated 180 degrees within the plane and superimposed upon itself, it is found to achieve closure at four adjacent points.

While this closure might logically be expected anywhere in the sequence, it in fact occurs at the conventional beginning and end of the sequence. While an arrangement with closure might have placed any two hexagrams opposite each other, what we in fact find is that the hexagrams opposite each other are such that the numbers of their positions in the King Wen sequence when summed is always equal to sixty-four.

Over twenty-seven thousand hexagram sequences were randomly generated by computer (all sequences having the property possessed by the King Wen sequence that every second hexagram is either the inverse or the complement of its predecessor). Of these twenty-seven-thousand-plus sequences only four were found to have the three properties of a 3:1 ratio of even to odd transitions, no transitions of value five, and the type of closure described above. Such sequences were found to be very rare, occurring in a ratio of 1 in 6,750.

For these reasons I was led to view the King Wen sequence as a profoundly artificial arrangement of the sixty-four hexagrams. Look

Figure 1

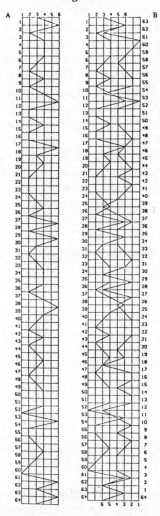

*Graphing the first order of difference of
the King Wen Sequence displays a singularity: the first and last three positions
have similar values. Thus closure occurs
at both ends of the graph when it is rotated in two dimensions and placed next
to itself.*

carefully at Figure 1. Review in your mind the steps from the King Wen
sequence that led to it. Notice that it is a complete set of the sixty-four
possible hexagrams, running both sequentially forward and backward.
Since it is composed of sixty-four hexagrams of six lines each, it is composed of 6 x 64, or 384 lines, or yao. One might make an analogy and say
that Figure 1 is to the King Wen sequence as a cube is to a square. Figure
1 is composed of the same elements as the King Wen sequence, but it has
more dimensions.

It is my assumption that the oracle-building pre-Han Chinese
viewed the forward- and backward-running double sequence of Figure
1B as a single yao, or line, and that it is therefore open to the same treat-

ment as lines are subject to in the *I Ching*, namely, multiplication by six and sixty-four. Since a hexagram has six lines, I visualized six double sequences in a linear order. But a hexagram is more than lines; a hexagram also contains two trigrams. Thus, over the six double sequences I overlaid two double sequences, each three times larger than the six double sequences. A hexagram also has an identity as a whole; thus, over the six and the two double sequences a single, larger double sequence is projected. The sets of double sequences of each level share a common point of origin and all return to a single endpoint. The resulting figure, too complex to show here, is to the original double sequence as a tesseract is to a cube, for again more dimensions have been added. This figure itself can then be imagined as a single hexagram, but one of a set of sixty-four.

The closure at the beginning and end of this figure suggested that it might be useful to model process. Its 384 subunits imply a calendar. Can it be coincidence that the length of a lunar month, 29.53 days, times 13 is 383.89? I believe that what we have here is a 384-day lunar calendar with resonances to other naked-eye astronomical phenomena known to be of interest to the ancient Chinese.

Figure 2

Permutations of I Ching Hexagrams

Base	Multiplier	Multiplicand	Astronomical unit
64 days (number of hexagrams in the *I Ching*)	× 6 (number of *yao* in a hexagram)	384 days	13 lunations
384 days	× 64 (number of hexagrams in a sequence)	67 solar years 104.25 days	6 minor sunspot cycles 11.2 years
67 solar years 104.25 days	× 64 (number of hexagrams in a sequence)	4306+ solar years	2 Zodiacal Ages 1 per trigram each 2200 years approx.
4306+ solar years	× 6 (number of *yao* in a hexagram)	25,836 solar years	1 complete precession of the equinoxes

Using standard techniques, the modular hierarchy I constructed out of Figure 1 by the method described above can be mathematically collapsed into a self-similar or fractal curve that can be used to map the unfolding of temporal variables and their resonances on all levels of duration.

In order to demonstrate this assertion it was necessary to write computer software that would allow easy manipulation of the fractal timewave and the quick comparison of various locations within it. This was done with the very skillful help of my colleague Peter Meyer, who is responsible for the computer implementation of my ideas.

Let us look at a screen, generated by computer, that shows a period of time familiar to most of us, the late fifteenth and early sixteenth

Figure 3*

135 years, from 1425 AD to 1560 AD

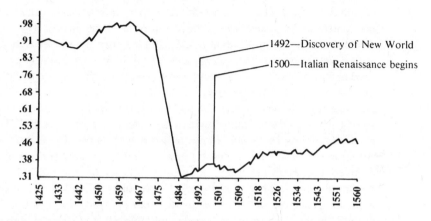

1492—Discovery of New World

1500—Italian Renaissance begins

century—a time distinguished by the invention of printing and the discovery of the New World.

It is screens such as this that are the primary experimental tools and experimental output of these ideas concerning the fractal structure of time. Here it is unnecessary to discuss the tools and options available within the software, but let us examine this small portion of the time-wave itself. The wave is shown by the wandering line. Clearly this line represents the ebb and flow of some process. But what process? My contention is that novelty is what is being portrayed. As the line moves toward the bottom of the figure, novelty is increasing; upward movement toward the top of the figure indicates a decrease of novelty. Novelty, then, is put forward as a primary term necessary to a description of any temporal system much in the way that spin, velocity, and angular momentum are primary terms necessary to the description of any physical system. Synonyms for "novelty" are "degree of connectedness" or "complexity." Note that these are not terms that make a moral judgment. Novelty is not "good" while entropy is "bad." Novelty is simply a situation of greater connectedness and complex organization, while entropy is the opposite of these qualities: it is less organized, less integrated, less complex.

I have deliberately chosen to use the word "novelty" for this concept in order to anchor these ideas in the metaphysics of Alfred North

*The values on the left of each graph (figures 3–8) are numerical quantifications of novelty. The maximum novel situation has a value of zero; hence, values tend toward zero as the end date is approached. In these graphs, the end date is assumed to be December 21, 2012 A.D.

Whitehead as presented in his *Process and Reality*. Whitehead has this to say:

> Creativity is the principle of novelty. Creativity introduces novelty into the content of the many, which are the universe disjunctively. The creative advance is the application of this ultimate principle of creativity to each novel situation which it originates. The ultimate metaphysical principle is the advance from disjunction to conjunction, creating a novel entity other than the entities given in disjunction. The novel entity is at once the togetherness of the "many" which it finds and also it is one among the disjunctive "many" which it leaves; it is a novel entity, disjunctively among the many entities which it synthesizes. The many become one, and are increased by one. In their natures, entities are disjunctively "many" in process of passage into conjunctive unity. Thus the "production of novel togetherness" is the ultimate notion embodied in the term concrescence. These ultimate notions of "production of novelty" and "concrete togetherness" are inexplicable either in terms of higher universals or in terms of the components participating in the concrescence. The analysis of the components abstracts from the concrescence. The sole appeal is to intuition. (1929, p. 26)

This notion of the ebb and flow of an invisible quality that integrates and disintegrates entities into the world is well established in Eastern thought as the idea of the Tao. What is unusual in this approach, if not unique, is the effort to give a formal mathematical description of the ebb and flow of this quality. I might have called it Tao, but I chose instead to call it novelty to stress the fact that it is process growing toward concrescence.

Within the timewave a variety of "resonance points" are recognized. Resonance points can be thought of as areas of the wave that are graphically the same as the wave at some other point within the wave, yet differ from it through having different quantified values. For example, if we choose an end date or zero date of December 21, 2012 A.D., then we find that the time we are living through is in resonance with late Roman times and the beginning of the Dark Ages in Europe.

Implicit in this theory of time is the notion that duration is like a tone in that one must assign a moment at which the damped oscillation is finally quenched and ceases. I chose the date December 21, 2012 A.D., as this point because with that assumption the wave seemed to be in the "best fit" configuration with regard to the recorded facts of the ebb and flow of historical advance into connectedness. Later I learned to my amazement that this same date, December 21, 2012, was the date assigned as the end of their calendrical cycle by the classic Maya, surely

Figure 4

4.2 years, from October 1986 to December 1990

Nov. 1988—American Presidential
Election

.0247
.0231
.0214
.0198
.0181
.0165
.0149
.0132
.0116

Oct. 1986 · Jan. 1987 · April 1987 · July 1987 · Oct. 1987 · Jan. 1988 · April 1988 · Aug. 1988 · Nov. 1988 · Feb. 1989 · May 1989 · Aug. 1989 · Nov. 1989 · Mar. 1990 · June 1990 · Sept. 1990 · Dec. 1990

Figure 5

475 AD—Final collapse of
Roman Empire

1.585
1.474
1.364
1.253
1.143
1.032
.922
.811
.701

340 · 357 · 374 · 390 · 407 · 424 · 441 · 458 · 475 · 491 · 508 · 525 · 542 · 559 · 575 · 592 · 609

one of the world's most time-obsessed cultures. However, the software that supports the timewave can accept any zero date and scale the timewave accordingly.

To see why I believe December 21, 2012 A.D., is a good candidate for the zero time, look at the wave signature for two rather long durations of time. Pay special attention to the congruence of the episodes of novelty during each duration and the way in which they are shown to be in very convincing resonance when December 21, 2012 A.D., is the common zero point.

Naturally, one cannot look at such wave signatures without wondering what the significance of the zero point is. My interpretation of the

Figure 6

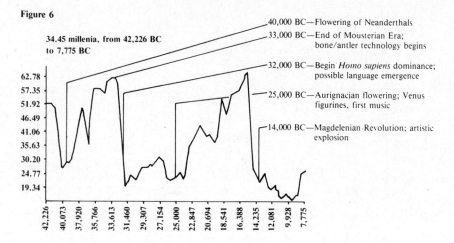

34.45 millenia, from 42,226 BC to 7,775 BC

40,000 BC—Flowering of Neanderthals

33,000 BC—End of Mousterian Era; bone/antler technology begins

32,000 BC—Begin *Homo sapiens* dominance; possible language emergence

25,000 BC—Aurignacian flowering; Venus figurines, first music

14,000 BC—Magdelenian Revolution; artistic explosion

Figure 7

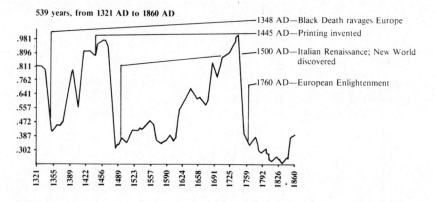

539 years, from 1321 AD to 1860 AD

1348 AD—Black Death ravages Europe

1445 AD—Printing invented

1500 AD—Italian Renaissance; New World discovered

1760 AD—European Enlightenment

Figure 8

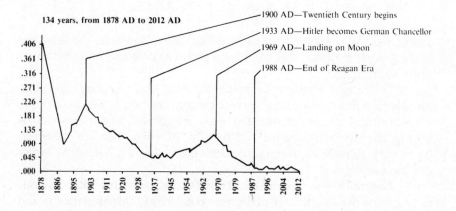

134 years, from 1878 AD to 2012 AD

1900 AD—Twentieth Century begins

1933 AD—Hitler becomes German Chancellor

1969 AD—Landing on Moon

1988 AD—End of Reagan Era

zero point is that it is the point at which the ingression into novelty and the degree of interconnectedness of the separate elements that comprise the concrescence will be such that the ontological nature of time itself will be transformed. History will end, and the transcendental object that has been drawing being into ever deeper reflections of itself since the first moments of the existence of the universe will finally be completely concrescent in the three-dimensional space–time continuum. Then the moving image of time will have discovered itself to be Eternity.[*]

---

[*] The reader who has found that this necessarily brief exposition of these ideas has whetted his or her appetite to know more should consult the book *The Invisible Landscape*, by Terence and Dennis McKenna. Readers interested in obtaining the software that allows exploration of the theory of time presented here should write for more information to Dolphin Software, 48 Shattuck Square #147, Berkeley, CA 94704.

9

Among *Ayahuasqueros*

NFORMATION flows through the multiple continuum of being, seeking equilibrium yet paradoxically carrying images of ways its flow toward entropy is locally reversed by a being or society or phenomenon. These images become concepts and discoveries. We are immersed in a holographic ocean of places and ideas. This ocean of images and the intricacy of their connections is infinite; we understand it to whatever depth we are able. This is perhaps why great genius proceeds by apparent leaps. The revolutionary idea that inspires the genius comes upon one complete and entire by itself from the ocean of speculative mind. We seek the intuitive leap that reveals the very mechanism of that other dimension. The need for such a leap for humanity will grow as we exhaust complexity in all realms save the microphysical and the psychological. At present my method is immersion in the images and self-examination of the phenomena—that is, taking psilocybin mushrooms and pondering just what this may all mean, with confidence that time will at least deepen understanding if not answer all questions.

My provisional acceptance of this view of the dimension "seen" in hallucinogenic trance approximates the worldwide "primitive" view that we are somehow comingled with a "spirit world."

Is the access to another dimension that the psilocybin mushroom makes available something so uniquely peculiar to it that it is reasonable to associate the phenomenon specifically with a single species of mushroom? Or is this strange world a thing unique to the chemical psilocy-

■■■

From *Gateway to Inner Space*, edited by Christian Rätsch (New York: Prism Books, 1989). This piece is a reflective diary of the search for *ayahuasca* that my partner Kat Harrison McKenna and I undertook in the Amazon in 1976.

bin, wherever it occurs in nature? Albert Hofmann has written in *LSD: My Problem Child* that when he presented tablets of psilocybin to the mushroom shaman of Huatla, Maria Sabina, the old *curandera* avowed, "The spirit of the mushroom is in the little pill" (1983, p.142).

In my confrontations with the personified Other that is resident in the mushroom, part of its message was its species-specific uniqueness and its desire for a symbiotic relationship with humans. At other times it presented itself not so much as a personage but as a giant network that many sorts of beings in different parts of the universe were using for their own purposes. I felt like a two-year-old child who struggles with the question, "Are there little people in the radio?" Perhaps the psilocybin-revealed dimension is a kind of network of information and images, or something even more substantial.

To answer such questions it seemed to me that it would be necessary to explore another plant hallucinogen, taxonomically unrelated to the psilocybin-containing fungi, yet chemically related to psilocybin at the level of molecular structure. The drug that I had in mind and that perfectly fits these criteria is *yagé*, or *ayahuasca*. This is a brew whose chief component is a huge jungle liana or vine, a woody creeper that attains to gigantic size in the Amazon Basin of the New World. The brews of the *Banisteriopsis* lianas have been known to science longer than have the mushroom cults of Mexico, but they are no less mysterious for that, even in today's overexplored world.

In 1851 the British botanist and explorer Richard Spruce, comrade of Alfred Russel Wallace, penetrated the upper Rio Negro Basin, heartland of Amazonas. He found the Tokanoan Indians of the Rio Vaupés using a strange drug to cause trances and prophetic divination. The drug was called *caapi*, and colorful and terrifying hallucinations were said to characterize its effects. Spruce made careful collections and later wrote: "I saw, not without surprise, that it belonged to the order *Malpighiaceae* and the genus *Banisteria*, of which I made it out to be an undescribed species and therefore called it *Banisteria caapi*" (Schultes, 1968, p. 318).

Fantastic accounts have characterized the *Banisteriopsis* drug since its discovery. The first description of the mysterious drug's effects was reported in 1858 when the explorer Villavincencio took it among the tribes of the upper Rio Napo in Amazonian Ecuador. This area is frequently implicated in reports of admixture plants, which are other plants added to the basic *Banisteriopsis* brew to strengthen the hallucinations.

Chemists who made the early attempts to isolate the alkaloids in *B. caapi* gave their compound the romantic name telepathine, reflecting the deep forest reputation of *yagé* as a genuinely telepathic drug. This is an idea most recently given impetus by F. Bruce Lamb in his *Wizard of the Upper Amazon,* in which Lamb's informant details collective trance sessions where all participants shared the same vision. So *yagé* is not without a gnosis of its own. Its has a reputation as a curing panacea and a powerful hallucinogen, bringing visions of strange cities, jungle beasts, and shamanic voyages to the heart of the Milky Way.

The great ethnobotanist Richard Evans Schultes inspired my decision to seek *ayahuasca* and to compare its experiential dimension to that of psilocybin when he wrote, "We stand merely on the threshold of our investigations into the botany, ethnology, history, pharmacology, chemistry and therapeutics of that complex of intoxicants known as *ayahuasca, caapi,* or *yagé*" (Schultes, 1968, p.12).

Our expedition to Peru would consist of just three persons: myself; Kat, who was our photographer, linguist, and botanical artist; and Richard, an old friend and a medical historian with a special interest in folk medicine and shamanistic curing. Neither Kat nor Richard had been into equatorial jungle before, but we prepared as carefully as possible and eagerly awaited the day when we would be whisked south to what we hoped would be warm jungles and high adventure.

Reality at last outran apprehension—on the morning of March 6, 1976, we arrived in Lima. As we flew south from Los Angeles that night, Comet West was impressively visible from 29,000 feet up. I took it as a good omen for our trip. Our arrival was typically rough—we were forced to linger several days in order to get our shotgun properly registered, a necessary ordeal since going unarmed into the forest only invites difficulties.

In a matter of days after arriving in Iquitos we found ourselves at the mouth of the Rio Napo, Loreto, Peru. Events moved very quickly. We unexpectedly encountered Lord Dark, nicknamed for his piercing stare. An old acquaintance of mine from Colombia, he was now a river pilot with his own boat. We accepted his offer of passage up the Napo. We, he and his female companion, and three young Germans traveled for three days before we came to the mouth of the Napo, with hopes of reaching Atun Cocha, a Yaqua village on an oxbow lake, later that day.

Our situation was an abyss of ambiguity. The strangeness of simply being in the Amazon in combination with the "chance" encounter with Lord Dark had made for a literary denseness of possibilities. I accepted the situation because hourly we moved farther up the Napo, deeper into *ayahuasca* country, and nearer to our own goals for the voyage. But I hoped we would be able to pleasantly part from this odd boatman, the same who accompanied me and my other companions nearly to La Chorrera on that previous trip into the jungle. Finally we parted company with our unkempt Charon. Fortunately we managed to part on strained good terms, so involved was he in a financial squabble with his

German passengers. The boat returned down the Napo, leaving us for the first time alone and without immediate onward transportation. We were at a small village some six hours downriver from Masan called Fancho Playa. There we dried our clothes and recovered from the ordeal of five days of cramped boat travel. The villagers had shown us a house with a sound roof and an attached cooking area, and there we were quite comfortable as we adapted and familiarized ourselves with the environs. I was disappointed in the degree of acculturation among the people living along the river. Though it is not a route of trade, traditional life-styles have either faded or moved deeper into the jungle.

The Amazon is full of reverses and surprises. Our stay in Fancho Playa was difficult. We were plagued by mosquitoes, chiggers, and biting black flies. Days of abuse by these pests brought us to long, fevered nights passed as in a waking dream. In spite of the difficulties, which were trials indeed and were to force us to new plans, we did learn that *brujos* with the ability to kill and cure and with knowledge of *ayahuasca* are common in that area. So well known are they that our informant was a child of six whom we met while walking in the forest with one of the men of the village, searching out *cumala* trees. *Cumala* is a generic term that includes the *Virola* species and related genera. We were too uncertain of how things stood to ask after *ayahuasca*.

Our difficulties with insects and dysentery forced us to reassess our first venture into the Rio Napo. There were many things we needed but did not have. Even though we had located a veritable nest of self-alleged *ayahuasqueros*, we could not do any work unless we equipped ourselves against the insects that accompanied the unseasonal persistence of the rains. Accordingly, we made plans to leave Fancho Playa shortly before dawn the next day on a *launcha* bound for Iquitos. On the eve of our departure we learned of an old woman in the village who had a knowledge of *ayahuasca*. In addition, the people with whom we shared some *aquardiente*, the local distilled alcohol, turned out to be village characters with a reputation for using *ayahuasca*. We were assured by the people that every settlement on these rivers has its own *ayahuasquero*.

After a rainy return to Iquitos and a number of days of wearing out our illness, we came to our lowest point. Our money was flowing away, and we had few hints as to where to contact anyone knowledgeable about *ayahuasca*. Finally, after several futile attempts, we were able to find someone who could point out to us the home of Manuel Cordova Rios, whose story is told in *Wizard of the Upper Amazon*. He was ninety-one but looked sixty, except for cataract-clouded eyes. He vehemently insisted that the *ayahuasqueros* of Iquitos are largely charlatans. Cordova Rios was quick to point out that it is not necessarily the deep forest Indian who is master of the *ayahuasca* knowledge—that it is simply a matter of finding someone who knows how to prepare it. He urged us to look into the Pucallpa area and gave us the name of a woman who had learned her art from him many years ago, Juana Gonzales Orbi, a leper whose affliction was arrested using jungle remedies, but not before she lost much of her hands and feet. Sr. Rios assured us that she loved to prepare *ayahuasca* for people and had helped *gringos* in the past. Since all other trails had grown cold, our meeting with Sr. Rios gave our quest a new direction. We decided to fly to Pucallpa, hoping to find this woman and to be found acceptable by her as observers.

We anticipated that a shift several hundred miles southward would shed some optimism on our somewhat illness-wearied and expense-riddled search. It was difficult amid the strain and bustle of travel to keep in mind the strangeness of the object of our search and the vision that would certainly be a part of our experience if we succeeded. Our meeting with Cordova Rios had seemed decisive, since he was the person who had described the telepathic collective trances that are a part of what we hoped to validate.

We arrived in Pucallpa shortly after dark. Our first impression was of a typical frontier town, more rough and ready than Iquitos, too raw and jumbled to have much charm. It is a sprawl of brick, mortar, and corrugated metal roof. But for its size it could be any of many river hamlets in the Amazon. No oil companies were yet active out of Pucallpa, so the clash of money and tradition was less noticeable than in Iquitos. The streets were unpaved, and we awoke the next morning to a cold rain (out of season, we were assured) that had turned the town to a sea of red mud. Our first round of inquiries was completely fruitless— whatever Juana Gonzales's situation was, it was not overly publicized. It seemed that so far our trip had been a series of wrong moves and wasted efforts. Even in Pucallpa we had no certitude that we would find what we were looking for. Yet we had decided to continue until all our money was spent if we could generate no other conclusion. We continued to hope to find an *ayahuasquero* and learn whatever we could of the craft.

After two days of fruitless searching, our morale had drifted even lower. It had remained impossible to locate Juana Gonzales, but in our search for her we inquired about other *ayahuasqueros* who might know of her. We were led to the Bar Huallaga, a country store at kilometer 12 on the highway to Lima, where we met Don Fidel Mosombite, a quiet but intense man whose home and chacra, a field of slash-and-burn cleared for growing food, were located nearby. As we climbed off the bus in the midday sun we were swept into the scene in progress on the dirt porch of the store. An older man was drunk and stood raving; first he greeted us, then sang the praises of our man, his *amigo*, a *maestro*, who sat silently nearby. "We are one blood. Today *la gente—un sangre. El maestro* brought me to my life. In Chiclayo, my home, *ayahuasca* brought no visions, but with this man . . ." And so on, very hard for me to follow.

The man we had come to see said nothing, but occasionally nodded agreement. His air of calm intelligence and disdain for the drinking going on was singular. He seemed near forty, powerfully built, his eyes so dark they appeared all pupil. My overall impression was of intelligence and self-control, nothing theatrical, nothing studied. The drunk older man told of *ayahuasca* journeys that Sr. Mosombite had made with Argentine doctors and other foreigners. The difference of the brews throughout Peru was mentioned, and I asked about the necessity of *chacruna* as part of the brew to produce visions. Sr. Mosombite confirmed this. *Chacruna* is the local term for a *Psychotria* species, *Psychotria viridis*, whose DMT potentiates intense hallucination in combination with harmine and other beta-carbolines.

Talk led to more talk, and gradually the impression grew that here was someone whose *ambiente* seemed correct for the mystery that he claimed to understand. I mused that this person, living peripherally to teeming Pucallpa and seeming an intellectual and respected professional to his peers, fit the typical profile of a shaman. We departed the small roadside bar and went alone with the *ayahuasquero* to the nearby house of the herb-dealing old woman at whose stall in a Pucallpa market we were first advised to seek Sr. Mosombite. As we walked, he openly discussed the plants we passed. "Specialities of the old woman, who grows them all near her house." Directly adjoining the house was a shed of bare-board construction, a place, we were told, where *ayahuasca* was taken every Saturday night. The room was not different from that of a small jungle church or school—it was in fact both. We talked at length with the old woman of the house and with the *ayahuasquero*. We spent the night and slept in an auditory environment of farm sounds, sounds of the nearby jungle, and the occasional passing of trucks on the highway. At the invitation of Sr. Mosombite we decided to return to take his *ayahuasca* with the group. The stress on visions led me to hope that we were closing distance with the experiences we sought in coming to Peru. The feeling then, since we had recently had so many disappointments, was one of expectation tinged with the nervousness that attends any challenging hallucinogen. If all went well we would stay with this new circle of people and gather as much plant material and information as we could. That became our firm intention.

Finally the night came when at the house of the herb woman and in the company of Don Fidel and another shaman, his nephew, we had our first *ayahuasca* experience. We arrived in the late afternoon and relaxed and made small talk until eight o'clock, when it was thoroughly dark. Then the shaman smoked a tobacco pipe of unusual construction, blowing smoke into a brown glass quart bottle that contained the *ayahuasca* and whistling through his teeth. The bottle was passed around, and we were assured that we would be sick in half an hour. Beyond slight discomfort, none of us had any stomach difficulties. We were all praised for having bodies so clean that we could hold the *ayahuasca*. Don Fidel and the old man that had been with him at our first meeting both vomited, the older man near the half hour mark and Don Fidel many hours later. At thirty minutes I felt myself slipping into a lulling numbness. My senses were alert, and I felt at ease and comfortable in the strange and unfamiliar surroundings. The singing began about ten minutes later, interwoven walls of sound by which the singer led and developed the hallucinations. As we were transported by the singing, sometimes Quechua, sometimes Spanish, sometimes monotonal chanting, hours passed.

My mood shifted from one of apprehension of a reputedly powerful psychedelic unknown to me to disappointment that the dose was apparently insufficient to trigger the anticipated flood of visions. At a pause in the singing we discussed our roughly similar states of mind with the maestros. We discussed the difficulties of a first "flight," differences of diet, or chemical poisons that might be interfering with *la purga*. Don Fidel questioned us about our drug use. Did we know marijuana? We described our devotion to cannabis and mushrooms and drew praise for our habit of taking only plant drugs. We again drank the *ayahuasca*. It was suggested that perhaps marijuana would help us concentrate on the *ayahuasca* even as the tobacco helped them to do so. We had previously been too uncertain of ourselves to smoke, but in a moment I hauled out our Oaxacan pollen and sent it around. Don Fidel abstained; his nephew Don Jose held his toke down and, eyes running tears, proclaimed it truly *fuerte*. We put the candle out and again the song-induced walls of nearly visible sound enwrapped us. Hours after the beginning of the trip, my mind, relaxed by the familiar taste of cannabis, flowed out into a hallucination-filled space. The synergistic effect of smoking cannabis is apparently necessary for deep rushes of visionary images on lower doses of *ayahuasca*, as it is with other hallucinogens. The singing showed the way through the billowing hypnagogia. I roved and scanned like a swimming fish caught in a spiral dance in a sea of tryptamine images, the mundane and the unimaginable crowding for my attention.

One moment among many of that first *ayahuasca* night is amusing to relate. In the nearly absolute darkness of our meeting place the singing was occasionally punctuated by popping mouth noises, strange expulsions of air. At one point I heard a low puff of air and immediately felt a sharp tingling on my right hand. I looked down and had the visual and tactile sensation of a blue tingling circle of light on my hand. I reached for the center of the sensation, expecting a sliver or quill. The thought of curare came and went in my mind, triggering a mild alarm easy to talk myself out of. But the sensation remained and grew: a spinning disc of blue foil hanging incandescent in the dark, growing larger, then gradually fading. It was a vision, of course, but it is not impossible that the sensation was caused by something like a *tsentsek*, a psychophysical power carrier moved by the will, and perhaps by the breath, of the shaman.

Don Fidel and his nephew are shamans who understand the vegetable psychedelics as a means to explore and understand the mechanics of the mind. Don Fidel especially seemed without elitism or any wish to obscure what he knew. They both unhesitatingly answered our every question. "Where are the old wild *ayahuasca* plants in virgin forest?" "At kilometer 29 and 32" was their open reply. What about admixture plants besides *chacruna*? Don Jose recognized my description of *Diploteris cabrerana*. He did not call it *oco-yagé* but knew it as *puca huasca*, and said he would try to get some. He was concerned that our hallucinations were not clear and definite. "We must concentrate on Jesus Christ," he said. "Concentrate on the fecund white stone filled with light." He knew a woman in Yarina Cocha who had *puca huasca*, a plant we would later explore in order to learn to cure.

The songs continued for many hours, songs declaiming the shaman's perceptions that we, like them, were sound and healthy, good persons for *ayahuasca*. There were songs for absent persons with problems; a song for a young woman present to have the dark effects of some dubious but unspecified act expunged; songs of marijuana, another curing plant to explore; songs of oration, invocation, and prayer. There were even songs asking the Lord to move the hearts of patients to pay their bills; these latter on the part of Don Jose, the nephew.

We paid 300 *soles* or six dollars for the songs of the *medicos* and for the *ayahuasca* itself. In Yarina Cocha, raw *ayahuasca* is 250 *soles* per kilo and *chacruna* is 150 *soles* per kilo. We were happy to divert our money from the overpriced accommodations of Pucallpa into the rural people's hands. They understood our sincerity and limitations. There was a sense of shared approach and of different kinds of understanding mutually reinforcing each other. "The understanding that comes from understanding" was a phrase that I heard in my mind many times that first *ayahuasca* night. It is a description of the gnosis that plant psychedelics bring; a standing within things yet somehow beyond them, an eidetic reduction that transcends subject and object. The *ayahuasca* way of understanding was opened before us. Though that night we only lightly brushed the power of *ayahuasca*, after I was able to relax I felt that, given sufficient opportunities, we would eventually be able to make our way deeply into the mystery.

The next day we would make collections of other medicinal plants, and on Saturday, two days later, we would photograph every stage in the preparation of a new batch of *ayahuasca* and again voyage with it that night. Eventually a number of possibilities would loom. We hoped to make a pilgrimage to an old wild grandfather plant in the forest. An attempt would be made to collect and try various admixture plants. The shaman claimed to be familiar with the use of the mushroom, although he preferred *ayahuasca*. Is the use of the psilocybin mushroom in the Pucallpa region a traditional folkway? Is it something learned recently from travelers familiar with the Mexican Indian use of the mushrooms? How long has the mushroom been taken in Peru? Is it possible it antedates the introduction of *Stropharia* in the New World? Is it possible that its use is pre-Conquest? If the latter, then it is the first time such an ancient folk use of psilocybin mushrooms has been suspected in South America, or anywhere outside of Mexico. These are fascinating questions, and the possibility exists of finding some concrete answers. Many experiences and much work lay ahead, but having found the path of *ayahuasca* and having been judged fit to follow it, we were filled with high anticipation of the things to be learned and seen in the weeks ahead. Our job was to refine our powers of observation so that we would make as much of the opportunity as possible.

Pucallpa is far more a jungle outpost than is Iquitos. Iquitos had a large mestizo population, while Pucallpa is a city built by the indigenous people as their population center. Such conditions explain the flourishing of jungle folkways in a modern rural and urban situation. *Ayahuasca* curing is deeply embedded in and respected by the mestizo culture. It flourishes among and is pursued experientially and intelligently by those who know and preserve the ancient New World *ayahuasca* cult.

It may be that the South American *yagé/ayahuasca* complex is the largest psychedelic cult in the world. From Panama to Bolivia, from the Pacific coast to deep into Brazil, these visions are regularly sought out, individual practitioners making their reputations on the quality of their brews, chants, and cures. Like all shamanic practices, the *ayahuasca* cult is the creation of highly individual personalities. For this reason, simple laboratory analysis of drug samples will not dispel the air of real mystery surrounding *ayahuasca*.

Ayahuasca is as good as the person who makes it is meticulous and demanding. The culture of rural Peru faces a shattered past and a turbulent future. The fate of the *ayahuasca* mystery hangs tremulously in the balance while at the collective level the culture gropes toward a decision to repress or reinforce the institution of hallucinogenic shamanism.

To truly understand *ayahuasca* would take years, for there are as many forms of *ayahuasca* as there are *Banisteriopsis* varieties plus admixtures. Local variations in ingredients and procedure should be systematically studied. It is an important task, reserved for one who wishes to give order to a particularly disordered set of ethnopharmacological issues. My own interest is the vision state and the contact dimension per se. I want to investigate these compounds as a means to those ends. For that, the tryptamine hallucinogens remain the most effective and impressive investigative tools that I am aware of. With them one can find oneself in the center of energies that lie present at hand but are normally unseen, pure image and imagination unconstrained by any limitations. The hallucinations are not limited to visions of a type or color or tone. It is as open a modality as, literally, it is possible to imagine.

The quality that permeated associating with the shaman Don Fidel was, at its best, a sense of mutual colleagueship. He was reverent in the face of the lux natura that his mystery revealed, but his understanding was that the operational basis of the experience was biochemical, subject to manipulation and open to theory making and shared collective validation. The *ayahuasqueros* are true technicians of psychedelic sacrality. Their approach—awed self-experiment and accumulation of a corpus of techniques experienced as valid—is no different from our own. Any approach that excludes these qualities will be too removed from the subject matter to offer a useful description. This is why anthropologists often miss the point. We should admit that we know no more of the topology of the collective unconsciousness than any other culture. No one is more knowledgeable in these things than a sincere person of any background can choose to become. It is shamanic personalities, grand exploring souls, who somehow rise above or find themselves beyond any but a universal set of values; they explore the deep waters of our collective being. They show the way, and to be with them is to be near the cutting edge. Shamanism in Peru is like European alchemy in that it utilizes psychic involvement in matter, but European alchemy became entrapped in a fascination with metals and purified elements. Psychedelic shamanism more happily centers its attention on living matter, specifically plants, where alkaloids and other biodynamic constituents congenial to the primate nervous system are encountered. *Ayahuasca* is such a plant, and its alchemy, jungle alchemy, is an immense panacea to those who use it regularly.

Hoping to observe the cooking of a batch of *ayahuasca*, we arranged to meet with Don Fidel early one morning at his home. Though we arrived an hour late, for unclear reasons he expressed amazement that we had made our way to his home so early. "Anyway," he told us, "it has not been possible to get *chacruna*, so there can be no cooking." He was not abrupt, and apparently that evening's *ayahuasca* session would still be held with previously prepared brew, which is supposedly good for six months—an *ayahuasca* vine being kept alive by being buried in wet sand. Don Fidel showed us a sprout-covered sandy stick that his child brought from nearby. We asked about *puca huasca*, which we assumed to be *Diploteris cabrerana*, and were unsettled when Don Fidel dismissed it as "food for dogs." When questioned he would say only that it was "too bizarre" and "not fit for Christians." When we had mentioned it to Don Jose he only said that he knew a woman in Yarina who could get it. Could this woman have been the mysterious Juana Gonzales Orbi? When questioned, Don Jose agreed in essence with Don Fidel that *puca huasca* (*D. cabrerana*) is too strong to use for curing. He also called it *comida del perro* (food for dogs), but it was less clear whether this was an expression of contempt or an actual description of some folk belief about the plants.

My attitude toward what we were and still are trying to find out is like that of a detective. We must simply work our way through each lead, each possibility, separating the wheat from the chaff. Does this rural *ayahuasca*-curing scene reflect the presence of practitioners who truly understand, control, and voyage into the borderland world that classical shamanism insists exists and whose parameters we are trying to define? A possible and unexpected conclusion that I can imagine now emerging from our trip to Peru is that while we can discover and even to some degree penetrate rural systems of psychedelic healing, we shall find it very hard to find people who look beyond the curing power to ask what is its basis and what is the meaning of hallucinogen-induced visions generally. The *ayahuasca* takers observe other worlds in space and time in their visions, but they feel a different sort of involvement in understanding what this may mean or in testing to validate what they believe. At the edge of things, where the really intense DMT-caused visions occur, it is hard for the shaman's personality not to be dissolved in a more primitive reaction of fear and unthinking awe. The curing shaman will not seek experiences in such titanic landscapes, and the researching shamanic explorer must step lightly, testing epistemological equipment at every step. Such a one is hard to find, since such a person will proceed by some theory of activity, and theories, especially concerning such arcane matters, do not travel well from one language to another.

I am left to conclude that we must remain our own guides into those still-elusive dimensions, more unexplored than we had previously imagined. This is what I have done for years, since each effort to find a preexisting tradition that made complete sense of the shamanic dimension as I personally know it has been less than successful. It may be that possession of pure chemicals in combination with collected living plants and the collected available data of ethnography put one in a better position to gain an overall sense of the importance of psychedelic visions than can be gotten from any particular informant, limited necessarily by adaptation to a single approach. What I really wish to know is whether we are alone at the edge of these mysteries, or whether there is a tradition of the hyperdimensions of gnosis. If the latter is true, what happens to one who gains admittance to its mysteries?

A hot and muggy equatorial afternoon found us awaiting with anticipation our second opportunity to take *ayahuasca*. We had moved to the home of the old woman where our first session took place. With our dwindling funds we were only too happy to accept living space and escape the tremendously inflated hotel prices in Pucallpa. The hospitality of the people was limitless, but the heat and the biting insects, about which we could do nothing, remained to wear us down.

The regular Saturday night *ayahuasca* session was canceled because our friends were unable to obtain *chacruna*, the *Psychotria* admixture. This disappointed many people, some of whom had come from Lima by bus. Conversation in the wake of that disappointment brought out the opinion that *chacruna* grew and could be obtained at kilometer 29—the same area where Don Jose indicated that the very old uncultivated *Banisteriopsis caapi* vines grow. We determined to make a trip there.

We spent a day in search of the admixture plant. We took a bus to kilometer 34 and arranged to purchase a substantial amount the following Sunday. Then, hoping to find a small supply to tide us over until then, we walked six kilometers off the main road on the road to Nueva Requena to the home of Don Fidel's uncle Don Juan. Don Juan occupies the elder uncle position in relation to Don Fidel, even as Don Fidel occupies the same position relative to Don Jose. At Don Juan's we were shown and allowed to photograph several small *chacruna* plants. They had been grown from cuttings and did not appear to be doing well. Perhaps these plants were in too dry a location, for according to the two dons, *chacruna* grows best in wet, swampy lowland. They were slow growing and were short. Don Juan also posed proudly with a meter-long piece of *ayahuasca*, almost as tall as he was. It had been gathered in primary forest some distance from his home; the old, wild-growing plants are preferred.

After we left Don Juan's and had stopped for a beer at the Bar Huallaga, Don Fidel held forth on many subjects: the sin of inducing abortions, the relations of some *curanderos* to God and of some to the devil. Don Fidel emphasized a kind of Manichaean view of good and evil in which the world is a mixture of things, some of which belong to God and some to the devil. Man has two bodies, one visible and associated with the physical and one invisible and associated with mind and thought. This second body is not destroyed by death, and it is the part of the shaman that cures and sees. Strange how close to the worldview of the *Corpus Hermeticum* his ideas are.

One morning, having slept well, we set off for Yarina, hoping to observe Don Jose making *ayahuasca*. We found him settled back with a couple of lady patients. Possibly they were smoking marijuana when we arrived, as there was some scrambling upon which Don Jose's monkey gazed restlessly. *Ayahuasca* was simmering in a shed not far away.

Don Jose gave us some *chacruna* leaves that he had managed to get to give to Don Fidel, and thus it was that we saw mature *chacruna* foliage at last. Its rubiaceous nature was clear, and the berries were about three-sixteenths of an inch in diameter and waxy green, just as Schultes had described. We obtained voucher specimens. Don Jose pointed out a taxonomic feature that he considered unique to *chacruna:* a double line of budlets or merestigmatic nodes that stud the underside of each mature leaf. Perhaps this has not been noticed before.

Events were punctuated by discussion whenever we spent time with Don Fidel. This particular day he was full of cosmology and metaphor. We further discussed *puca huasca*, and I learned that not all visions are human visions; some that are meaningless to human beings are visions meant for animals. *Puca huasca* carried the vision best understood by dogs. Though he may have been pulling our leg a bit with this, the traditional avoidance of *Diploteris cabrerana* is curious. Meanwhile, the *chacruna* market is booming—a kilo packet costs 250 soles. Apparently *chacruna* grows well only in wet lowland, and those lucky enough to have a source sell it at a dear price to less fortunate *ayahuasqueros*.

It was on that same excursion to Yarina that we ran to ground the search for Juana Gonzales Orbi. We inquired after her in a part of Yarina that we were told on a previous visit was her home, but the trail was cold. The good woman had been away for four months and was not expected soon. We spoke with her middle-aged brother and learned that she now practices out of Tingo Maria and travels between there and Lima. It appeared that Juana Gonzales Orbi was not to be encountered on this visit.

On April 7 we had another try at Don Jose's *ayahuasca*. Again, while there was a buildup of psychedelic potential, there was no outbreak of deep visions. Several people complained of the weak brew. This session ended any further dealings with Don Jose, for he was apparently not really able to prepare *ayahuasca*, even though he had the traditional recipes and materials. He represents the vitiated tradition. Financial success, or more properly the search for it, has caused him to forget the basics. *Ayahuasca* is in large measure dependent for its strength on the even and smooth rhythm of preparation. Don Jose is slapdash, and hence his *purga* is *el poco purga*, as Don Fidel said. It is Don Fidel's expectation that when the *ayahuasca* is made properly, there is no difficulty in getting off. We were eager to try Don Juan's brew. We had tried just a sip on our visit to his house, and it certainly tasted stronger than any other we had been offered.

During this time we were definitely moving closer to Don Fidel and his uncle and away from the *sobrino* (nephew), Don Jose, who was younger, eager, and, as Don Fidel said, "ambitious." Don Jose eventually went off to Lima on a reputation-building errand and so faded as naturally as did Juana Gonzales. Thus we were left with the older, poorer, more rural of the *ayahuasqueros* we had met. Both Don Fidel and Don Juan gave us a feeling of solidity and trustworthiness. We had really yet to get to know Don Juan, who on our first visit to his home showed us harvested *ayahuasca* and young *chacruna* bushes. With Don Fidel we had long, groping talks. He sees his immediate surroundings as transformed. He lives in "an earthly paradise," and the muddy trail winding past his thatched home is "the path that Christ walked on earth." He says he leads a clean life and can cure—it is his gift. His real interest is the invisible body that persists after death and that is the mental vehicle of those who travel on *ayahuasca*. This is an idea that I relate to the modern notion of UFOs.

A day was spent with Don Fidel at his house watching and photographing how he prepares his *ayahuasca*. The *chacruna* is placed at the bottom of a two-gallon enameled metal pot and is covered by pieces of *ayahuasca* that have been crushed by being beaten with a hardwood club against a log. The crushed stems, some nearly two inches in diameter, are arranged in layers until the pot is filled; then the material is covered with water and boiled, none too gently, until the volume of water appears to be cut in half. The plant material is then removed, and the remaining liquid, perhaps one and a half quarts, is poured into a smaller pot to cool while the larger, now empty, enameled pot is refilled with a load of *chacruna*, *ayahuasca*, and water, exactly as before. This second load is boiled down just as the first was. The two liquid fractions are combined in the enamel pot, and the boiling down continues until about one liter of café au lait–colored liquid is obtained. Sometimes the *ayahuasca* is further refined to a paste. Don Fidel's brew is twice as dark as the rather weak beverage prepared by Don Jose.

There came a day in April that began with the realization that Kat and I were ill with salmonella. Our hope was to hold our guts sufficiently together to be able to do justice to the *ayahuasca* that we had seen prepared the day before at Don Fidel's house. Since the brew was twice as dark as the other *ayahuasca* brews we had seen, I hoped that it would be twice as strong. We arranged to have two liters of *ayahuasca* prepared for us, it being our hope that analysis of this and of our sample of each brew we encountered would give us an idea, once back in the United States, of their nearness to the ethnopharmacological ideal. In spite of our two ambiguous experiences, I was hopeful that we would find a compelling psychedelic dimension in the next experience of *ayahuasca*.

While Don Fidel was brewing, a man stopped by for some medical consultation. When the subject changed to *ayahuasca* the visitor avowed that he had taken it and had "seen nothing." Since it is regarded as a health restorative as well as a hallucinogen, seeing visions seems to be the icing on the cake for many who occasionally take *ayahuasca*— while for us hallucinations are a sine qua non.

The factors that had previously impeded our getting off were perhaps minor: the dose may have been insufficient or we may have been resisting the effects, unconsciously unwilling to allow ourselves the psychic vulnerability that would accompany getting wildly intoxicated with a room full of unfamiliar people. I leaned to the idea that the dose was insufficient, and later events proved that true.

We took *ayahuasca* five times with the shamans of Pucallpa, the third time using *ayahuasca* made by Don Fidel and doled out by him. This time Kat and Richard got psychedelically stoned. By their testimony, the brew worked. I, on the other hand, spent a very hot, sticky night meditating on the threshold of an intense psychedelic experience. Because of the rigid control of the dose by the shamans, it is nearly impossible for a person of large stature to get an effective dose. There is nothing to be done in such a situation, but it was ironic to unwillingly become a mere spectator to the drug experience in which I had hoped to participate and for which I had come so far.

On the day following that evening we went with Don Fidel to kilometer 29 to collect *ayahuasca*, with hopes of getting voucher specimens of the plants comprising the brew. We found the *ayahuasca*. It was a grand specimen—several vines twisted into a cable nearly eight inches in diameter. But it was tragically damaged. A ten-foot section had been removed between where the plant left the ground and the highest point that a standing person could reach with a machete. Nearly all of the hundreds of pounds of *ayahuasca* above the cut were so dried out as to be deemed useless. Nonetheless, we managed to fill a burlap bag with this low-quality material. We had found the ancient *Banisteriopsis*, only to find it vandalized.

Because of the size and growth conditions of the *Banisteriopsis* plant, it is very difficult to introduce it into new areas or indeed even to preserve it in areas where it is now indigenous. Because so much biomass is necessary for the *ayahuasca* brew, *Banisteriopsis* species are particularly susceptible to being overharvested and often therefore are in short supply. These huge old vines are certainly growing rarer and rarer around population centers, and those who use them must inevitably seek farther and farther afield, which presages a day when their scarcity will seriously threaten the *ayahuasca* cults.

Many of the early and uncertain reports of *ayahuasca*'s effectiveness have been due, I believe, to the higher body weight of explorers relative to the body weights of their hosts. Of the brews we took, only Don Fidel's had been truly effective. All of the inferior *ayahuasca* that we saw was an opaque liquid looking like well-milked coffee that did not settle or clear, while Don Fidel's brew was a rich coffee color that after a day or so settled out and became a clear, dark tea- or amber-colored liquid. How did these other brews manage to appear so different, since Don Fidel's method of preparation appears as direct and simple as one could imagine? I suspect that since *ayahuasca* is sold by the bottle, these other practitioners are very lax. They fail to boil off excess water to obtain a really effective concentration. The proper preparation of *ayahuasca* may well be a dying art.

What we see is a tradition growing vitiated and sterile before our eyes. People here brew and take *ayahuasca* regularly, but rarely is it prepared with sufficient care and at sufficient concentrations to allow one to enter trance on the dose apportioned out at a curing meeting. So the usual story is one of exaggerated claims and minimum effectiveness. All these difficulties are only compounded for a person with an above-average body weight. As a consequence, outsiders have given, and continue to give, very different descriptions of the effects.

Mysteries abounded at even the most mundane level. Don Juan arrived late one afternoon, expecting to share with us the bottle of *ayahuasca* we had paid him to prepare and that had served as an untapped reserve bottle at our last session with Don Fidel's brew. No one had seen that bottle since that evening, everyone assuming that Don Fidel had transported it to his house. Such was not the case, so grave suspicion came to rest on the *sobrino*, Don Jose. He had slouched into the session late, sung badly and loudly and against everyone else's song, and left in the early morning hours without a word to anyone. Don Juan was certain that the *sobrino* had stolen the missing bottle. He rushed to Don Fidel's and confronted him, saying that Don Fidel's practice was in disarray and that taking on the *sobrino* had been a mistake. It may have been that Don Fidel, for reasons unclear, was very reluctant to expel his nephew from the *ayahuasca* sessions. The fate of the missing bottle was obscure enough, though we could not even be sure that the outrage would rid us of the presence of the *sobrino*.

Don Juan finished his description of his visit to Don Fidel's and then promised that Friday, Good Friday, we would do a bottle that he would prepare. Naturally, we agreed; we always availed ourselves of every opportunity to take the brew. Kat was eager to advance into it, and I, while holding no great hopes for any particular occasion, still hoped to experience the full effects of *ayahuasca* before we departed.

At Don Fidel's house we prepared two kilos of the concentrated *ayahuasca* honey to take with us to the States for use there. This cooking project occupied the better part of three days. Don Fidel prepared four enormous pots, each boiled three hours and drained, then combined and reduced to two liters. At its conclusion we had a material of which, we were later to learn, two tablespoons was sufficient for visions. My own point of view had improved during this cooking, since I found respite from a wracking bout of salmonella that left me weakened but still game.

In that rather calmer moment between bouts of illness and *ayahuasca* taking, I assessed what we had accomplished. We had been accepted into a particular *ayahuasca*-taking circle and had enough exposure to the brew to know that effectiveness depends entirely on the care used in making it and on the knowledge and personality of the shaman-chemist. The person we met who brewed best was the person to whom we were closest. He seemed to hold nothing back in matters of locating and identifying plants or in making the brew. For him the heart of *la ciencia* lay in the mystery of the songs and the cures, and of these things we were very ignorant. But we were free to return and to learn as much as we wished to absorb. Don Fidel knows well the correct way to prepare *ayahuasca*, and this in itself is a great secret today. He doubtless knows much more that he would share over time.

Even at that time, without having yet felt the full effects of *ayahuasca*, there were nevertheless things I noticed that seemed to set it apart from other hallucinogens. As it comes on it is mildly anesthetic, so that the rush is not accompanied by restlessness or any sense of energy moving up the spine. Rather, the visions appear without any particular somatic effect accompanying them. Generally, except for the vomiting it sometimes triggers, *ayahuasca* seems very smooth, with a very pleasant comedown that leaves one invigorated instead of exhausted. In the initial rush it is like DMT; later it exhibits the long, coherent visions that make its reputation unique. The experience of curing, the vast landscapes, and the communication at a distance are effects that have made *ayahuasca* legendary.

Don Fidel had said to us in essence that we should use well the many *ayahuasca* trips he was making available to us to take home. If, after thirty or more trips, we had been carried to a place where we wished to learn more, then we should return here. He was wise to urge us to explore *ayahuasca* against the background of our own culture and expectations. For all the interest that the shamanic performances we had witnessed had held for us, they had necessitated that we behave as spectators; yet real understanding of *ayahuasca* doubtlessly comes from entering into it as a participant. This can only be done by repeated and careful observation, once in a familiar environment and free to experiment with dosage, setting, and other parameters.

Don Fidel finished cooking the large batch of *ayahuasca* that we had contracted for. And we made reservations to return to California, thus setting an end to our period of field exploration into the phenomenon of *ayahuasca*. Once in California we would be able to examine the effects of the brew away from the setting that is its natural home and in the setting that is our home. Purists might object, but recurring bouts of salmonella and various water fevers endemic to jungle Peru had nearly broken our hold on health. These things cannot be avoided when one lives as the people live. And of course, we had no resistance acquired through long exposure to these diseases. The situation in Amazonian Peru is as funky as I found rural Nepal in 1969, the previous record holder in these matters. Don Fidel seemed in agreement with our decision to depart. He knew we would be better able to gauge the personal importance of *ayahuasca* once we had taken fifteen or twenty flights inside the normal flow and structure of our lives.

There were many around less sympathetic to *gringos* than Don Fidel. He had really risen to a universal humanism in his dealings with people. He invited us to return and allowed himself to boast of strange, strong brews he knows how to prepare. What few details could be gotten about these imply no known drugs and so are especially tantalizing. "Next time," said Don Fidel, "when you are familiar with *ayahuasca* and have your tape recorder."

We had hoped to duplicate the *ayahuasca* brew in California from *Banisteriopsis* plants that we had under cultivation there. But if, as the *ayahuasqueros* maintain, the plants must be at least five years old to produce the desired effect, then we were naive to take this approach. Perhaps these plants as cultivars in temperate-zone greenhouses will remain merely scientific curiosities and cannot ever become the source of a substantial amount of *ayahuasca*. Probably only a synthetic duplication of *ayahuasca* compounded with the correct percentages of DMT and beta-carbolines will ever make the experience available outside the area where it is endemic.

Hallucinogens reveal to the human psyche holographic images from all parts of our continuum. Though humanity as a whole may not yet be able to integrate these images by undergoing evolutionary waves of advancement, our role as investigators is to immerse ourselves in this revelation of atemporal images. We need to make deep voyages through clear mind space to contemplate the source of these mysteries. This is what was elusive during our trip in Peru—the turbulence of physical travel made the crystalline mental dimensions we sought all the more distant. In Peru we lived the life, saw the plants, met the people, and shared all the joys and discomforts—but this, however it may seem, was not fieldwork. True fieldwork for us meant being psychedelically ecstatic and at play in the fields of the Lord in search of the shamanic dimension where contact with the Other is likely.

Once back and among familiar things, we could more clearly make comparisons and distinctions. Hallucinogens are a finite set of compounds, and by acquiring experience of the effects of the various chemically possible hallucinogens it is possible to zero in on those compounds most reactive with one's own highly individualistic set of physical drug receptors. Thus we can slowly learn the chemical route to just that set of effects most personally useful and beautiful. Obviously this cannot be taught, but must be learned through persistence in attempting to define the self in the hallucinogenic dimension. Probably no two routes are the same—and different people have different methods, though they may use the same plant or substance. Finally, it is the person and his or her unique place in nature and time that determines the depth of the vision vouchsafed. Many have sought to understand the way in which persons and families evolve special drug receptors and thus special relationships to certain botanical drugs. Choosing an ally means finding a physiologically neutral way of repeatedly triggering the ecstatic mind state in which contact with the alien modality is possible.

We anticipated something special at the gathering on the night of Holy Saturday. Both Don Fidel and Don Juan would be bringing bottles, and the *sobrino* would not be present. There would be enough *ayahuasca* for everyone to have a proper dose. It was to be our last opportunity to take *ayahuasca* in its native setting. The experience nearly ten days in the past had given way to a calm awaiting of whatever this last experience would be. I had given up anticipating the content of these experiences. I was interested, almost as an outsider, in whether before we departed Pucallpa we would meet the visions.

Our fourth *ayahuasca* trip made many things appear more clear, and a few things less so. Both Kat and I managed to get off, though she less than the previous time. My deepest immersion in hallucination occurred that night, a full-field hallucination of a kind of flowing magenta liquid. It seemed very promising but then slowly faded away as quickly as it had appeared. A few minutes later I walked outside to get some fresh air, and to my surprise I became suddenly sick. I thought that this would surely be followed by an intense wave of hallucinations, but nothing as strong as the first magenta wave was repeated. I was pleasantly, somatically stoned. I affirmed to Don Fidel that it was good, and he seemed gratified. There is no doubt that one can take flight with Don Fidel's brew if one is free to increase the dosage until the connection is achieved.

That night I glimpsed a set of issues not explainable by the social context in which the brew is taken, adumbrations of the idea that there is a vast difference between naturally occurring, one-plant, full-spectrum hallucinogens and prepared hallucinogens, even if the latter are compounded of local plant materials. The unprepared, naturally occurring drug is a mystery, stabilized in the genetic component of the plant itself. The composition of the active compound remains virtually the same over thousands of years—untroubled and uncompromised by the migrations, epidemics, and vicissitudes that occasionally disrupt the society of its practitioners.

The case of a difficult-to-prepare combination drug is quite different. For the tradition to remain intact, the correct understanding must be preserved and handed on. In such a case the plants themselves lose some of their mystery, and that mystery is transferred to the persons who prepare and control the power of the drug. Thus the way is open for a cult of personality to intrude itself between the hallucinogen and the practitioner. The efficacy of a preparation may last only as long as the lifetime of the practitioner, and the mystery becomes a hollow sham if the drug is not correctly made.

The night's imagery was drifting and incoherent, comparable to the effects of a small amount of mescaline. *Ayahuasca* seemed a hallucinogen with less of the internally self-organized quality that characterizes mushroom psilocybin, which seems to show that the psilocybin experience is not so much self-exploration as an encounter with an organized Other. I don't know whether this is a distinction most people in my situation would make or whether my long and intense involvement with the mushrooms has allowed me, almost without realizing, to develop an empathy so deep that it has become for me another personality— not a chemical substance at all. Though this question hinges on a number of subjective factors, it is an important one to answer. It has implications for another question: whether we are pursuing a phenomenon uniquely personal and therefore forever private, or whether there is a special mental experience encountered at great depth in the psychedelic experience that is qualitatively different and truly hyperdimensional.

The encounter with the Other seems to occur in fairly deep water. Shamans, at least the *ayahuasca* shamans, are quick to call such autonomous power complexes evil or demonic. Their approach to *ayahuasca*

is usually to dose themselves so as to only slightly exceed the hallucinogenic threshold. The more disorienting and profound forms of intoxication are kept out of the ceremonies we have seen, probably because these
are social events and some sort of collective ambience must be maintained. And certainly these states are strange—they are not mere phan-
tasms drifting before closed eyes, but complete immersions in higher
topological manifolds and experiences potentially incomprehensible or
frightening. Individuals may take power to themselves by boldly, even
recklessly, exploring these dimensions, but even though these places are
the heart and soul of shamanism, they are too numinous and energy-
laden to be accessible through a tradition. Instead they must be personally discovered in the depths of the psychedelically intoxicated soul. It
almost requires a modern mentality—or great courage alone—to probe
this area unflinchingly, for it is the demon-haunted bedrock of being.

Our trip to Peru and our experiences with *ayahuasca* convince me
that even with our modern methods of scientific analysis it is going to
take courage to understand what these plants show. We have reached
the point where we must accept all responsibility for the direction we
follow and then go alone without the comforting delusion that what we
are trying to define is not unique and unprecedented. These are the
realms of chaos into which one can go only as deep as one's understanding shows the way. We each have different capacities to understand and
different forces driving us toward or away from these mysteries; finally,
when one finds the edge of what one knows and even the edge of what
anyone knows, then perhaps one has reached the point where the real
contact begins.

Immense novelty is not something guarded by a shamanic guild
that understands what it guards. Rather, all groups that claim certain
knowledge of anything are shams. Science and religion are such shams.
Novelty is unguarded because its domain is everywhere. It presses in on
the seeker often most obtrusively when he is furthest from the secrets
that tight-fisted lineages hover over. The power of the Other is humbling
and magnificent, but because it cannot be bent into power in this world,
priestcraft turns away from it. It is the "thrown away knowledge" of the
Luis Senyo Indians of Baja California. It is only seeing and knowing. It
informs the blessed and abides with them. It is the Logos, the faint outlines of humanity's evolving Overmind casting the enormous shock
wave of its shadow out over the chaotic centuries that immediately pre-
cede its rising out of the long cosmic night of human hopes to end profane history.

Under the effects of *ayahuasca* I often found myself reflecting on
the phenomenology of the hallucinatory state in general. While the literature speaks of the effects of hallucinogenic drugs as lasting for hours, in

my experience it is actually only the peripheral effects that endure so long. The period of intense visual activity behind closed eyelids lasts more nearly forty minutes to an hour, almost as though the episode of hallucination corresponded to the temporary perturbation of some brain subsystem by the presence of the psychoactive compound. As soon as the brain is able to enzymatically respond to damp the drug-induced perturbation, the episode of hallucination ends, though other somatic effects may persist for some time. Hallucinations are in part neural phenomena accompanying an internal fluctuation of the brain state of an organism. This internal fluctuation is of an extraordinary sort, since it is of a quantum-mechanically delicate enough order to be partially influenced by will and cognition.

A few days before we left Peru and at Don Fidel's wife Rosabina's urging, we asked Don Fidel about the possibility of taking *ayahuasca* once more. He seemed completely amenable to the notion, so we scheduled the event for the next evening. We would use the same bottle that had been drawn from at the last session.

This would be our fifth *ayahuasca* voyage in three weeks—an unusually intensive exposure for most hallucinogens, but *ayahuasca*, aside from causing vomiting, seems to have no adverse side effects. In fact, each day following a session I felt clarified and revitalized. Such is not the case with the frequent use of other hallucinogens. *Ayahuasca* seems benign in the body, but perhaps at higher doses this would be less true. Psilocybin is also benign upon early exposure, but done at the frequency we had been doing *ayahuasca* even it would be followed by aching muscles and enervation on the following day.

Our fifth trip occurred in the same situation as the others; semipublic and in the shed directly adjoining Sra. Angulo's house. Nothing radically different could be expected—all the constraints of the earlier sessions were in force. On that last *ayahuasca* voyage an event occurred that has returned to my mind again and again. We were joined that last night for the second time by a man who was an aficionado of *ayahuasca*. He had spent some time on the Rio Negro and in Brazil, always pursuing the better brew. He sang a song—which he described as *de los brassleros*—that was almost a miracle. Through the rhyme and rhythm each word seemed to have a galaxy of relationship to all the words around it. Long warbling runs alternated with pleasing whimsical stops and glides. Some Indian languages sound as close to the tryptamine glossolalia as anything I have encountered. It was high art— a rupture of the mundane plane.

These *ayahuasca* experiences seemed to have resolved themselves into a series of perspective-widening disillusions. During my last voyage with Don Fidel I was not sick and became approximately as intoxicated as on the previous two trips. The dose stuck with me all night long, but again the period of even mild hallucination could not have lasted more than fifteen minutes. After we returned to Berkeley we would find that a larger dosage level of *ayahuasca* delivered the experience we had expected from *ayahuasca* in its jungle habitat. The shamanic curing context is perhaps not the ideal context for determining the parameters of any hallucinogen.

On the brink of return to California, we said our last good-byes to the people in the *ayahuasca* circle. As we were leaving, Don Juan showed up with the bottle intended for that night's regular session, and we were able to get a sample for analysis from his controversial brew. On our last visit to Don Fidel he also gave us a bit more of the *esencia,* the syrup that finally precipitates to the bottom of a well-made bottle of *ayahuasca.* We had learned much and gathered much hallucinogenic material.

Cities pass like billboards in the night of the mind, one night Lima, the next night home. I could not but think as we crossed over the Andes of the little circle of people back at Sra. Angulo's house whistling and chanting. How strange to have shared their mystery with them and to be returning to our own frenzied society that knows nothing of *ayahuasca.* How strange a creature is man; with religion, intoxication, dream, and poetry we try to take the measure of the shifting levels of self and world. It is a grand enterprise, hedged about with tautology but no less grand for that. I hoped that the sense of the special worth of all plant hallucinogens that this trip reinforced so unexpectedly would not be lost once we had returned to a world whose familiarity should not be taken for the merely mundane.

It had been barely seven weeks since Comet West glowed outside the window of our airliner flying south toward Lima, hardly a month since Lord Dark left us at Fancho Playa on the Rio Napo. Worlds seemed to have come and gone, yet friends who stayed behind in the United States hardly realized that any time at all had passed, emphasizing the bewildering sense of a density of experience that the traveler is always able to make his own. We were not unlike the psychedelic voyager who may be absent from company only a single evening and yet may fill that evening with years-long odysseys in strange and enchanted worlds, may in fact explore strange times and worlds of alternate possibilities in a single long silence.

Once we returned to the States, our *ayahuasca* would serve as the basis for experiments that shed light on its possible ability to synergize psilocybin. We worked through those experiments with a sense of their place in the context of hallucinogens generally. We needed to reflect on the strangeness of the possibilities that the magical plants had made familiar to us. We must chart further directions of research that hew to deep waters yet minimize risk.

People in the Amazon insist on the importance of chanting as a vehicle of expression when on tryptamine hallucinogens. This is a vital point, since in some way sound can control the topology of the hallucinations. We need to shed our inhibitions and experiment with sound and tone in the presence of these compounds. I have long felt this but have been uncertain as to how to proceed; the style of chanting of the *ayahuasqueros* is a beginning.

As I had anticipated during the visit to Peru, I was able to find my way into the confidence of the *ayahuasca* mystery once I was free to experiment with dosage and setting. Twice since returning from the Peruvian Amazon, Kat and I have taken Don Fidel's brew. Neither of these trips was as intense for Kat as her most intense experience in the Amazon. I, on the other hand, got much deeper into it than I had ever done before.

The first of these experiments was elusive and unsatisfying. We each took fifty milliliters of *ayahuasca*, which looked to us like the approximate dose that we had been given in Peru. I experienced a brief surge of hallucinations, but of a very banal sort, rather like being lost in a vast supermarket. We concluded from this experience that we had somehow become inundated by the telepathic background noise of the hillside suburban community in which we lived. It made us reluctant to repeat the experiment, since a psychedelic brush with the subliminal vulgarity of our own culture was somehow much more disturbing than had been regular sessions with people who had a whole different language and worldview than our own.

During that first trip, the subject of the flow of images was shifting and seemed impersonal and removed from me: thinking of the impersonal aspect of these images encountered in myself, I formed the aphorism "Sailing the ocean of the self; every wave cut by my prow is myself." There was a tendency to be drawn into emotional involvement with the scenes at once removed from myself. Twice I reminded myself that feeling frustration at the direction in which the images were flowing was inappropriate, and that I should be open to what is shown me no matter how different it may be from my expectations. Kat was as usual more affected than I. She had audible hallucinations—a strange voice speaking a futuristic kind of musical English. Toward the end of her visions she saw people in poverty-stricken and sleazy conditions. This may have been the DMT in action, since subthreshold DMT experiences often do dissolve into squalid or banal images as the experience fades away.

A few weeks later, and in the company of a friend who, like ourselves, had considerable experience with psychedelic agents, we decided to try again. This time we each took sixty milliliters initially and then about an hour later twenty milliliters more. At last I completely broke through. It was a dimension very similar to the state invoked by the mushroom psilocybin, leading me to harden my opinion that active compounds in *Stropharia cubensis* must metabolize to some near relative of dimethyltryptamine before the effect can take hold. At one point I was given a kind of motto, which came unbidden: "Mind conjures miracles out of time." It was like a Zen *koan* holding perhaps a clue to the nature of reality. There were long bursts of science-fiction-related images and beautiful hallucinations against a black background, a seeming characteristic of the *ayahuasca* visions. The message from this trip, which came as a very deeply felt gestalt perception, was that the Other is in man. I felt this more clearly than ever before. Unlike the psilocybin rapture, which presents itself as an alien intelligence, the *ayahuasca* seemed to have a kind of psychiatric presence that urged the recognition that all images and powers of the Other spring from our confrontation with ourselves. Like the psilocybin mushrooms, it displayed a network of information that seemed to make accessible the experiences and images of many worlds, but *ayahuasca* insisted that in some sense still unrevealed these were ultimately human worlds.

10

Mushrooms and Evolution

OR PERHAPS tens of millennia human beings have been utilizing hallucinogenic mushrooms to divine and to induce shamanic ecstasy. I propose to show that the human/mushroom interaction is not a static symbiotic relationship, but rather a dynamic one through which at least one of the parties has been bootstrapped to higher and higher cultural levels. The impact of hallucinogenic plants on the evolution and emergence of human beings is a heretofore unexamined phenomenon, yet it promises to provide an understanding of not only primate evolution but also the emergence of the cultural forms unique to Homo sapiens.

At Gome National Park in Tanzania, primatologists found that one particular species of leaf kept appearing undigested in chimpanzee dung. They found that every few days the chimps would vary from their usual pattern of eating wild fruit. Instead, they would walk for twenty minutes or longer to the site where a species of *Aspilia* was growing. They would repeatedly place their lips over an *Aspilia* leaf and hold it in their mouths. Chimps were seen to pluck a leaf, place it in their mouths, roll it around for a few moments, then swallow it whole. In this way as many as thirty small leaves might be eaten.

Biochemist Eloy Rodriguez of the University of California, Irvine, isolated the active principle from the *Aspilia*—a reddish oil now named thiarubrine-A. Working with the same substance, Neil Towers of the

■■

This article appeared in *Revision*, vol. 10, no. 4, spring 1988. I regard it as potentially significant because it proposes a radical new theory of human evolution.

University of British Columbia found that this compound can kill common bacteria in concentrations of less than one part per million. Herbarium records studied by Rodriguez and Towers (1985) showed that African peoples used the same leaves to treat wounds and stomachaches. Of the four species of *Aspilia* native to Africa the indigenous peoples used only three; the same three species were the ones utilized by the chimpanzees.

These findings show clearly the way in which a beneficial plant, once discovered by an animal or a person, can be included in the diet and thus confer an adaptive advantage. The animal or person is no longer threatened by certain factors in the environment, such as diseases that may have previously set constraints on the life span of individuals or perhaps upon the growth of the population as a whole. This type of adaptive advantage is easily understood. Less easy to understand is the way in which plant hallucinogens might have provided similar yet different adaptive advantages. These compounds do not catalyze the immune system into higher states of activity, although this may be a secondary effect. Rather, they catalyze consciousness, that peculiar, self-reflecting ability that has reached its greatest apparent expression in human beings. One can hardly doubt that consciousness, like the ability to resist disease, confers an immense adaptive advantage on any individual who possesses it.

Consciousness has been called "awareness of awareness" (Guenther, 1966) and is characterized by novel connections among the various data of experience. Consciousness is like a super nonspecific immune response. There is no evolutionary limit to how much consciousness can be acquired by a species. And there is no end to the degree of adaptive advantage the acquisition of consciousness will confer upon the individual or the species in which it resides.

There is reason to question the scenario that physical anthropologists present us regarding the emergence of human consciousness out of binocular, bipedal primates. The amount of time allotted to this ontological transformation of animal organization is excessively brief. Evolution in higher animals takes a very long time to occur. For example, the biologist who studies the evolution of the early amphibians operates in time spans of rarely less than a million years and often speaks in terms of tens of millions of years. But the emergence of humans from the higher primates is something that has gone on in less than a million years. Physically, humans have apparently changed very little in the last million years. But the amazing proliferation of consciousness, of social institutions, of coding practices, of cultures, has come so quickly that it is difficult for modern evolutionary biologists to account for it. Most do not even attempt an explanation.

There is a hidden factor in the evolution of human beings that is neither a "missing link" nor a telos imparted from on high. I suggest that this hidden factor in the evolution of human beings, the factor that called human consciousness forth from a bipedal ape with binocular vision, involved a feedback loop with plant hallucinogens. This is not an idea that has been widely explored, though a very conservative form of this notion appears in R. Gordon Wasson's *Soma: Divine Mushroom of Immortality*. Wasson does not comment on the emergence of humanness out of the primates, but he does suggest hallucinogenic mushrooms as the causal agent in the appearance of spiritually aware human beings and the genesis of religion. Wasson feels that omnivorous foraging humans would have sooner or later encountered hallucinogenic mushrooms or other psychoactive plants in their environment.

The strategy of these early human omnivores was to eat everything and to vomit whatever was unpalatable. Plants found to be edible by this method were then inculcated into their diet. The mushrooms would be especially noticeable because of their unusual form and color. The state of consciousness induced by the mushrooms or other hallucinogens would provide a reason for foraging humans to return repeatedly to those plants, in order to reexperience their bewitching novelty. This process would create what C. H. Waddington (1961) called a "creode," a pathway of developmental activity (in other words, a habit).

Habituation to the experience was ensured simply because it was ecstatic. "Ecstatic" is a word unnecessary to define except operationally: an ecstatic experience is one that one wishes to have over and over again. It has been shown in experimental situations that if one creates a situation in which N,N-dimethyltryptamine (DMT) can be delivered to a monkey on demand, then a large number of monkeys exposed to that experimental apparatus will prefer the DMT over food and water. DMT was used in these experiments because it is a very short-acting, overt hallucinogen that occurs in many different plant species (Jacobs, 1984). Though we cannot analyze the laboratory monkeys' state of mind, it is very clear that something in the experience impels them to return to the stimulus again and again.

Wasson's idea that religion originated when an omnivorous proto-human encountered alkaloids in the environment was countered by Mircea Eliade, the most brilliant expositor of the anthropology of shamanism and the author of *Shamanism: Archaic Techniques of Ecstasy*. Eliade considers what he calls "narcotic" shamanism to be decadent. He feels that if one cannot achieve ecstasy without drugs, then one's culture is probably in a decadent phase. The use of the word "narcotic"—a term usually used for soporifics—to describe this form of shamanism betrays an unsettling botanical and pharmacological naiveté. Wasson's notion, which I share, is precisely the opposite: it is the presence of a hallucinogen in a shamanistic culture that indicates its shamanism is authentic and alive. It is the late and decadent phase of shamanism that is characterized by elaborate rituals, ordeals, and reliance on pathological personalities. Where these latter phenomena are central, shamanism is well on its way to becoming simply "religion."

One view of plant hallucinogens is to see them as interspecies pheromones or exopheromones. Pheromones are chemical compounds exuded by an organism for the purpose of carrying messages between organisms of the same species. The meaning of the message is not intrinsic in the pheromone's chemical structure, but in evolutionarily established convention. Ants, for instance, produce a number of secretions with very specific meanings for other ants. However, these chemical "languages" are species-specific; the ant of one species cannot "read" the pheromones of another species. In fact, there is one known case where a pheromone means one thing to one ant species and yet bears a completely different meaning to another ant species, much in the same way that the English word "no" means "yes" in Greek.

If hallucinogens are operating as exopheromones, then the dynamic symbiotic relationship between primate and hallucinogenic plant is actually a transfer of information from one species to another. The primate gains increased visual acuity and access to the transcendent Other, while the benefits to the mushroom arise out of the primate domestication of previously wild cattle and hence the expansion of the niche occupied by the mushroom. Where plant hallucinogens do not occur, such processes cannot take place, but in the presence of hallucinogens a culture is slowly introduced to ever more novel information, sensory input, and behavior and thus is bootstrapped to higher and higher states of self-reflection.

It is reasonable to suggest that human language arose out of the synergy of primate organizational potential by plant hallucinogens. Indeed, this possibility was brilliantly anticipated by Henry Munn in his essay "The Mushrooms of Language" (1973). Munn writes:

> Language is an ecstatic activity of signification. Intoxicated by the mushrooms, the fluency, the ease, the aptness of expression one becomes capable of are such that one is astounded by the words that issue forth from the contact of the intention of articulation with the matter of experience. The spontaneity the mushrooms liberate is not only perceptual, but linguistic. For the shaman, it is as if existence were uttering itself through him.

Other writers have sensed the importance of hallucinations as catalysts of human psychic organization. Julian Jaynes, in his controversial book *The Origins of Consciousness in the Breakdown of the Bicameral Mind*

(1977), makes the point that there may have been major shifts in human self-definition even in historical times. He proposes that through Homeric times people did not have the kind of interior psychic organization that we take for granted. What we call ego was for pre-Homeric people what they called a "god." When danger threatened suddenly and unbidden, the god's voice was heard in the individual's mind, a kind of metaprogram for survival called forth under great stress. This integrative psychic function was perceived by those experiencing it to be either the direct voice of a god; the direct voice of the leader of the society, the king; or the direct voice of the dead king, the king in the afterlife. Merchants and traders moving from one society to another brought the unwelcome news that the gods were saying different things in different places, and so cast early seeds of doubt. At some point people integrated (in the Jungian sense) this previously autonomous function, and each person *became* the god and reinterpreted the inner voice as the "self" or, as it was later called, the "ego."

Hallucinogenic plants may have been the catalysts for everything about us that distinguishes us from other primates, except perhaps the loss of body hair. All of the mental functions that we associate with humanness, including recall, projective imagination, language, naming, magical speech, dance, and a sense of *religio* may have emerged out of interaction with hallucinogenic plants. Our society more than others will find this theory difficult to accept, because we have made pharmacologically obtained ecstasy a taboo. Sexuality is a taboo for the same reason: such things are consciously or unconsciously sensed to be entwined with the mysteries of where we came from and how we got to be the way we are. A theory of plant hallucinogens as central to the origin of mind suggests a scenario such as the following:

We know that the Sahara was much wetter as recently as four or five thousand years ago. The Roman historian Pliny referred to North Africa as "Rome's breadbasket." The presumption is that over the last one hundred and fifty thousand years the Sahara has grown gradually drier, changing from a subtropical forest to grasslands and, recently, to desert. When the grasslands first appeared, the arboreal adaptation of the primates ill served their continued survival. They left the trees and began to foray onto the grasslands. Their arboreally evolved repertoire of troop signals came under pressure to further expand. It has been suggested that it was the generation of hunting-pack signaling such as occurs in wolves and dogs that served as the basis for language. But another result of moving out of the trees and onto the grasslands was the likelihood of encountering the manure of ungulate herbivores, and in the same situation coprophilic (dung-loving) mushrooms. Several species of psilocybin-containing mushrooms are coprophilic; *Amanita muscaria*, which has a symbiotic relationship to birch and fir trees, is not.

The far fewer number of plant species that characterizes grass-lands in contrast with forests makes it highly likely that any grassland plant encountered would be tested for its food potential. The eminent geographer Carl Saur (1973) feels that there is no such thing as a natural grassland. He suggests that all grasslands are human artifacts resulting from burning. He bases this argument on the fact that all grassland species can be found present in the understory of the forests at the edge of the grasslands, but a very high percentage of the forest species are ab-sent in the grasslands. From this he argues that the grasslands are so re-cent that they must be seen as concomitant with the rise of large human populations.

The next step in the cultural evolution of the bipedal pack-hunting primates was the domestication of some of the browsing herbivores. With the animals and their manure came the mushrooms, and the human–mushroom relationship was further enhanced and deepened.

Evidence for these speculations can be found in southern Algeria. There is an area called the Tassili Plateau, a curious geological forma-tion. It is like a labyrinth, a vast badlands of stone escarpments that have been cut by the wind into many perpendicular narrow corridors, almost like an abandoned city. And in the Tassili there are rock paintings that date from the late neolithic to as recently as two thousand years ago. Here are the earliest known depictions of shamans in coincidence with large numbers of grazing animals, specifically, cattle (Lhote, 1959; Lajoux, 1963). The shamans, dancing and holding fistfuls of mushrooms, also have mushrooms sprouting out of their bodies.* Similar images oc-cur in pre-Columbian Peruvian textiles wherein the shaman is shown holding an object that has been identified as either a chopper or a mush-room. Chopping tools have been found that resemble the depicted ob-ject. Unlike the Peruvian images, with the Tassili frescoes the case is clear. Here we see dancing shamans with six, eight, ten mushrooms clutched in their hands and sprouting from their bodies.

The herding peoples who produced the Tassili paintings moved out of Africa over a long period of time, perhaps from twenty thousand to five thousand years ago. Wherever they went, their pastoral life-style went with them. The Red Sea was landlocked at that time. The boot of Arabia was backed up against the African continent. The land bridge there was utilized by some of these African pastoralists to enter the fer-tile crescent and later Asia Minor, where they intermingled with popula-tions already present and became well established by twelve thousand

*This connection between the Tassili art and mushroom use was discovered and pointed out to me by Jeff Gaines, an ethnomycologist and art historian living in Boulder, Colorado. It was he who recognized the implications of the Tassili images for the role of mushroom use in human prehistory.

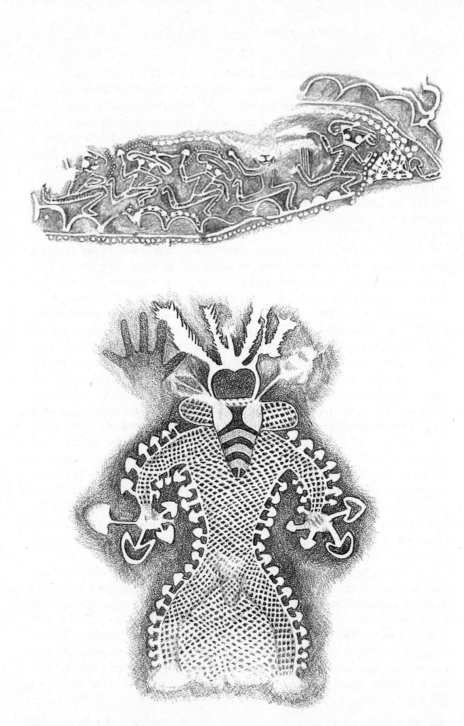

Mushroom shamans from Matalen-Amazar on the Tassili Plateau. Done in the Round-Head style, these rock paintings date from sometime before 6000 B.C. (Pencil sketches by Kathleen Harrison McKenna.)

years ago. These pastoral people had a cult of cattle and a cult of the Great Goddess. The evidence for this comes from a number of sites in Southern Anatolia, the best researched being Çatal Hüyük, a site dated to eight to nine thousand B.P. Çatal Hüyük has only begun to be excavated and contains amazing shrines with cattle bas-reliefs and heads of the cattle covered with ocher designs—the very complex paintings of a very complicated civilization (Mellaart, 1965, 1967).

It is possible to see in the confluence of the cult of the Great Goddess and the cattle cult a recognition and an awareness of the mushroom as the third and chthonic member of a kind of late Neolithic trinity. For the mushroom, seen to be as much a product of the cattle as milk, meat, and manure, was the pipeline to the presence of the Goddess. Recently Riane Eisler in her important revisioning of history, The Chalice and the Blade, has advanced the important notion of "partnership" models of society being in competition and oppressed by "dominator" forms of social organization. These latter are hierarchical, paternalistic, materialistic, and male dominated. Her position is that it is the tension between these two forms of social organization and the overexpression of the dominator model that is responsible for our alienation. I am in complete agreement with Eisler's view. In fact, this essay asks a question that is an extension of her argument. What was the factor that maintained the equilibrium of the partnership societies of the late Neolithic, and what factor faded and in fading set the stage for the emergence of the evolutionarily maladaptive dominator model?

I believe that it is the depth of the relationship of a human group to the gnosis of the vegetable mind, the Gaian collectivity of organic life, that determines the strength of the group's connection to the archetype of the Goddess and hence to the partnership style of social organization. The last time that the mainstream of Western thought was refreshed by the gnosis of the vegetable mind was at the close of the Hellenistic Era, when the Eleusinian mysteries were finally suppressed by enthusiastic Christian barbarians (Wasson et al., 1978).

The late Medieval church that conducted the great witch burnings was very concerned that all credit for episodes of magic and derangement should be given to the devil—hence, the church suppressed knowledge of plants such as datura, deadly nightshade, and monkshood and the role that they were playing in the nocturnal gatherings and activities of the practitioners of the craft. After all, we cannot have a devil who is such a diminished figure that he must rely on mere herbs to work his wiles. The devil must be a worthy foe of the Christos, and hence nearly coequal (Duerr, 1985).

My conclusion is that taking the next evolutionary step, the Archaic Revival, the rebirth of the Goddess, and the ending of profane history are agendas that implicitly contain within themselves the notion

of our reinvolvement with and the emergence of the vegetable mind.
That same mind that coaxed us into self-reflecting language now offers
us the boundless landscapes of the imagination. Without such a relationship to psychedelic exopheromones regulating our symbiotic relationship with the plant kingdom, we stand outside of an understanding of
planetary purpose. And understanding of planetary purpose may be the
major contribution that we can make to the evolutionary process.
Returning to the bosom of the planetary partnership means trading the
point of view of the ego for the intuitional translinguistic understanding
of the maternal matrix.

The people of Çatal Hüyük and other Mesopotamian peoples existed undisturbed in the ancient Middle East for a long time, practicing
their Mother Goddess religion. Then, around five to seven thousand B.P.,
a different kind of people with wheeled chariots, patriarchy, and a ritual
involving horse sacrifice swept down from north of the Caspian Sea into
Turkey and Anatolia, and what is now Iraq and Iran, encountering the
pastoral, mushroom-using lowlanders. These invaders are the people
that Wasson has suggested were the bearers of soma. He felt that soma,
the intoxicating plant of the Vedic hymns, may have been the mushroom
Amanita muscaria. A mushroom mystery cult was carried out of the
forests of Central Asia by Aryan people who eventually settled in India.

The problem with this hypothesis is that *A. muscaria* is not a reliable visionary hallucinogen. It has proven difficult to obtain a consis-
tently ecstatic intoxication from *Amanita muscaria.* Much ink has been
shed over this problem. Some have suggested that *A. muscaria* must be
pounded with milk curd in order to decarboxylate muscarine, the active
toxin, into muscamol, the hallucinogenic constituent. Others have suggested that the *Amanita* must be dried or roasted and aged before it is
rendered nontoxic and effective. The fact of the matter is that muscamol
is not a deep hallucinogen even when used as a pure compound.
Wasson was on the right track, correctly recognizing the potential of
Amanita muscaria to induce religious feeling and ecstasy, but he did not
take into account the imagination and linguistic stimulation imparted by
the input of African psilocybin-containing mushrooms into the evolution of Old World mycolatry.

We know that at least one psilocybin mushroom, *Psilocybe cubensis* or *Stropharia cubensis,* is circumtropical in its distribution, occurring
throughout the warm, wet tropics wherever cattle of the *Bos indicus* type
are present. This raises a number of questions. Is *P. cubensis* exclusively a
creature of the manure of *Bos indicus,* or can it occur in the manure of
other cattle? How recently has it reached its various habitats? The first
specimen of *Psilocybe cubensis* was collected by Earle in Cuba in 1906, yet
current botanical theory places the actual point of origin for the species
in Kampuchea. An archaeological dig in Thailand at a place called Non

Nak Tha has been dated to 15,000 B.P., and there the bones of *Bos indicus* have been found coincident with human graves. Some of the bones have burnt-out centers, indicating that they had been used as chillums to burn and presumably smoke vegetable material. Chillums of the Non Nak Tha type are used even today among yoga-sadhus throughout India. *Psilocybe cubensis* is common in the Non Nak Tha area today.

At what point, then, did *P. cubensis* enter the New World? In Southern Mexico coincident with the Mayan cultural area, natives use a number of psilocybin-containing mushrooms: *Psilocybe mexicana*, *P. aztecorum*, *P. maztecorum*, and others. These mushrooms constitute the Mexican mushroom complex discovered by Valentina and Gordon Wasson in the early fifties. *Psilocybe cubensis* also occurs in these areas, being especially prolific at Palenque. Palenque is the site of the ruins of one of the most exquisite cities of the Mayan climax. Many people have taken the mushrooms at Palenque and have had the impression that they were ingesting the sacred sacrament of the people who built this fabulous abandoned seventh-century Mayan city, but this notion is disputed by modern botanists. We cannot be certain that *P. cubensis* was the mushroom sacrament of the Maya. Most orthodox botanists argue that *P. cubensis* entered the New World with the Conquest, transported by the Spanish and their cattle. In the absence of a decipherment of the Mayan glyphs, it is not easy to imagine how such a matter could be proved or disproved. In my opinion, given the long viability of the spores and the generally prevailing winds at the equator, the circumtropical distribution of *P. cubensis* is probably a very old fact of the ecology of the planet.

What seems reasonable to suggest is that the Indo-European people coming out of central Asia contacted valley-dwelling, pastoral, partnership cultures and assimilated from them the cult of the coprophilic psilocybin-containing mushroom, carrying it eastward into India. The evidence is thin, but, on the other hand, the evidence has not been sought. After all, the current desert climate of the region encompassing Iraq, Iran, southern Turkey, Jordan, and Saudi Arabia makes this a very unlikely place to look for archaeological evidence of a mushroom cult. However, Robert Graves's *Food for Centaurs* discusses how a taboo usually indicates an earlier historical involvement with the forbidden item in the inventory of the culture. And mushrooms, which are hardly to be found in the contemporary environment where these religions are practiced, are very taboo in the substratum of primitive Zoroastrianism, Mandaeanism, and the undifferentiated cult religions that preceded them. Mandaeanism specifically forbids the eating of mushrooms, according to Wasson (Wasson, Hofmann, and Ruck, 1978).

In *The Sacred Mushroom and the Cross*, John Allegro, concentrating on post-exilic Judaism in Palestine, makes a controversial case that can

be judged only by Sumerian philologists. He posits that there are mushroom words, phrases, and symbols that can be traced through Akkadian
into old Akkadian, back into Sumerian, and that mushrooms were used
very early in this area. My own approach has been to work forward
from the Vedas. The Vedas are hymns that the Indo-European people
composed somewhere along their millennia-long peregrinations to
India. The Ninth Mandala of the *Rig Veda* especially goes into great detail about soma and states that soma stands above the gods. Soma is the
supreme entity. Soma is the moon; soma is masculine. Here we have a
rare phenomenon: a male lunar deity. The connection between the feminine and the moon is so deep and obvious that a lunar male deity stands
out, making its traditional history in the region easy to trace.

I reexamined the mythologies of the Near East, trying to find a lunar god that would prove that this idea had been imported to India from
the West. I found that the Sumerian civilization's northernmost outpost
was a city called Harran, a city traditionally associated with the beginning of astrology. Invented in Harran, astrology spread to China, later to
Egypt and throughout the ancient world. The patron deity of the city of
Harran was a moon god, Sin or Nannar. Sin was male and wears a cap
that looks like a mushroom. No other deity in that pantheon has this
headgear. I found three examples of Sin or Nannar on cylinder seals,
and in each case the headgear was prominent. In one instance the accompanying text by a nineteenth-century scholar mentions that this
headgear was in fact the identifier for the god (Maspero, 1894).

Why was the Aryan deity connected with the mushroom perceived as male? Though this is a problem for folklorists and mytholo-
gists, certain points are obvious. German folklore has always associated
the moon with the masculine, and the mushroom will take the projection
of masculinity or femininity with equal ease. It is obviously connected to
the moon: it has a lustrous, silvery appearance in certain forms, and it
seems to appear at night when the moon rules the heavens. On the other
hand, one can shift the point of view and suddenly see the mushroom as
masculine: it is solar in color, phallic in appearance, and imparts a great
energy. The mushroom is actually an androgynous shape-shifting deity
that can take various forms relative to the predisposition of the culture
encountering it. One can almost say that it is a mirror of cultural expectations. That is why for the Indo-Europeans it took on a masculine quality and why in other situations it seems to have a very lunar quality.
Either way, it is a hallucinogen that is not wild, that is associated with
the domestication of animals and with human culture. This association
with domesticated animals implicates the mushrooms in the cultural development of the Indo-Europeans, the people who wrote the Vedas.

These same Indo-Europeans were the authors of a breakthrough
in religious ontology. For them there were no sacred rivers, no sacred

trees, no holy mountains. They transcended geography in their notion of deity. They built a fire, and where the fire was kindled the center of the universe came to rest. They had discovered the transcendence of time and space. A sacramental plant hallucinogen that is linked to the dung of domesticated animals means that the sacrament is as nomadic as the people and animals that provide its favored milieu.

There are a number of problems with this theory, one of which is the lack of confirmation in India of the presence of *Psilocybe cubensis* or other psilocybin-containing mushrooms. *Amanita muscaria* is also rare in India. I predict, however, that a careful search of the flora of India will reveal *P. cubensis* as an indigenous component of the biome of the subcontinent. And I maintain that the desertification of the entire area from North Africa to the Tarr region around Delhi has distorted our conception of what occurred in the prehistoric evolution of religious ontology when these civilizations were in their infancy and the area was much wetter. It is my suggestion that the mushroom religion is actually the generic religion of human beings and that all later adumbrations of religion stem from the cult of ritual ingestion of mushrooms to induce ecstasy.

A rethinking of the role that hallucinogenic plants and fungi have played in the promotion of human emergence from the substrata of primate organization can help to lay the basis for a new appreciation of the unique confluence of factors responsible and necessary for the evolution of human beings. The widely felt intuition of the presence of the Other as a female companion to the human navigation of history can, I believe, be traced back to the immersion in the vegetable mind that provided the ritual context in which human consciousness emerged into the light of self-awareness, self-reflection, and self-articulation: the light of the Great Goddess.

Please see my *Food of the Gods: The Search for the Original Tree of Knowledge* (New York: Bantam, 1992) for a fuller discussion of the relationship between hallucinogenic mushrooms and human evolution.

11

"New Dimensions" Interview

MT: THE SEARCH for self-knowledge has occupied humanity for millennia, assuming many different guises. In our modern technical information culture the deeper meaning is often overlooked as we race helter-skelter toward an unknown end. Questions of values, ethics, and personal meaning are repressed under the holy banner of practicality and living in the real world. John Naisbitt, the author of *Megatrends*, points out that we are drowning in information but starved for knowledge. And yet, at the same time, one researcher has estimated that 80 percent of the public is involved in some aspect of self-fulfillment. Another paradox to ponder, since both may be true. The quest for liberation is a journey through paradox, and perhaps by noticing how other cultures and social milieus have incorporated the search, we can learn more about our own. We live in exciting times, in which the external reality we perceive is catalyzing a renewed momentum toward exploring our internal reality.

Our guest today, Terence McKenna, is one of those cultural point writers who commands our attention, not so much for the answers he has found, but rather because of the questions he poses. He is the coauthor, with his brother Dennis, of *The Invisible Landscape: Mind, Hallucinogens, and the* I Ching, and generally functions as a freelance writer, reading and researching.

My name is Michael Toms. I'll be your host for the next hour.

Terence, welcome.

■■

Michael Toms interviewed me for his "New Dimensions" radio show sometime in 1985. What follows is an edited transcript.

TM: Thank you very much; it's a pleasure to be here.

MT: Well, do you think we're in a state of transition? Are we moving from one culture to another?

TM: We are certainly in a state of transition; we have arrived at nothing less than the end of history. However, it is not something to be alarmed about. I imagine it's simply the normal situation that prevails when a species is preparing to depart for the stars.

MT: Do you think we're preparing to depart for the stars?

TM: On the scale of a hundred or a thousand years, I think it's an unavoidable conclusion. That span of time in geological terms is hardly the wink of an eye. In fact, from that perspective, all of human history appears as a preparation for human transcendence of planetary existence.

MT: Do we want to get away from the planet?

TM: I think you have to take the view that certainly the planet is the cradle of mankind, but, inevitably, one cannot remain in the cradle forever. The human imagination, in conjunction with technology, has become a force so potent that it really can no longer be unleashed on the surface of the planet with safety. The human imagination has gained such an immense power that the only environment that is friendly to it is the vacuum of deep space. It is there that we can erect the architectonic dreams that drive us to produce a Los Angeles or a Tokyo, and do it on a scale and in such a way that it will be fulfilling rather than degrading. So, yes, I think we cannot move forward in understanding without accepting as a consequence that we have to leave the planet. We are no longer the bipedal monkeys we once were. We have become almost a new force in nature. I think of language and cybernetics as an amalgam of computers and human brains and societal structures that has such an enormous forward momentum that the only place where it can express itself without destroying itself is, as James Joyce says, "up n'ent."

MT: So long, long ago, in a faraway galaxy, a Star Wars–style society may be in our future? As opposed to our past?

TM: It's in our present, I think. Our future is probably almost unimaginable. I think the transformation that leaving the planet will bring will also involve a transformation of our consciousness. We are not going as 1950s-style human beings; we are going to have to transform our minds before we are going to be able to leave the planet with any amount of grace. This is where I think the psychedelics come in, because they are anticipations of the future. They seem to channel information that is not available by the laws of normal causality, so the experience is really that of a prophetic dimension—a glimpse of the potential of the far centuries of the future through these compounds. No cultural shift of this magnitude can be unambiguous. The very idea that as a species we would leave the earth behind us must be as rending an idea as that a child would leave its childhood home. Obviously, it's a turning away from something that, once left behind, can never be recaptured. However, this is the nature of going forward into being: a series of self-transformations, a sense of level shifting. And we now simply happen to have reached the moment of ascent to a new level that is linked to leaving the planetary surface physically and to reconnecting with the contents of the unconscious collectivity of our minds. These two things will be done simultaneously. This is what the last half of the twentieth century, it seems to me, is all about.

MT: By and large, psychedelics have really not been accepted into the mainstream. Do you see a change in that?

TM: Not particularly. They hold a certain fascination for a persistent minority, and in that way they do their catalytic work upon society, which is to introduce new ideas and to release a certain kind of creative energy into society. I certainly would not like to see a return to the psychedelic hysterias of the 1960s. I think it's fine that these things are now the subject of interest of a much smaller group of people, but perhaps a group of people with a greater commitment, a better idea of exactly what these things are. It's really the same people; it's just a smaller group of them, and they have accumulated experience over the past twenty years, though I certainly don't think all psychedelic frontiers are conquered.

One of the subjects that I write and speak about is a phenomenon many people experience with the psilocybin family of hallucinogens that has not been included in the standard model of psychedelic substances. I am referring to the Logos-like phenomenon of an interior voice that seems to be almost a superhuman agency—a kind of *genus loci*. I consider this an alien intelligence—an entity so beyond the normal structure of the ego that if it is not an extraterrestrial it might as well be. Its bizarreness and its distance from ordinary expectations about reality is so great that if flying saucers arrived here tomorrow from the Pleiades it would make this mystery no less compelling in comparison. It amuses me that the scientific community has taken over the search for extrater-

restrial intelligence and defined it as they care to define it and have dedicated radio telescopes to search the galaxy for signals. The world's
largest radio telescope is at Arecibo in Puerto Rico, and within the shadow of that installation, psychedelic mushrooms grow in the fields and
the cows graze quietly in the sunshine. It's a marvelous interpenetration
of the near and the faraway. I believe that the place to search for extraterrestrials is in the psychic dimension, and there the problem is not
the absence of communication but an abundance of signals that must be
sifted through, because the fact of the matter is that shamans and mystics and seers have been hearing voices and talking to gods and demons
since Paleolithic times and probably before. We shouldn't rule out this
approach to communication. It seems to me far more likely that an advanced civilization would communicate interdimensionally and tele-
pathically, and the amounts of time available for an intelligent species to
have evolved these kinds of communication are vast.

I think that it's very interesting then that the tryptamines, psilocybin and DMT, at effective doses, very reliably trigger what could only be
described as contactlike phenomena, not only the interior voice in the
head, but also the classical flying saucer motifs of the whirling disc, the
lens-shaped object, the alien approach. This seems to be something hard-
wired into the human psyche, and I would like to find out why. I think
it's a very odd fact of human psychology, and I don't buy any of the current theories, ranging from that nothing at all is happening to that this
is, in fact, a species from a world around another star that is getting in
touch with us. I think this alien intelligence is something so bizarre that
it actually masquerades as an extraterrestrial so as not to alarm us by the
true implications of what it is.

MT: Your statement implies that it's something external to ourselves, and I wonder about that.

TM: This dualism of the interior and the exterior may have to be
overcome. It obviously transcends the individual. But I suspect it is
something like an Overmind of the species and that the highest form of
human organization is not realized in the democratic individual. It is realized in a dimension none of us has ever penetrated—the mind of the
species. It is the hand at the tiller of history. It is no government, no religious group, but actually what we call the human unconscious; however, it is not unconscious, and it is not simply a cybernetic repository of
myth and memory. It is an organized entelechy of some sort, and
though human history is its signature on the primates, it is very different
from the primates. It is like a creature of pure information. It is made of
language. It releases ideas into the flowing stream of history to boost the
primates toward higher and higher levels of self-reflection. We have

now reached the point where the masks are beginning to fall away and we are discovering that there is an angel within the monkey, struggling to get free. This is what the historical crisis is all about. I am very optimistic. I see it as a necessary chaos that will lead to a new and more attractive order.

MT: Terence, you were talking about extraordinary realities, and it occurs to me that there is an enormous amount of prejudice against the psychedelics and the use of hallucinogenic substances, almost as if there's an inordinate fear to open up the closet that these substances reveal. What about that prejudice? How is it going to be resolved? What is the resolution of that?

TM: I think it's more complicated than a prejudice. It's a prejudice born of respect, because most people sense that these compounds probably actually do what their adherents claim they do. It's possible to see the whole human growth movement of the 1970s as a wish to continue the inward quest without having to put yourself on the line the way you had to when you took 250 gamma of LSD. I think all these other methods are efficacious, but I think it's the sheer power of hallucinogens that puts people off. You either love them or you hate them, and that's because they dissolve worldviews. If you like the experience of having your entire ontological structure disappear out from under you—if you think that's a thrill—you'll probably love psychedelics. On the other hand, for some people that's the most horrible thing they can possibly imagine. They navigate reality through various forms of faith; whereas with the psychedelics the doors of perception are cleansed and you see very, very deeply.

I spent time in India and I always visited the local sadhus of great reputation. I met many people who possessed what I call wise-old-man wisdom, but wise-old-man wisdom is a kind of Tao of how to live. It has nothing to say about the dimensions that the psychedelics reveal. For that you have to go places where hallucinogenic shamanism is practiced, specifically the Amazon Basin, and there you discover that beyond the wisdom of simply how to live in ordinary reality there is a gnosis of how to navigate in extraordinary reality. This reality is so extraordinary that we cannot approach what these people are doing with any degree of smugness, because the frank fact of the matter is that we have no more viable theory of what Mind is than they. The beliefs of a Witoto shaman and the beliefs of a Princeton phenomenologist have an equal chance of being correct, and there are no arbiters of who is right. Here is something we have not assimilated. We have been to the moon, we have charted the depths of the ocean and the heart of the atom, but we have a fear of looking inward to ourselves because we sense that is where all the contradictions flow together. The kind of prejudice leveled against psychedelics attended psychoanalysis during the twenties and thirties when it was thought to be superfluous or some kind of fad. Psychedelics touch a very sensitive nerve. They touch the issue of the nature of humans, and some people are uncomfortable with this.

MT: What is the value of exploring extraordinary realities?

TM: I believe it's the same value that attends the exploration of ordinary realities. There's an alchemical saying that one should read the oldest books, climb the highest mountains, and visit the broadest deserts. I think that being imposes some kind of obligation to find out what's going on, and since all primary information about what is going on comes through the senses, any plant or any compound that alters that sensory input has to be looked at very carefully. I've often made the point that, chemically speaking, you can take a molecule that is completely inactive as a psychedelic, reposition a single atom on one of its rings, and suddenly it's a powerful psychedelic. Now it seems to me that this is a perfect proof of the interpenetration of matter and mind. The movement of a single atom from one known position to another known position changes an experience from nothing to overwhelming. This means that mind and matter, at the quantum-mechanical level, are all spun together. This means in a sense that the term *extraordinary reality* is not correct if it implies a division of category from ordinary reality. It is simply that there is more and more and more of reality, and some of it is inside our heads and some of it is deployed out through three-dimensional Newtonian space.

MT: I think most of us just simply accept the everyday reality as the only one. You're talking about journeys into nether regions far beyond most people's conception or desire.

TM: I think there's a shamanic temperament that is characterized by a craving for knowledge—knowledge in the Greek sense of gnosis. In other words, knowledge not of the sort where one subscribes to *Scientific American* and it validates what you believe, but cosmologies constructed out of immediate experiences that are always found to be applicable. You see, I don't believe that the world is made of quarks or electromagnetic waves, or stars or planets, or any of these things. I believe the world is made of language and that this is the primary fact that has been overlooked. The construction of the flying saucer is not so much a dilemma of hardware as it is a poetic challenge. People find it very hard to imagine exactly what I'm talking about. What I'm saying is that the leading edge of reality is mind, and that mind is the primary substratum of

being. We in the West have had it the wrong way around for over a millennium, but once this is clearly understood, using what we have
learned in our little excursion through three-dimensional space and matter, we will create a new vision of humanity that will be a fusion of the
East and the West.

MT: You suggest that the world is made of language, yet I think
of these extraordinary realities that are totally beyond any language that
we use in any ordinary sense.

TM: Yes, they are beyond ordinary language. I always think of
Philo Judaeus writing on the Logos. He posed to himself the question,
"What would be a more perfect Logos?" and then he answered, saying it
would be a Logos that is not heard but beheld. And he imagined a form
of communication where the ears would not be the primary receptors,
but the eyes would be. A language where meaning was not constructed
through a dictionary of spoken words, but where three-dimensional objects were actually generated with a kind of hyperlanguage so that there
was perfect understanding between people. This may sound bizarre in
ordinary reality, but these forms of synesthesia and synesthesic glossolalia are commonplace in psychedelic states.

MT: Terence, could you identify Philo for us and tell us who he
was?

TM: He was an Alexandrian Jew of the second century who
made it his business to travel around the Hellenistic world discussing all
the major cults and religious and cosmogonic theories of his day. So he's
a major source of Hellenistic data for us.

MT: How would you relate to Socrates' view of the world?

TM: I think that it's hard not to be a Platonist, but it's something
that perhaps we should struggle against, or at least struggle to modify. I
think of myself as sort of a Whiteheadian Platonist. Certainly the central
Platonic notion, that of the Ideas—archetypal forms that stand outside of
time—is one that is confirmed by the psychedelic experience. The
Neoplatonists—the school of Plotinus and Porphyry—are psychedelic
philosophers. Their idea of an ascending hierarchy of increasingly more
rarified states is a sophisticated presentation of the shamanic cosmology
that one experientially discovers when one is involved with psychedelics.

MT: What I think most of us don't realize is that Greek culture
and the Eleusinian mysteries incorporated the use of something very

akin to psychedelics. Essentially Western civilization is based on a culture that had at its core an experience and a ritual that used
psychedelics.

TM: Yes, for over two thousand years everyone who was anyone
in the ancient world made the pilgrimage to Eleusis and had this experience that Gordon Wasson and Carl Ruck have argued very convincingly
was a hallucinogenic intoxication produced by ergot. But of course, as
soon as the church solidified its power, it closed these Platonic academies
and moved against so-called pagan and heretical knowledge. Not only
the Platonists but all the Gnostic sects and mystery schools were repressed. I like to think that this repression ended in a very odd way when
in 1953 Gordon Wasson and his wife, Valentina, discovered the psilocybin mushroom cult in the village of Huatla de Jimenez. It was as if Eros,
who had been martyred in the Old World, was found sleeping in the
mountains of Mexico and resurrected. The experience of the mushroom
is very much the experience of a *genus loci*, a god on the Grecian model—
not the god who hung the stars in heaven, but a local god, a pre-
Christian, bacchanalian nature power that is very alien and yet resonates
with our expectations of what that experience would be like.

MT: Interesting that the mushroom is a symbol in our culture of
death and destruction—the symbol of the nuclear explosion.

TM: Yes, my brother has made the point, asking, "What mushroom is it that grows at the end of history? Is it the mushroom of Fermi
and Oppenheimer and Teller, or is it the mushroom of Wasson and
Albert Hofmann and Humphrey Osmond?"

MT: Somehow I think the latter is safer.

TM: It may not only be safer; it may open the way to escape from
the former. It's like a pun of physics that the force of liberation and the
force of destruction could take the same form. It's what alchemists call
the *coincidencia oppositorum.*

MT: It seems an amazing synchronicity. I was interested in talking with Andy Weil, the author of *The Natural Mind,* about the fact that
a new genus of psilocybin-containing mushrooms is appearing that has
never been seen before. It's almost as if they're appearing now for a
reason.

TM: It's amazing how many new species have been discovered
since people have bent their attention to hallucinogenic mushrooms.

There have been psilocybin mushrooms reported from England and France, localities where, so far as we know, there is no cultural history of usage at all. However, it's interesting that cultural usage seems to come very early in human history. Hallucinogens are hardly welcome in agricultural societies. I think it was Weston La Barre who made the point that once one learns how to grow plants one's gods shift from the ecstatic gods of the hallucinogens to the corn god or the food god, and life is no longer about divining the hunt and the weather through the ecstatic use of hallucinogens. Rather it becomes about being able to get up every morning and go to work and hoe the crop. You mentioned earlier the prejudice against hallucinogens. I think cultural suppression of hallucinogens reaches back to the beginning of agriculture when there was competition among plant gods that exemplified life-styles that were alien to each other.

MT: Is psilocybin illegal?

TM: Yes, it's a Schedule One drug. It was placed on the list at the same time as LSD, even though the issue was presented to the public in terms of LSD being made illegal. Actually, at that time a number of compounds were made illegal, yet there was never any public debate. All psychedelics were viewed the same way, and LSD was used as the model. Actually, these compounds vary widely. There is a spectrum of psychedelic effects, and certain compounds trigger some of them. But, yes, psilocybin is illegal.

MT: Are the mushrooms illegal?

TM: The mushrooms also are illegal, as they contain psilocybin.

MT: You recall Andy Weil saying that he walked along a downtown Seattle residential street picking up psilocybin mushrooms from the front yards of residential homes.

TM: English law took the view that it was preposterous to try to outlaw a naturally occurring plant. They took the position that only the chemical was illegal, which I think is a very wise position. But I notice that Canada recently chose the American interpretation over the British one.

MT: The kind of knowledge and the kind of information you're putting forward is not generally available. It's not the kind of information and knowledge that one would find in the typical academic anthropology curriculum, yet it seems to be a knowledge that is ever expanding.

Somehow it's outside of the cultural institutional entities. Number one, why do you think that is the case? Of course there's a logical answer to that one, but what do you see as the future of this kind of information and knowledge?

TM: I think in a sense it signals the rebirth of the institution of shamanism in the context of modern society. Anthropologists have always made the point about shamans that they were very important social catalysts in their groups, but they were always peripheral to them—peripheral to the political power and, actually, usually physically peripheral, living some distance from the villages. I think the electronic shaman—the person who pursues the exploration of these spaces—exists to return to tell the rest of us about it.

Hopefully we are now coming into a period of maturity as a species. We can no longer have forbidden areas of the human mind or mindless cultural machinery. We have taken upon ourselves the acquisition of so much power that we must now understand what we are. We cannot travel much further with definitions of humanity inherited from the Judeo-Christian tradition. We need to truly explore the problem of consciousness, because as human beings gain power they are becoming the defining factor on the planet. The questions that loom are, "Is man good?" and then, if the answer is yes, "What is man good for?"

The shamans will point the way because they are visionaries, poets, cultural architects, forecasters—all these roles that we understand in more conventional terms rolled into one and raised to the nth power. They are cultural models for the rest of us. It has always been true that the shaman has access to a superhuman dimension and a superhuman condition and thereby affirms the potential for transcendence in all people. The shaman is an exemplar, if you will, and I see the new attention that's being given to these things signaling a sense on the part of society that we need to return to these models. This is why, for instance, in the *Star Wars* phenomenon Skywalker, the name of a major character, is a direct translation of the word "shaman" out of the Tungusic, which is where Siberian shamanism comes from. So these heroes that are being instilled in the heart of the culture are shamanic heroes; they control a force that is bigger than everybody and holds the galaxy together; this is true, as a matter of fact. As we explore how true this is, the limitations of our previous worldview will be exposed for all to see. I think it was J. B. S. Haldane who said, "The world may not only be stranger than we suppose, it may be stranger than we *can* suppose."

MT: I think that the character Yoda is a shamanic-type character.

TM: Very much so.

MT: As we talk about shamans and shamanism, again that brings up cross-cultural currents. Do you see shamanism taking on a new form?

TM: I believe, along with Gordon Wasson and others, but in distinction to Mircea Eliade, who is a major writer on shamanism, that it is hallucinogenic shamanism that is primary. Where shamanic techniques are used to the exclusion of hallucinogenic plant ingestion, the shamanism tends to be vitiated; it is more like a ritual enactment of what real shamanism is. The shamanism that is coming to be is coming to be within people in our culture who feel comfortable with psychedelic plants and who, by going into those spaces and then returning with works of art or poetic accounts or scientific ideas, are actually changing the face of the culture.

I connect the psychedelic dimension to the dimension of inspiration and dream, and I think history has always progressed by the bubbling up of ideas from these nether dimensions into the minds of receptive men and women. It is simply that now, with the hallucinogens, we actually have a tool to push the button. We are no longer dependent upon whatever factors previously controlled the ingression of novelty into human history. We have taken that function to ourselves, and this will intensify and accelerate the cultural crisis toward its ultimate resolution.

MT: So as we continue to move toward the further exploration of these spaces, we can expect social change as a result of personal change?

TM: Tremendous social change. In fact, what is happening is a tendency toward what I call turning the body inside out. Through our media and cybernetics, we are actually approaching the point where consciousness can be experienced in a state of disconnection from the body. We have changed. We are no longer bipedal monkeys. We are instead a kind of cybernetic coral reef of organic components and inorganic technological components. We have become a force that takes unorganized raw material and excretes technical objects; we have transcended the normal definitions of humans. We are like an enormous collective organism with our data banks, our forecasting agencies, and our computer networks, and the many levels at which we are connected into the universe. Our self-image is changing; the monkey has been all but left behind and, shortly, *will* be left behind.

Again, I take the flying saucer to be an image of the future state of humanity. It is a kind of millenarian transformation of the human where the soul is exteriorized as the apotheosis of technology. It is that eschatological event that is casting enormous shadows backward through time over the historical landscape. That is the siren singing at the end of time, calling all humanity across the last hundred millennia toward it. Calling us out of the trees and into history, and through this series of multileveled cultural transitions to the point where the thing within the monkeys—the creature of pure language and pure imagination whose aspirations are entirely titanic in terms of self-transformation—that thing is now emerging, and it will emerge as humanity leaves the planet. It's not something quantized and clearly defined. Nevertheless, it is what the next fifty or so years will be about. At the end of it, the species will be off-planet and transformed and fully wired from the depths to the heights.

MT: Are we talking about another version of the Christian death, resurrection, ascension into heaven?

TM: Except that it is coming into history. What is happening is that the paradise promised the soul is actually going to enter into history. Technological man took the apocalyptic aspirations of Christianity so seriously that we are going to realize them. It has become the guiding image of what we want to be. I'm reminded of the poem by William Butler Yeats, "Sailing to Byzantium," where he speaks of the artifice of eternity and says:

> Once out of nature I shall never take
> My bodily form from any natural thing,
> But such a form as Grecian goldsmiths make
> Of hammered gold and gold enamelling
> To keep a drowsy Emperor awake;
> Or set upon a golden bough to sing
> To lords and ladies of Byzantium
> Of what is past, or passing, or to come.

This is the image of the human body become an indestructible cybernetic object; yet within that indestructible cybernetic object there is a holographic transform of the body that is released into the dream. It is an image of the human transformed and released into a hyperspace of information, where one is a thing of eternal circuitry but one appears to be walking along an unspoiled beach in Paradise. We are going to find the power to realize our deepest cultural aspirations. This is why we must find out what our deepest cultural aspirations are.

MT: What about the idea that these spaces that we've been talking about—that you've been illuminating—are spaces that can be achieved without the use of psychedelics?

TM: I scoured India, and my humble, personal opinion is that it is highly unlikely. I've always approached people of spiritual accomplishment with the question "What can you show me?" Wise-old-man wisdom is one thing, but the hallucinogen-using shaman of the Amazon seems to be able to go far beyond that. There may be physical techniques for duplicating this, but the efficacy and the dependability of the hallucinogens seems to me to make them the obvious choice. Only a series of cultural taboos would cause one to engineer around hallucinogenic shamanism. It is the obvious path to transcendence. People must face the fact that, at one level, we are chemical machines. That doesn't mean we are that at every level, but it does mean that there is a chemical level where we can intervene to change the pictures that are coming in and going out at higher levels.

MT: You're not suggesting that people should do this by themselves?

TM: Take hallucinogens? Well, I don't know about taking them by themselves—probably not, although I always prefer to. What I am suggesting is that hallucinogens be taken in a situation of minimum sensory input. Lying down in darkness with eyes closed cannot be surpassed. People want music; they want to walk around in nature and all these things. Nature and music are beautiful in their own right; they are the adumbrations of the psychedelic experience that we deal with in ordinary reality. In confrontation with the deep psychedelic experience these things are hardly more than impediments. Very interesting things are happening in the utter blackness behind your eyelids while lying still in silent darkness, and that is where the mystery comes from and goes to.

MT: My question had to do with use or nonuse of a guide.

TM: Oh, I don't think people should do this without a guide unless they feel confident from long experience that they don't need a guide.

MT: Terence, it's been fascinating. I think we could probably go on for another few hours if we had time.

TM: It's a pleasure to talk with you about this. I like to have these ideas get out. I think it's important that we discuss all this in a way that is only now becoming possible because of the situation in the 1960s. Now we need to shed all that and look back and look forward and try to make a mature judgment for our culture based on the facts of the matter.

MT: Thank you for being with us, Terence.

TM: Thank you.

12

The *Voynich Manuscript*

THE *VOYNICH MANUSCRIPT* has been called the most mysterious manuscript in the world. Dating at least to 1586, the manuscript is written in a language of which no other example is known to exist. It is an alphabetic script, but of an alphabet variously reckoned to have from nineteen to twenty-eight letters, none of which bear any relationship to any English or European letter system. The manuscript is small, seven by ten inches, but thick, nearly 170 pages. It is closely written in a free-running hand and copiously illustrated with bizarre line drawings that have been water-colored: drawings of plants, drawings of little naked ladies appearing to take showers in a strange system of plumbing (variously identified as organs of the body or a primitive set of fountains), and astrological drawings— or what have been interpreted as astrological drawings. Since the *Voynich Manuscript* is at the Beinecke Rare Book Room at Yale, it is accessible to any serious scholar. *The Most Mysterious Manuscript*, edited by Robert Brumbaugh, reproduces a number of the folios from the manuscript that readily convey the weirdness of it all. It is quite unearthly and does not fit into the context of late medieval alchemical manuscripts or late medieval manuscripts of any other kind.

The known facts about the manuscript are few. Historically, it first appears in 1586 at the court of Rudolph II of Bohemia, who was one of the most eccentric European monarchs of that or any other period. Rudolph collected dwarfs and had a regiment of giants in his army. He

■■■

Portions of this article appeared as a book review in *Gnosis*, no. 7, spring 1988.

was surrounded by astrologers, and he was fascinated by games and codes and music. He was typical of the occult-oriented, Protestant noblemen of this period and epitomized the liberated northern European prince. He was a patron of alchemy and supported the printing of alchemical literature. The Rosicrucian conspiracy (about which I will say more later) was being quietly fomented during this same period.

To Rudolph's court came an unknown person who sold this manuscript to the king for three hundred gold ducats, which, translated into modern monetary units, is about fourteen thousand dollars. This is an astonishing amount of money to have paid for a manuscript at that time, which indicates that the Emperor must have been highly impressed by it. Accompanying the manuscript was a letter that stated that it was the work of the Englishman Roger Bacon, who flourished in the thirteenth century and who was a noted pre-Copernican astronomer.

Prague, where Emperor Rudolph held his court, was a hotbed of alchemists who esteemed the reputation of Roger Bacon. Only two years before the appearance of the *Voynich Manuscript*, John Dee, the great English navigator, astrologer, magician, intelligence agent, and occultist had lectured in Prague on Bacon. John Dee had an unexpectedly long stay in Prague because his companion, Edward Kelley, had publicly claimed to be able to perform the alchemical opus, and the emperor more or less placed the pair under house arrest and asked them to perform the opus for him as a favor for his generous patronage. When they were unable to produce, Dee was able to talk his way out of it since it was Kelley who had made the major claims. Kelley was detained and actually died when the slate roofing on a high parapet of the castle slid underneath his feet one moonlit night during a frantic bid for freedom, making him one of alchemy's rare martyrs. I shall demonstrate directly why the relationship between Dee, Kelley, and Rudolph has direct bearing on the mystery of the *Voynich Manuscript*, for it is my opinion that Dee was involved in its sale.

Today the *Voynich Manuscript* is still accompanied by the letter that attributes it to Roger Bacon. Rudolph's best astrologers and cryptographers could make nothing out of the manuscript. It entered a vast collection of weird artifacts and curiosities that Rudolph had gathered together from all over the world that were dispersed to diverse people after his death. The *Voynich Manuscript*, because it contained botanical illustrations, passed to his botanist, a man named Marceci. He kept it for twenty years; then it passed to an unnamed party who had it for another twenty years, bringing its history up to the 1620s. It then passed to Athanasius Kircher, who was one of the great polymaths of the mid-seventeenth century. He was a Catholic intellectual and alchemist, and the first to systematically study artificial languages. We know of letters of his to various people asking about the *Voynich Manuscript*, written before he obtained it. He was even sent small portions of it, reproduced, that he struggled over. But once he actually had the manuscript in his possession, his diaries are silent about it. Five years after he acquired it he published *A Universal Study of Artificial Languages*, which nowhere mentions the *Voynich Manuscript*.

Kircher decided to become a Jesuit in about 1660 and had to give away all of his worldly goods. He gave his library to a Jesuit seminary south of Rome, and among his books was the *Voynich Manuscript*. It sat on a shelf in the seminary for over 250 years, until Alfred Voynich, a New York rare book dealer, bought the entire library on a trip to Europe in 1912. When Voynich got the library back to New York and sorted through it, he found among all the easily catalogued late-Renaissance Italian theological material a peculiar, totally anomalous book. Even as late as the period from which we have the first historical record of the *Voynich Manuscript*, the 1580s, the store of images in the European mind was very limited. There were only ten or fifteen herbals in circulation among the educated people of Europe at that time, and none of the *Voynich* images can be directly traced to any of these previously printed or circulated sources. Yet the biological sections of the *Voynich Manuscript* contain over 120 drawings of plants. Likewise, the script itself has no antecedents, and it spawned no imitators. Codes from the early sixteenth century onward in Europe were all derived from *The Stenographica* of Johannes Trethemius, Bishop of Sponheim, an alchemist who wrote on the encipherment of secret messages. He had a limited number of methods, and no military, alchemical, religious, or political code was composed by any other means throughout a period that lasted well into the seventeenth century. Yet the *Voynich Manuscript* does not appear to have any relationship to the codes derivative of Johannes Trethemius, Bishop of Sponheim.

I shall now offer an explanation of why I think that John Dee is the obvious candidate for being the purveyor, if not the author, of the *Voynich Manuscript*. First of all, Trethemius's book, *The Stenographica*, didn't circulate as a printed book until the 1580s, but it circulated in manuscript from about 1530 onward. When Dee visited the continent as a fairly young man, he recorded in his diary that he spent three days hand-copying the relevant chapters of a manuscript copy of *The Stenographica* that he was shown in Paris, so from very early in his intellectual life he was in possession of the Trethemian code-making machinery.

The next important event in his life with regard to the *Voynich Manuscript*, and one of the most puzzling events in the whole history of science, took place on an afternoon in July 1582. While in his study at Mortlake, John Dee was distracted by a brilliant light outside his window and stepped outside to receive from a creature he described as the Angel Gabriel a polished lens of New World obsidian, which he described in his diary thenceforward as "the Shew Stone." He was able, by meditating on this stone, to induce visions and dialogues with spirits, but this ability seemed to fade in the months after he received the stone until a strange personage came into his life in the spring of 1584. This was Edward Kelley.

Kelley was a much younger man than Dee, and Dee was married to a much younger woman, Ann. Kelley was of the rascal type; in one account, he is even described as being earless, having had his ears removed for some petty crime in the provinces. He arrived at Dee's place in Mortlake, pop-eyed and breathless, with a wild story about how he had fallen asleep in a ransacked tomb in a monastery in Wales. When he awakened, he found beneath him in the tomb a vial of red powder that was the transformative elixir, and a book in an undecipherable language that he called the *Gospel of St. Dunstable*. Kelley claimed that he had been told in the village nearby that this book was enciphered Welsh. We actually hear no more in anybody's diaries of the *Gospel of St. Dunstable*; however, Arthur Dee, the son of John Dee, writing some thirty years later and reminiscing about his father, said that from the time John Dee met Kelley he spent a great deal of time trying to unravel a book "covered all over with hieroglyphiks." Perhaps this is the *Gospel of St. Dunstable*, and perhaps the *Gospel of St. Dunstable* and the *Voynich Manuscript* are one and the same.

In any case, Kelley's entree to Dee was the undecipherable manuscript and the alchemical potion. Kelley quickly learned from his conversations with Dee the story of the Shew Stone, and together they set up a séance during which Kelley proved himself to be a very adept scryer of the stone. From the very first instance, he could describe vast theatrical undertakings and speak all the parts of the characters. (The Shew Stone is in the British Museum, where one can see it today.)

John Dee's meeting with Edward Kelley began a new period in Dee's diaries. They were published in 1658 by Meric Casaubon as *A True and Faithful Relation, etc.* In the series of entries that span the next ten years, there are recorded hundreds of spirit conversations, including the delivery to Dee and Kelley of an angelic language called Enochian, composed of non-English letters, but which computer analysis has recently shown to have a curious grammatical relationship to English. Over four thousand words are known in Enochian, transmitted by the ghostly apparitions that Kelley channeled to Dee. Some of the messages were theological or political in nature and came to the two as they traveled about Europe visiting such places as the court of Rudolph. They were responsible for spreading the fame of the alchemist Roger Bacon, which laid the public relations groundwork for sale of the *Voynich Manuscript* at a high premium.

The manuscript, which would have been written in the thirteenth century if it were by Roger Bacon, definitely shows all the physical signs of a sixteenth-century origin. I estimate it was written sometime around 1540, indicating that Kelley obtained it somewhere. If Kelley wrote it himself, it would have to have been done later—as late as the early 1580s. If Dee actually wrote it, then it should be possible to determine this by comparing it to his other writings. The several groups that have studied the *Voynich Manuscript* have not been familiar with the large amounts of encrypted material in John Dee's diaries. There are over ninety-two pages of strings of numbers and letters. If the method of encryption utilized by Dee could be related in some way to the encoding of the Voynich material, the problem of its authorship would be solved.

During the height of his creativity, Dee wrote a strange book called *The Hieroglyphic Monad (Monas Hieroglyphicam)*, containing thirty-six quasi-geometric theorems. This book hints at some kind of mystical doctrine yet remains utterly obscure. In the early 1580s it circulated in manuscript form, and it was printed a few years later.

In 1604, and again in 1608, the primary Rosicrucian documents, *The Fama* and *The Confessio*, were anonymously circulated in Europe. They came out of nowhere, broadsheets distributed in the middle of the night from street corners. They said, "We are a secret society and who we are ye may not know, but if you're ready you'll be contacted and asked to join." Robert Fludd, the heir of the Dee tradition in English occultism and science, practically put out an advertisement saying, "If I am not good enough, nobody's good enough. Why haven't you people contacted me?" The fact is that the Rosicrucians, meaning the authors of *The Fama* and *The Confessio*, never contacted anybody. Their claim was basically fraudulent: that the tomb of Christian Rosenkrantz, a great knight who had gone on the last Crusade in the fourteenth century, had been discovered. This was rather like harking back to Roger Bacon, invoking a mythical personage who had lived two centuries previously. Inside the tomb there were said to have been alchemical books with a quasi-political overtone, definitely favoring the court of Frederick V, the Elector Palatine. All this was disseminated as gospel in a kind of alchemical Protestant revival. Curiously, these texts, *The Fama* and *The Confessio*, had many doctrinal similarities to Dee's *Hieroglyphic Monad*, so that it appears that Dee's earlier work was used as the model for the Rosicrucian broadsheets by their authors. Though these authors were unnamed, I suspect the Bohemian alchemist Johannes Andreä. Andreä and fellow alchemist Michael Maier were old enough to have been involved in Dee's earlier visits to Prague and to have been at the peak of their intellectual powers when the episode of the Winter King and Queen occurred in 1620 and briefly brought Frederick the Elector and his wife to Prague as alchemical rulers.

Dee died an old and broken-hearted man under the reign of James I in 1608, many years after the sale of the *Voynich Manuscript*. Dee had been the court astrologer of Elizabeth, a friend of Sir Philip Sidney, and the most educated man in England until James came to power. James had a horror of the whole magical side of the Elizabethan court. He didn't want astrologers around him. He was a rationalist, and his anti-Catholicism extended to a mistrust of the entire occult tradition.

Previously I mentioned that when Rudolph died and his court fell into disarray, the *Voynich Manuscript* passed to his botanist. The old emperor was dying at a great age, and was unquestionably mad as a damned hatter. Meanwhile, to the west of Prague, in Heidelberg, Frederick the Elector wed Elizabeth, the daughter of Dee's nemesis, James I of England. Frederick was everything a Protestant alchemical prince could hope to be: young, brilliant, scheming, and totally in command of his lords. Frederick took the king's decision to give his daughter's hand in marriage as tacit approval for Frederick's plan to establish a Protestant alchemical kingdom in central Europe. Actually, James—being the plotting conservative that he was—had a far more Machiavellian purpose in wedding his daughter to Frederick. He also had it in his mind to wed one of his sons to a Spanish Catholic Hapsburg princess and was trying to steer a neutral course. When he realized that Frederick and Elizabeth had gone off to their court in Heidelberg to patronize alchemists and astrologers like Michael Maier, Gerhart Dorn, and Johannes Andreä, James was much alarmed, but by that time it was too late to reverse his decision and he realized that Frederick was a wild card. When Rudolph finally did die, the princes of the Northern League gathered to choose his successor by secret ballot. Frederick won, and so in the late fall of 1619 he and Elizabeth transferred their court to Prague and ruled for one winter, until May of 1620. To provide historical context, recall that the Mayflower was setting sail that same year. By May, the Hapsburgs had mounted an army and were able to crush the Winter Kingdom.

In a sense, that incident can be seen as the opening shot of the Thirty Years' War. One of the young French soldiers in the Hapsburg army laying siege to the city was the nineteen-year-old René Descartes, who, under the influence of a dream he would have only a few months later, would mature into the great proponent of modern French materialism. Michael Maier, one of the last great synthesizers of the late medieval alchemical vision, died in the siege of the city. Frederick was killed and Elizabeth fled into exile in the Hague for many years. The

Voynich Manuscript was forgotten. Modern times overtook Europe, and the secret of the manuscript drifted further and further into the past.

The hope of establishing an alchemical political union in Central Europe was, in the context of what followed (the Thirty Years' War and modern times), a channel where the river of history chose not to run. It was a path not taken, but had things turned out differently, for instance had the king of England been behind the union wholeheartedly, events might have unraveled somewhat differently.

My reconstruction of the unknown part of the story is this:

When Dee and Kelley were entertaining Emperor Rudolph with tales of the alchemical prowess of Roger Bacon, they had the *Voynich Manuscript* in mind. Either they wrote it or they had it with them. If they had it with them, the story becomes more interesting, because then perhaps they are not its authors. If they *are* its authors, then it merely reveals the grammatical deep structure of the deranged minds of two Elizabethan magicians and would explain to some degree why it has defied decipherment. If Dee and Kelley didn't write it, if they only had it in their possession, then the mystery continues. Where did they get it and what was it?

It is true that Dee was under the patronage of the Earl of Northumberland, who, when Henry VIII broke with Rome, sacked English monasteries that had large repositories of Roger Bacon material. Dee's library at Mortlake was known to have fifty-three Baconian manuscripts, of which only forty-one have survived into modern times. They now reside at the Bodleian Library at Oxford and at the British Museum. In the truly compendious *A True And Faithful Relation, etc.*, Dee recorded the day-by-day séances with spirits as he and Kelley traveled all over Europe. In the very month that the emperor paid the three hundred gold ducats for a manuscript, Dee recorded in his diary that he and Kelley received three hundred gold ducats from a mysterious source.

Some biographers have taken the position that Dee didn't believe in magic at all, and that he only posed as an occultist to conceal the fact that he was an intelligence agent for the British crown. According to this interpretation, he was visiting the courts of Europe as an astrologer, necromancer, and alchemist, while actually encrypting very succinct military, strategic, and diplomatic information into letters, which he then sent home. Because he could cast the finest horoscope in Europe, he had an entree into the lives of nobility. Doubtless the truth lies somewhere in between. He was an agent of the British crown, but he was also the finest flower of the medieval mind. He was used by Shakespeare as the model for Prospero in *The Tempest*, and was the model for Dr. Faustus in Christopher Marlowe's play of the same name.

Many careers have floundered on the basis of alleged decipherments of the *Voynich Manuscript*. Some scholars have come forward with very bold claims. In the 1920s, William Romaine Newbold, a classics scholar, a medievalist, and by all accounts a very brilliant man, announced that he had a complete decipherment of the *Voynich Manuscript*. He claimed that the key was tiny shorthand strokes that were components of each letter in the manuscript, and he maintained that by staring through a magnifying loupe one could see that, encoded into each character, were the distorted remains of a Roman shorthand system that had been lost for six hundred years. He produced astonishing decipherments of Roger Bacon–related material. His decoded passages dealt with student uprisings at Oxford at Christmastime in 1291, when riots between the Black Friars and the town would not have been uncommon. The problem with all of this was that no one else could extract the same plaintext using Professor Newbold's method. It involved so many choices from pools of letters at every given point along the way that one could demonstrate that hundreds of different messages could be extracted from the same passages. Newbold died a broken man, disgraced, his career shattered. He had gone too far, and the *Voynich Manuscript* had claimed its first victim.

The next person to propose a decipherment of the *Voynich Manuscript* was Robert S. Brumbaugh, also of Yale University, and his decipherment is, in some ways, almost as puzzling as the encryption. He would have us believe that the *Voynich Manuscript* says things like "liquid Cerian matter, liquid matter, plus Cerian Sicilian, plus Cerian salt European Swedish Sicilian plus Cerian, plus Russian Asian Sicilian salt, liquid liquid Asian Italian Cerian salt, liquid Sicilian Italian plus Sicilian, plus salt," and so on. When his method was examined by others attempting to reproduce the same plaintext, they got nowhere, and his effort has not been taken seriously.

Another effort at decipherment, which is minor, perhaps, in comparison to the other two, but which provides an interesting anecdote, was by a man named Strong at the University of California at San Diego. He claimed decipherment of certain of the labels of the *Voynich Manuscript's* illustrations. When Paul Lee formed a working group to look into the *Manuscript*, Dr. Strong was one of the people they wanted to interview, and a member of the group who is a friend of mine, Ralph Abraham, a mathematician at the University of California at Santa Cruz, had photostats made of certain folios of the *Voynich Manuscript*. He sent these folios along with very detailed letters to Strong with questions such as, "It is alleged that on folio 9B you translated a certain word as 'uterus.' Here is a photostat of folio 9B; please circle the word you translated." Strong's secretary wrote Ralph back saying that Strong was very

old, in his nineties, and he didn't feel he could compose a letter to address all these questions, but that if Ralph would come to San Diego he
would satisfy him completely. That was a Thursday. Ralph got a reser-
vation to fly down on the following Monday. Sunday night the secretary
called to say that Dr. Strong had died of a heart attack that evening. The
Voynich Manuscript has bedeviled people's careers, and people who have
claimed to understand it have died with the secret untransmitted to the
rest of us.

The United States government intelligence community has spent
a fair bit of time looking into the *Voynich Manuscript*, simply because it is
unheard of that a sixteenth-century manuscript should resist decipherment by modern methods. The single most interesting writing about the
Voynich Manuscript is a Department of Commerce publication called *The
Voynich Manuscript: An Elegant Enigma*, by Mary D'Empirio. It is a colla-
tion of everything known about the manuscript, commissioned by the
United States government.

Many interesting facts have been established, and there is hope
that the manuscript may eventually be deciphered. Computer analysis
of the handwriting shows that two hands are involved. Does this mean
it was written by Dee and Kelley? If so, can we get a better idea of their
role in its creation by comparing the handwriting in the manuscript with
that of Dee and Kelley?

D'Empirio discusses many magical alphabets, many different
forms of shorthand and specialized note-keeping scripts that were current in Europe throughout the Middle Ages. None of them look particularly like the *Voynich* script. Ralph Abraham made a suggestion that the
Voynich script had some relation to early Brahmanic number systems.
He thought perhaps that it was a string of numbers that would have to
be decoded and the resulting string further deciphered to extract the literal message.

One possibility is that we moderns simply overrate the sophistication of our code-breaking machinery. Perhaps there are simple ways
of encoding material that simply have not occurred to the CIA, and
when the *Voynich* code is finally broken, the solution will prove trivial,
but unexpected in some way. For instance, Ralph made the suggestion
to me that grids with holes cut in them might have been used. When
such a grid was laid over a page, it separated the message parts of the
text from the nonsensical noise.

If the grid changes from page to page and is completely irrational
in the way that it changes, then no computer program imaginable could
separate the plaintext from the noise. A recursive formula could not de-
duce an ever-changing variable based on whim, and this would preclude any machine-oriented effort to decipher the manuscript. This grid
method is well known and represents a standard method of hiding a

message, embedding it in great amounts of garbled material. It would have appealed to the alchemical imagination of Dee or Kelley or any of their educated occult contemporaries. If this notion is the key, it may mean that somewhere there exist either the grids or the instructions for building them.

In the summation of her book, D'Empirio suggests ideas for further research. The *Voynich Manuscript* has never been physically analyzed, which would settle once and for all at least the century of its origin. The libraries of the world should be searched for other examples of Voynich script. After all, are we really sure that there's no other extant example of this strange writing? Computer analysis, the approach of the Santa Cruz group, could settle on a standard alphabet for the manuscript and then catalog every character, the number of times it occurs, and in what combinations it occurs with other characters. From this data a preliminary grammar might be deduced.

None of the illustrations have ever been satisfactorily interpreted. What are called the astrological illustrations are only nominally astrological. They seem to have stars and circles in them, but otherwise they are not particularly referent to the sky. The so-called pharmaceutical section, which depicts little canisters and strange little naked women bathing in curious, convoluted plumbing, could be anything—an obscure form of central German hydrotherapy, or the doodlings of a deranged imagination. When you only have one of something, it is quite difficult to place it in the correct context of cultural history, especially since there was a lot of secrecy in this period, faking of manuscripts and spurious attributions, use of secret cover languages, communication in secret codes, plotting of secret societies.

If my analysis of the *Voynich Manuscript* as the product of Dee and Kelley has seemed too facile, let me assure my reader that it is, and that not all the facts are covered by this theory. What fascinates me most about the *Voynich Manuscript*, above and beyond the historical puzzle and above and beyond how interesting it would be to know what it actually says, is the idea of an unreadable book. It is a kind of Borgesian concept that there must be, somewhere, an unreadable book, and perhaps this is it. The unreadable book hints at the idea that the world is information. We have cognizance of the world by ordering all the information we come upon in relation to information that we have already accumulated—through patterns. An unreadable book in a non-English script, with no dictionary attached, is very puzzling. We become like linguistic oysters, we secrete around it, we encyst it into our metaphysic. But we don't know what it says, which always carries with it the possibility that it says something that would unhinge our conceptions of things or that its real message is its unreadability. It points to the Otherness of the nature of information, and is what is called in structuralism a "limit text." Certainly the *Voynich Manuscript* is the limit text of Western occultism. It is truly an occult book—one that no one can read. It is a making literal of the mythical book in H. P. Lovecraft's work *The Necronomicon*, the writings of the mad Arab, Alhazrad; in fact, Colin Wilson, in his book *The Philosopher's Stone*, connects the *Voynich Manuscript* to *The Necronomicon* and the Shew Stone used for scraying by Dee with the Philosopher's Stone.

O

And there the matter rested until 1987, and might have rested forever but for the questing curiosity of one man. Enter Dr. Leo Levitov, author of *Solution of the Voynich Manuscript*; a man who claims a complete understanding of the dynamics of *Voynich* and translation of the manuscript. He gives us the good news in his subtitle: *A Liturgical Manual for the Endura Rite of the Cathari Heresy, The Cult of Isis*. Levitov's thesis is that the *Voynich* is nothing less than the only surviving primary document of the Great Heresy that arose in Italy and flourished in Languedoc until ruthlessly exterminated by the Albigensian Crusade in the 1230s. Very little is known about the beliefs of the Catharite faith, and all the knowledge we do have of it is secondhand, obtained from the records of the Inquisition, whose task was the destruction of Cathar society. Levitov's translation, if substantiated, would throw new light on the puzzling rise and extermination of the greatest heretical challenge that the Roman church ever faced.

There are a number of problems with Levitov's notions, but there are also triumphs. He makes several startling claims that he supports very well. The little women in the baths who puzzled so many are for Levitov a Cathar sacrament, the Endura, "or death by venesection [cutting a vein] in order to bleed to death in a warm bath." The plant drawings that refused to resolve themselves into botanically identifiable species are no problem for Levitov: "Actually, there is not a single so-called botanical illustration that does not contain some Cathari symbol or Isis' symbol." The astrological drawings are likewise easy to deal with: "The innumerable stars are representative of the stars in Isis' mantle."

Levitov's strong hand is translation. He asserts that the reason it has been so difficult to decipher the *Voynich Manuscript* is that it is not encrypted at all, but merely written in a special script, and is "an adaptation of a polyglot oral tongue into a literary language which would be understandable to people who did not understand Latin and to whom this language could be read." Specifically, a highly polyglot form of medieval Flemish with a large number of Old French and Old High German loan words. Good. So now we know.

Where there is danger for Levitov is in the contents of the translated material. Levitov freely admits that he is convinced from his translation that Catharism is a religion of Isis, a religion of the great Goddess. Apparently he is alone in this belief, although A. E. Waite says in his discussion of the Cathars and The Holy Grail (1961), "The Grail Mythos is . . . like the Veil of Isis, which no man can raise rather than tolerate the suggestion that these nightmare faiths are behind it." Save for Waite's lucky turn of phrase, no commentator, ancient or modern, has ever breathed a word concerning Isis in connection with the Cathars. At one point the Cathars became a focus of latter-day occultists, but not even their literature mentioned Isis.

Levitov is almost casual in his presentation of his work, questioning at one point whether now that he has figured out how to translate the manuscript, it is worth actually doing. "A complete translation of the more than 200 pages waits in the wings—a long, arduous and possibly unrewarding task." For Levitov the problem seemed to be one of solving the language problem, but larger problems are now raised if in fact the Voynich is to be seen as a primary source showing the Cathars to be not at all as we have come to think of them. Students of Gnosticism, paganism, and the Goddess will all have to digest this new slant on the role of the Cathars.

As for what the manuscript actually says, it is a gloomy and repetitive work, made partly so by Levitov's decision to present it in a rather raw state, as its sense requires scholarly interpretation. At its most lyrical the translation is quite interesting:

> The person who is knowledgeable about aid, knows there is only one way to treat agonizing pain. He treats each one by putting them through the Endura. It is the one way that helps Death. Not everyone knows how to assist the one with pain. The one who is with death, and does not die will have pain. But those who have such pain of death, need his help. He understands the need. He is also aware that the person who needs help does not know that he needs it. We all know that everyone of them needs help and each of us will be available to help.

The passage refers to the Cathar sacrament for the dying, a form of euthanasia in which pious Cathars were helped to die by specially trained perfecti.

Levitov mentions extensive personal research into the Cathar material, but cites none of it. I cannot tell if he was aware of H. J. Warner's The Albigensian Heresy or W. L. Wakefield's Heresy, Crusade and Inquisition in Southern France. He states that the Voynich Manuscript is the only primary Catharite document in existence. However, A. E. Waite in his *Holy Grail* mentions, "There is fortunately one fragmentary record of Albigensian belief which has survived. . . . I refer to the *Cathar Ritual of Lyons* which is now well known having been published in 1898 by Mr. F. C. Conybeare." Waite goes on to mention that part of the Lyons Codex contains "certain prayers for the dying." The codex is in the langue d'oc. Does it resemble the *Voynich* material? We are not told.

If Levitov is right, we moderns simply overrated the sophistication of our code-breaking machinery and overlooked the possibility that the manuscript was not in code at all.

Levitov fails to mention the physical manuscript. Yet it seems obvious that one of the first steps that should be taken would be to attempt to confirm the thirteenth-century origin date for the manuscript. If the manuscript was written before 1250, then it is older than was claimed by even the adherents of the Roger Bacon theory of its authorship. Surely it should be possible to determine whether the manuscript was written in the thirteenth or the sixteenth century!

If it was a product of the thirteenth century, then my own efforts to see the hand of John Dee in its composition are immediately rendered futile, although it is still quite possible that Dee was involved in the manuscript's finding its way to Rudolph's court. Until Levitov, most scholars have been confident in placing the origin of the manuscript in the early fifteenth century.

Therefore, Leo Levitov is to be congratulated. He has made a persuasive case and remained modest doing it. Now we need to hear from the experts, the medievalists, linguists, and scholars of heresy, for it will be through the consensus and judgment of the community of scholars that Levitov's claim to have translated the world's most mysterious manuscript will stand or fall.

13

Wasson's Literary Precursors

THERE can be no doubt that the modern era of ethnomycology begins with the work of Gordon and Valentina Wasson. The late Mr. Wasson is the Abraham of the reborn awareness in Western civilization of the presence of the shamanically empowering mushroom. Yet, like all great innovative thinkers, the Wassons had their precursors. Before the Wassons there were those who had stumbled onto an awareness of the visionary potential of fungi. Their experiences, their findings, did not become a cause célèbre or an academic discipline. Many simply chose to keep secret what they had discovered—a sensible response to Western society's long-standing bias against these mushrooms, which was reinforced by frightening reports of "mushroom intoxication" that never acknowledged anything salutary about the experience. A good example, set down in *Science*, September 18, 1914, is by A. E. Merrill of Yale University. Merrill described the hallucinogenic effects of an accidental ingestion of *Panaeolus papilionaceus* from Oxford County, Maine. Although the identification of the mushroom may have been in error, the effects described are very likely due to psilocybin. Robert Graves has offered a summary of the incident in his *Food for Centaurs:*

> Mr. W. gathered about a pound of *panaeolus papilionaceus* mushrooms, and fried them in butter for himself and his niece. The immediate effect was that both felt a bit tipsy, and soon their surroundings seemed to take on bright colours, in which a vivid green predominated. Next both expe-

A shortened version of this essay first appeared in *The Divine Mushroom Seeker*, a festschrift for Gordon Wasson, edited by Tom Riedlinger, published by Dioscorides Press, 1990.

rienced an irresistible impulse to run and jump, which they did hilari-
ously, laughing almost to the point of hysteria at the witty remarks they
exchanged. . . . When they left the house to take a walk, they lost all sense
of time—a long period seemed short and contrariwise; the same with distances. . . . Wallpaper patterns appeared to creep and crawl about,
though at first remaining two dimensional; then began to grow out toward him from the walls with uncanny motions. He looked at a bunch of
large red roses, all of one kind, which lay on the table; and at another on
a writing-desk. At once the room seemed to fill with roses of various red
colours and many sizes in lavish bunches, wreaths and chains.

Feeling a sudden rush of blood to his head, he lay down. Then followed
an illusion of countless hideous faces of every sort and extending in mul-
titudes over endless distances, all grimacing at him rapidly and horribly,
and coloured like fireworks—intense reds, purples, greens, and yellows.
(1960, pp. 277–78)

It would be difficult indeed for any voluntary user of hallucinogenic fungi to openly defend such effects as desirable, even for artistic
inspiration. Instead, the inclination was for the mushroom *cognoscente* to
keep silent.

Yet some, it appears, found a way to safely publicize their personal familiarity with psychoactive mushrooms, by disguising it as literary
fiction. It is useful for us now, in the expanded intellectual arena that
ethnomycology has created for itself, to examine those brave futurists of
the past who anticipated what Gordon Wasson made explicit—that is,
the presence of an awesome spiritual power resident in the visionary
fungi, resident in psilocybin.

The Wassons acknowledged a few of these "literary precursors"
in *Mushrooms, Russia and History*. One was Lewis Carroll, whose 1865
masterpiece *Alice's Adventures in Wonderland* includes an interesting section in which Alice eats pieces of a mushroom that causes her to alter-
nately shrink and grow. The Wassons observed:

All of Alice's subsequent distortions, softened by the loving irony of
Lewis Carroll's imagination, retain the flavor of mushroomic hallucinations. Is there not something uncanny about the injection of this mushroom into Alice's story? What led the quiet Oxford don to hit on a device
so felicitous, but at the same time sinister for the initiated readers, when
he launched his maiden on her way? Did he dredge up this curious specimen of wondrous and even fearsome lore from some deep well of half-
conscious folk-knowledge? (1957, pp. 194–195)

The possibility that Carroll may have drawn on a personal experience with psychoactive mushrooms is not acknowledged by the

Wassons. Instead they proceed to develop convincingly their thesis that he got his inspiration from a different source: Mordecai Cooke's *Plain and Easy Account of British Fungi* (1862). This book included what the Wassons call "horrifying accounts of the amanita-eating Korjaks" of Siberia, who, upon eating this mushroom (*Amanita muscaria*), experienced "erroneous impressions of size and distance" among other psychoactive effects.

Interestingly, the Wassons ignored a significant piece of evidence that strengthens the case for their thesis considerably. It is found in the beginning of the scene in which Alice encounters the magical mushroom:

> There was a large mushroom growing near her, about the same height as herself; and, when she had looked under it, and on both sides of it, and behind it, it occurred to her that she might as well look and see what was on the top of it.
>
> She stretched herself up on tiptoe, and peeped over the edge of the mushroom, and her eyes immediately met those of a large blue caterpillar, that was sitting on the top, with its arms folded, quietly smoking a long hookah, and taking not the smallest notice of her or of anything else. (Carroll, 1960, p. 66)

At the time the Wassons wrote *Mushrooms, Russia and History* they did not know of another, more relevant book by Mordecai Cooke, *The Seven Sisters of Sleep* (1852), which discussed seven major varieties of psychoactive substances. Included among them are both *Amanita muscaria* and cannabis, united by Carroll in one striking image of a hookah-smoking caterpillar perched on a mushroom with magical properties.

Also in *Mushrooms, Russia and History*, the Wassons acknowledged an interesting psychoactive mushroom story written by H. G. Wells in the late nineteenth century. "The Purple Pileus" tells the ostensibly fictional tale of one Mr. Coombes, a meek, henpecked man who tries to kill himself by eating what he thinks to be a poisonous mushroom he finds in the forest. This mushroom, writes Wells, is "a peculiarly poisonous-looking purple: slimy, shiny, and emitting a sour odor" (1966, pp. 191–200). When broken by Coombes, its creamy white inner flesh changes "like magic in the space of ten seconds to a yellowish-green colour." Its taste is so pungent he almost spits it out. Within minutes, his pulse starts to race and he feels a tingling sensation in his fingertips and toes. Then, before he can pick more purple pilei from a cluster he sees in the distance, Coombes is distracted by the mushroom's full effect. It induces a powerful change in his psychology for several hours, transforming him into a veritable lion. He rushes home, gaily singing and dancing, to confront his wife. His eyes as he enters the house are described as "unnaturally large and bright." After frightening off his wife's boyfriend and earning her lasting respect, he falls into a "deep and healing sleep."

The Wassons make it clear, in their analysis of Wells's story, that Coombes had not eaten *Amanita muscaria*. Instead, they conclude, Wells had "filled out the necessities of a given plot by inventing the needed mushroom" (1957, pp. 50–51). They do not suggest, and apparently never considered, that Wells's purple pileus may have been a thinly disguised *Psilocybe* mushroom. Like *Psilocybe*, it changes color when broken; has a markedly pungent taste when eaten fresh; often grows in clusters; quickly causes profound psychological and somatic effects, including dilation of the pupils; and induces deep sleep as an aftereffect. Also worth noting is that Wasson later, in 1978, made much of a psychoactive fungus's purple color in *The Road to Eleusis: Unveiling the Secret of the Mysteries*, where he and coauthors Albert Hofmann and Carl A. P. Ruck argued convincingly that the sacramental drink imbibed at Eleusis contained the psychoactive fungus *Claviceps purpurea*. According to them, the purple color of the vestments of the priests who conducted the mysteries was identical to, and therefore emblematic of, this fungus, which grows throughout Europe.

Could Wells have been personally familiar with the effects of *Psilocybe*, *Claviceps*, or some other species of hallucinogenic mushroom? Certain others of his stories seem to resonate with insights that may well have been derived from such experience. In "The Platter Story," for example, the title character finds himself transported to an eerie, hallucinatory "Other-world" with a green sun, where the left and right side of his body are transposed. The green illumination is consistent with the previously cited experience of Graves's Mr. W., whose "surroundings seemed to take on bright colors, in which a vivid green predominated" when he ate what were reported to be *Panaeolus papilionaceus* mushrooms. The transposition of Plattner's body reminds one of Alice's adventures "through the looking glass," since mirrors cause a similar transposition; modern theories are that hallucinogens shift emphasis from left- to right-brain thinking. Of equal interest, this "Other-world" coexists with ours and is accessible to us when our perceptions are enhanced. "It seems quite possible," wrote Wells, "that people with unusually keen eyesight may occasionally catch a glimpse of this strange Other-world about us" (1966, pp. 141–157). Another Wells story, "The New Accelerator," tells of a man who takes a drug that speeds his metabolism to such a degree that the world around him appears to be standing still. The impression of "stopping the world" is another effect that occurs with hallucinogens, though Wells compares it instead to the effect of nitrous oxide: "You know that blank nonexistence into which one drops when one has taken 'gas,'" says his protagonist. "For an indefinite interval it was like that" (pp. 165–176). The possibility that Wells experienced psychoactive substances is therefore compelling.

An even stronger case can be made for Wells's contemporary John Uri Lloyd, who almost certainly had personal awareness of the psychoactivity of psilocybin-containing mushrooms. The first publication date of his crypto-discourse on psilocybin, *Etidorhpa*, is 1895, nearly sixty years before the Wassons' first trip to Huatla.

There is ample evidence, both circumstantial and *prima facie*, that Lloyd had experienced intoxication by psilocybin. Lloyd was a *fin de siècle* character, both a competent pharmaceutical chemist and a man with a passion for occult literature and speculation. According to Neal Wilgas, author of the introduction to both later editions of *Etidorhpa* (1976, 1978),[*] Lloyd was born in West Bloomfield, New York, on April 19, 1849—the eldest son of a civil engineer and a descendant of Governor John Webster of Massachusetts. His family moved to Kentucky and then to Cincinnati. It was there, at the age of fifteen, that John Uri Lloyd began to learn the drug trade. He became the laboratory manager of a drug firm and later became a partner in the company. Lloyd and his brothers published a quarterly journal, *Drugs and Medicines of North America*. Later he was to participate in the establishment of the Lloyd Library of Botany and Pharmacy. To this day, in the field of phytochemistry, the preeminence of the journal *Lloydia* is a testament to the Lloyd brothers' passion for pharmacology and pharmacognosy.

John Uri's brother, Curtis Gates Lloyd, is described by one source as one of the leading fungi botanists of his time. C. G. Lloyd made extensive collections of fungi in the Gulf states and the Deep South; there can be little doubt that if a mushroom species such as *Stropharia cubensis* was present then in those places with even a fraction of the frequency that it is encountered today, then Curtis Gates Lloyd would have collected and been familiar with it. Lloyd's specimen collections deposited with the Smithsonian number several thousands. Perhaps an examination of those collections would yield specimens of psychoactive fungi and field notes concerning them.

In any case it seems clear that John Uri Lloyd's bizarre hollow-earth novel *Etidorhpa* was for him a kind of labyrinth at whose center he wished to place the apotheosis that he had personally experienced in his

---

[*]I have listed all known editions of Lloyd's *Etidorhpa* in the bibliography to this book. The introduction by Neal Wilgas, titled "The Pharmaceutical Alchemist," that accompanies both later editions is scholarly and informative and discusses the psychedelic interests of Lloyd.

own peregrinations in the realm of gigantic fungi. For forty-one pages (from page 235 to page 276 in the 1895, privately printed author's edition), Lloyd raves. He gives us not only his encounter with the anagrammatic mother goddess Etidorhpa (she is "Aphrodite" backward), but a theory of time that bears the unmistakable imprint of the mushroom *philosophe*. At the end of seven chapters devoted to a classic psychopompic initiation via visionary fungi, Lloyd places a footnote that lets the cat out of the bag:

> If, in the course of experimentation, a chemist should strike upon a compound that in traces only would subject his mind and drive his pen to record such seemingly extravagant ideas as are found in the hallucinations herein pictured, or to frame word-sentences foreign to normal conditions, and beyond his natural ability, and yet could he not know the end of such a drug, would it not be his duty to bury the discovery from others, to cover from mankind the existence of such a noxious fruit of the chemist's or pharmaceutist's art? To sip once or twice of such a potent liquid, and then to write lines that tell the story of its power may do no harm to an individual on his guard, but mankind in common should never possess such a penetrating essence. Introduce such an intoxicant, and start it to ferment in humanity's blood, and it may spread from soul to soul, until, before the world is advised of its possible results, the ever increasing potency will gain such headway as to destroy, or debase, our civilization, and even to exterminate mankind. (1895, p. 276)

And what are the extravagant ideas and hallucinations of which John Uri Lloyd wishes to speak? At the close of chapter 23, the hero of *Etidorhpa* is told to drink the juice of "a peculiar fungus." Our hero's guide minces no words: "He spoke the single word, 'Drink,' and I did as directed." The following three chapters are a virtual monologue on the methods of intoxication known to humanity worldwide and throughout history. The horror of inebriation and addiction is graphically depicted and reaches a climax in chapter 39, "Among the Drunkards." If these chapters are the obligatory hell experience of nineteenth-century drug reportage, then chapter 40 is the paradisiacal apotheosis. It is also the climax of the book and contains the incident in which the hero confronts Etidorhpa. Indeed, J. Augustus Knapp's beautiful etching of her is tipped into this chapter. Her appearance and retinue sets off a cascade of florid (and psychedelic) Victorian prose:

> Could any man from the data of my past experiences have predicted such a scene? Never before had the semblance of a woman appeared, never before had an intimation been given that the gentle sex existed in

these silent chambers. Now, from the grotesque figures and horrible cries of the former occupants of this same cavern, the scene had changed to a conception of the beautiful and artistic, such as a poetic spirit might evolve in an extravagant dream of higher fairy land. I glanced above; the great hall was clothed in brilliant colors, the bare rocks had disappeared, the dome of that vast arch, reaching to an immeasurable height, was decorated in all the colors of the rainbow. Flags and streamers fluttered in breezes that also moved the garments of the angelic throng about me, but which I could not sense.

The band of spirits or fairy forms reached the rock at my feet, but I did not know how long a time they consumed in doing this; it may have been a second, and it may have been an eternity. Neither did I care. A single moment of existence such as I experienced, seemed worth an age of any other pleasure. (1895, p. 253)

The appearance of the goddess is quickly followed by reestablishment of the theme of suffering and terror as the hero imagines himself lost and wandering for days in an arid wasteland, at first tormented by the sun, later frozen by its absence. As this hallucination fades:

The ice scene dissolved, the enveloped frozen form of myself faded from view, the sand shrunk into nothingness, and with my natural body, and in normal condition, I found myself back in the earth cavern, on my knees, beside the curious inverted fungus, of which fruit I had eaten in obedience to my guide's directions. (1895, p. 270)

At the beginning of chapter 42 the hero argues with his guide concerning the nature of what he has just experienced. The psychopomp speaks first:

"You ate of the narcotic fungus; you have been intoxicated."

"I have not," I retorted. "I have been through your accursed caverns and into hell beyond. I have been consumed by eternal damnation in the journey, have experienced a heaven of delight, and also an eternity of misery."

"Upon the contrary, the time that has passed since you drank the liquid contents of that fungus fruit has only been that which permitted you to fall upon your knees. You swallowed the liquor when I handed you the shell cup; you dropped upon your knees and then instantly awoke. See," he said; "in corroboration of my assertion the shell of the fungus fruit at your feet is still dripping with the liquid you did not drink. Time has been annihilated. Under the influence of this potent earth-bread narcoto-intoxicant, your dream began inside of eternity; you did not pass into it." (1895, pp. 272–273)

These passages are more than sufficient to convince the open-minded reader that John Uri Lloyd, nineteenth-century savant, pharmacist, occultist, and author, had discovered the consciousness-expanding properties of psilocybin mushrooms, experienced them, and then decided to suppress his discovery. Given Lloyd's obvious ambiguity toward the visionary state, evinced by his diatribes against intoxication, and his love of word play, evinced by his reversing the letters in the name Aphrodite to create the title of his masterpiece, I am emboldened to put forth evidence that argues that Lloyd had a particular species of mushroom in mind, one that must have been very familiar to his botanist brother Curtis.

Facing page 116 in the author's 1895 edition is a magnificent full-page illustration of the hero and his guide making their way through a forest of enormous mushrooms. The caption reads "I was in a forest of colossal fungi." While examining this illustration and thinking about the letter reversal used to form the book's title, it occurred to me that perhaps the clue to the identity of the intoxicant that Lloyd was so concerned to suppress might be hidden anagramatically in the captions of the full-page illustrations.

"If such were the case," came the unbidden thought, "then the following full-page illustration may have a caption that can be manipulated to give the name of the secret source of the intoxicant."

That illustration (opposite page 130) again shows hero and guide, this time examining the face of a stony cliff of a crystalline mineral. The caption reads, "Monstrous Cubical Crystals." Annagramatic manipulation is unnecessary. Out of the caption the letter groups STRO CUB jump out at any one with any interest in ethnomycology. *Stropharia cubensis* is the species most likely to have been known to the botanical Lloyds!

Does this mean that the mystery has been solved? That all the pieces neatly fall into place? Quite the contrary. *Stropharia cubensis* was supposedly not named until its discovery in Cuba by the botanist Earle in 1906. Nine years *after* the first publication of *Etidorhpa!*

Are we dealing with an instance of prophetic vision, or an outlandishly improbable coincidence? Or would research show that the Lloyd brothers knew the work of Earle, knew even the name he would eventually propose for a new species of mushroom flourishing in the pastures of the American South and the Caribbean Islands? It is the kind of mystery that haunts research into the world of mycolatry, the kind of mystery that Gordon Wasson loved.

"MONSTROUS CUBICAL CRYSTALS."

Wasson's interest in Lloyd is a matter of record, though he never, to my knowledge, wrote about him in his books. There is a file at the Valentina and Gordon Wasson Ethno-mycological Collection at Harvard's Botanical Museum where Wasson saved newspaper clippings, letters, notes, and other information for a second edition of *Mushrooms, Russia and History* that never materialized. In this file is a letter from a Mr. Bernard Lentz dated May 16, 1957, recommending that Wasson read *Etidorhpa*. A copy of Wasson's reply, dated June 4, 1957, is also on file. It reads in part: "I shall try to look the matter up, when I have time. John Uri Lloyd—a well known name." Years later, in his forward to a bookseller's catalog, Wasson (1979) wrote the following:

> There is one item in it [the catalog] that interests me especially: *Etidorpha* ("Aphrodite" spelled backwards), by J. U. Lloyd, a strange novel, or better a fantasy, first published in 1895, a novel that Michael Horowitz (the cataloguer) rightly says was a psychoactive mushroom tale. Where did Lloyd's ideas come from? He must have read carefully Captain John G. Bourke's *Scatalogic Rites of All Nations*, published in 1891, that immense and amazing collection of scatological materials. Lloyd's mushrooms are clearly not *Amanita muscaria*. Did he possess a copy of that rarest of all entheogenic books, by the famous English Mycologist M. C. Cooke, *The Seven Sisters of Sleep*, a book that Cooke never referred to in his later mycological writings? Here is indeed a manual of psychoactive drugs, published almost 120 years ago! Nor was it included in the bibliography of his writings published on his death. How did Lloyd hit on this mushroom fantasy? Is there latent in our society a memory of mushroom use, long long ago, a subliminal memory that crops out in Lloyd's tale, also in *Alice in Wonderland*? The suggestive shapes and delicate changing colors of mushrooms, their sudden appearance and disappearance, the endless diversity in their odors, one for each species—all support a mushroom mythology that is backed up, when one knows about it, by the compelling entheogenic potency residing in some of them. (1979, p. 6)

Again, as with Carroll and Wells, Wasson failed to admit the possibility that Lloyd's insights were based on personal experience. But neither did he rule it out. The matter thus remains to be resolved by a new generation of ethno-mycologists—or literary archaeologists.

Finally, we turn to a work of the twentieth century overlooked by Wasson. In the May 1915 issue of the *Irish Ecclestical Record* a piece appeared, written by an A. Newman, titled "Monsieur Among the Mushrooms." This piece purports to be a nonfiction recollection of a person known to the author. "Monsieur Among the Mushrooms" was reprinted in 1917, one piece among many, in a book titled *Unknown Immortals—In the Northern City of Success* by one Herbert Moore Pim, apparently a minor essayist and journalist of the time. Pim in his preface thanks the editors of the *Irish Ecclestical Record* for permission to reprint "Monsieur," so we can be confident that Pim is A. Newman.[*]

While the mushrooms described in "Monsieur" are not overtly psychoactive (except, perhaps, as a fetish), the story is relevant to our discussion for being (1) the record of a person with an appreciation of mushrooms on a cosmic scale and (2) the earliest known instance of a modern cult of mushroom users. Pim says in his preface:

> The original of "Monsieur Among the Mushrooms" is alive and prosperous. He is a perfectly amazing person, a man of considerable fortune, who has, I believe, been detained in an asylum on several occasions. He conducts a large business during the day-time; but he may be discovered at four or five o'clock in the morning, pouring forth a stream of brilliance, and holding men in the cold street against their will. His brain works with such rapidity that he has constructed a language of his own, by means of which only the absolutely essential thought is presented to the hearer. I have seen calm men whipped into fury when they found themselves simply swept off their feet in argument with my model.
>
> In "Monsieur" I have drawn him exactly as he exists, save in the matter of the physical description. Apart from that fact, there is nothing exaggerated; and the debate between Monsieur and the members of the committee is almost as true as a description of such a debate could be. There you see my model and his method (1917, p. 604)

"Monsieur Among the Mushrooms" is a recollection of a remarkable personality, we might say an obsessed personality, who has been committed to an asylum because of his unusual ideas concerning fungi. In the piece, Monsieur argues that he is sane before the release committee of the asylum in which he resides. But before that Pim informs us of the remarkable philosophy and history of his model, as he calls him:

> Here it was that Monsieur learned how the mushroom might be persuaded to grow; and here it was that for many days he toiled unobserved, appropriately attired in black, with a light heart and a somewhat lightened purse. And in those first, fresh, active days he found time

[*]In the bibliography to this work, I have included citations for both instances in which "Monsieur Among the Mushrooms" was printed, since both are obscure and difficult to obtain. The 1915 version has extensive footnotes, which were dropped from the 1917 reprinting. Special deep thanks to Michael Horowitz of Flashback Books in Petaluma, California for calling my attention to the work of Herbert Moore Pim.

even to press his theory upon others as a physic to be received in small measures, while the giver retains something, if it even be the bottle. And so it came that, in a little while, there arose a respectful company of believers.

"How great, indeed," Monsieur would exclaim, "is the mushroom! it has claimed the round world for its habitation; and when man rears his cities of stone it demands of him that even in the heart of cities it shall be given space to express itself in silence."

There was the world itself to be considered. For presently it put its claw into its own stomach, where Monsieur and his disciples were digesting wisdom, and demanded to know the reason for an aesthetic appreciation of a commodity interesting only for its commercial value. (1915, p. 588)

Needless to say, a hearing was held, its conclusions forgone:

And who can forget the genial and superior smile which rested upon the faces of his judges? The mushroom was the all-powerful exception! Just so. Who could doubt it? But for such as believed in it there had been made complete provision.

"But how," exclaimed Monsieur, "shall I make progress in my investigation?"

He was assured with gentleness that, even though placed *extra muros*, he should have "every facility," "ample scope," and that, above all, he might hope to be well again.

"But to what end?" he interrupted.

"In order," it was explained to him, "that you may be in harmony with the majority."

"But the majority here are mushrooms! Man, their toy, is nowhere. It is he who is *extra muros!*" (1915, p. 590)

A virtual prisoner, Monsieur spends his days in the asylum contemplating the irony of his situation and ultimately hatches a plan of escape. His asylum musings revolve around only one theme:

With his knowledge of the mushroom he was all-powerful. Behind the material which witnessed to a supremely strong exception, there was the energy of mind that drove and guided, swept aside and conquered. And in the mushroom itself there was unity without contact. The mushroom was, indeed, a giant body torn and strewn over the earth. There was the fungus of the hair. There was that which, by its shape, clearly proved the existence of the brain. There was a form which made certain that the egg was the origin of that which it contained. There was the manifestation of that which generates. And there was a growth which appertained to the lower animals. There were many things besides: the star-like eyes, from which the sun and moon derived their radiance; the great masses of body and limb; the fingers and the features; the mouth that devoured. There was the warrior from whose wounds blood could flow. There was that which indicated the cellular structure of the human body, and indeed of all living things. And yet all this was incalculably strong, and all this was inexplicably united. (1915, p. 592)

Eventually Monsieur effects a daring, mushroom-assisted escape. Then we are told in a footnote:

He lived for some time under the protection of the keeper of a plant nursery, who had become so enthusiastic a believer in the doctrine of the Mushroom that he painted his glass-houses with a black light-excluding fluid, and cultivated the mushroom reverently. A primitive worship had already developed when Monsieur was restored to his followers. I have reason to believe that he prepared to encourage this, and, in some respects to modify it. But the world interfered. There is a journal before me which records frequent attacks upon the glass-houses; and there are references to search parties from the asylum. I am enabled to trace the purchase of a sailing ship by the keeper of the plant nursery, and the embarkation of Monsieur and his followers upon this ship, the hold of which contained mushroom-spore bricks. After that I have no reliable evidence. (1915, p. 605)

Aside from the early date of its composition, what makes "Monsieur Among the Mushrooms" so interesting is that it purports to be a factual account of a group of people, informed as to the transformative power of the mushroom and united around a leader and a set of cult practices. It is difficult to believe that Pim would have given such a central philosophical role to mushrooms had he not been aware of the visionary experience imparted by psilocybin-containing species.

Perhaps Pim had read *Etidorhpa*. The book was very popular in its time, having influenced no less a personage that Howard Phillips Lovecraft, the inventor of "cosmic horror" science fiction and the Chthulu mythos. Lovecraft makes reference to *Etidorhpa* in material contained in his *Selected Letters* and *Marginalia*, noting for instance that his visit to the Endless Caverns in Virginia made him think "above all else, of that strange old novel *Etidorhpa* once pass'd around our Kleicomolo circle."

Ultimately we are left with a number of unanswered questions: Who was the mysterious Monsieur and where and how did he discover the psychoactive properties of mushrooms? Was Monsieur actually Herbert Moore Pim himself?* Are there other written records concerning this remarkable career? Into what asylum was Monsieur placed? What "journals" did Pim refer to as describing the attacks on the glasshouses of Monsieur's benefactor? And finally, what became of Monsieur, his writings, and his disciples?

All fascinating questions, answers to which would serve to illuminate the real status of awareness of psilocybin in the pre-Wasson era.

O

Finally we come to the notion of those precursors of Wasson who were his peers. For no one's thought grows in a world devoid of its self-reflections. The most apparent initiatory influence on Gordon Wasson in the matter of mushrooms was certainly his wife, partner, and codiscoverer Valentina:

> Suddenly, before I knew it, my bride threw down my hand roughly and ran up into the forest, with cries of ecstasy. She had seen toadstools growing, many kinds of toadstools. She had not seen the like since Russia, since 1917. She was in a delirium of excitement and began gathering them right and left in her shirt. From the path I called to her, admonished her not to gather them: they were toadstools, I said, they were poisonous . . . I acted the perfect Anglo-Saxon oaf confronting a wood nymph I had never before laid eyes on. (Wasson et al., 1986, p. 17)

Valentina and Gordon Wasson were influenced in the direction of their mushroom studies by Robert Graves, quoted above. Graves discusses Wasson in a number of essays published together as *Difficult Questions, Easy Answers*. In one of these, "The Two Births of Dionysus," Graves writes:

> Wasson began his career as a journalist without any university education (which may account for the preservation of his genius), became a Wall Street reporter, was taken over by J. P. Morgan & Co. as their press agent, and soon elevated to Vice-President when his extraordinary understanding of business became apparent. Similarly with his second profession: he began as an amateur mycologist and has since become the acknowl-

---

*A respectable precedent for this was set by William James when he published a description of his own severe attacks of melancholia attributed to someone else in *Varieties of Religious Experience* (1902).

edged founder of the huge, immensely important new science, ethnomycology. Whenever I pick up strange news of mushrooms, as often happens, I send it to him for filing. It had been a chance bit of information
that I passed on to him in the early fifties that prompted him to investigate the mushroom oracles of Mexico. (1964, pp. 108–9)

Robert Graves's writings on mushrooms, poetry, and mythology
deserve a wider audience. His thought runs in a parallel stream to that
of Wasson, and each illuminates the other. Graves's *Food for Centaurs*
and *Difficult Questions, Easy Answers* are rich with thought and imagery
directed toward understanding the psychedelic experience.

Graves's last sentence above is fascinating. "It had been a chance
bit of information that I passed on to him in the early fifties that prompted him to investigate the mushroom oracles of Mexico." Graves is casu-
ally referring to the pivotal incident in the reemergence of Western
civilization's discovery of visionary ecstasy through psilocybin. One can
only wonder just where Robert Graves had picked up this "chance bit of
information." Quite by coincidence I ran across a passage in an unlikely
source that may shed light on this.

In discussing Sufi techniques of word play, Idris Shah in his book
The Sufis makes the following comments:

> The Arabic word for a hallucinogenic fungus is from the root GHRB.
> Words derived from the GHRB root indicate a knowledge of the strange
> influence of hallucinogenic fungi. (1964, p.129)

Shah goes on to quote from the Sufi ecstatic Mast Qalandar. After
analyzing the text, Shah concludes:

> The usages of these words, though not incorrect, are so unusual (because
> there is so often a conventional word more apt in such a context) that
> there is absolutely no doubt that a message is being conveyed to the ef-
> fect that chemical hallucinogens derived from fungi provide an undeni-
> able but counterfeit experience. (1964, p. 129)

In the world of ethnomycology the news of an Arabic or Sufi
mushroom cult, ancient or modern, would be of great interest. Shah de-
nies the possibility that Sufis used mushrooms, but his very denial is the
first time I have heard such a thing suggested. The gentleman doth
protest too much. Something in this reminded me of a passage in
Graves's essay "The Two Births of Dionysus" mentioned above, wherein
he explicitly mentions his own awareness of *Stropharia*:

[Wasson] with his Russian wife, had made me aware that stropharia, a small [sic] mushroom growing on cow dung, possesses much the same properties, and whispered news comes to me that this was still used for sacred purposes in India where it grew on the dung of sacred cows. (1964, p. 107)

It appears to me that Graves learned about mushrooms from Idris Shah. Indeed the introduction to Shah's book, *The Sufis*, is written by Robert Graves! At one point Graves writes "I wrote to Idris Shah and he replied" (1964, p. xiii). In another place he remarks, speaking of an emblem, "Idris Shah Sayed has explained its symbolism to me" (1964, p. xv).

Idris Shah Sayed happens to be in the senior male line of descent from the Prophet Mohammed and to have inherited the secret mysteries from the Caliphs, his ancestors. He is, in fact, a Grand Sheikh of the Sufi *Tariqa*.

Here then is the place to leave this scholarly reminiscence, having shown earnestly but light-heartedly that our beloved Valentina and Gordon Wasson, when they went to Mexico in search of magic mushrooms, may have been acting on a hint dropped to an Irish poet by a great-grandson of Mohammed. The Wassons thereby gave meaning to the otherwise premature and incomprehensible discoveries of John Uri Lloyd and Herbert Moore Pim. And more than all that: they thereby gave psilocybin to the modern world.

14

Critique Interview

**B:** IT'S A pleasure to be here with you again, Terence. We'd like to begin by asking you to tell us how you became interested in shamanism and the exploration of consciousness.

TM: I discovered shamanism through an interest in Tibetan folk religion. Bon-Po, the pre-Buddhist religion of Tibet, is a kind of shamanism. In going from the particular to the general with that concern, I studied shamanism as a general phenomenon. It all started out as an art historical interest in the pre-Buddhist iconography of *thankas.*

DB: This was how long ago?

TM: This was in '67, when I was just a sophomore in college. And the interest in altered states of consciousness came simply from, I don't know whether I was a precocious kid or what, but I was very early into the New York literary scene, and even though I lived in a small town in Colorado, I subscribed to the *Village Voice* and *The Evergreen Review,* where I encountered propaganda about LSD, mescaline, and all these experiments that the late beatniks were involved in. Then I read *The Doors of Perception* and *Heaven and Hell,* and it just rolled from there. That was what really put me over. I respected Huxley as a novelist, and I was slowly reading everything he'd ever written, and when I got to *The*

■■

This interview by David Jay Brown and Rebecca McClen appeared in *Critique,* summer 1989. *Critique* has since changed its name to *Sacred Fire.*

Doors of Perception I said to myself, "There's something going on here for sure."

DB: Recently you personally addressed close to two thousand people at the John Anson Ford Theater in Los Angeles. To what do you attribute your increasing popularity, and what role do you see yourself playing in the social sphere?

TM: Well, without being cynical, the main thing I attribute to my increasing popularity is better public relations. As far as what role I'll play, I don't know. I mean, I assume that anyone who has anything constructive to say about our relationship to chemical substances, natural and synthetic, is going to have a role to play, because this drug issue is going to loom larger and larger on the social agenda until we get some resolution of it—and by resolution I don't mean suppression or just saying no. I anticipate a new open-mindedness born of desperation on the part of the Establishment. Drugs are part of the human experience, and we have got to create a more sophisticated way of dealing with them than exhortations to abstinence, because that has failed.

RM: You have said that the term New Age trivializes the significance of the next phase in human evolution and have referred instead to the emergence of an Archaic Revival. How do you differentiate between these two expressions?

TM: The New Age is essentially humanistic psychology eighties style, with the addition of neo-shamanism, channeling, crystal and herbal healing, and this sort of thing. The Archaic Revival is a much larger, more global phenomenon that assumes that we are recovering the social forms of the late neolithic, and the Archaic Revival reaches far back in the twentieth century to Freud, to surrealism, to abstract expressionism, even to a phenomenon like National Socialism, which is a negative force. But the stress on ritual, on organized activity, on race/ancestor consciousness—these are themes that have been worked out throughout the entire twentieth century, and the Archaic Revival is an expression of that.

RM: In the book you wrote with your brother Dennis, *The Invisible Landscape,* and in recent lectures and workshops, you've spoken of a new model of time and your efforts to model the evolution of novelty based on the ancient Oriental system of divination, the *I Ching.* Can you briefly explain how you developed this model, and how an individual can utilize this system to modulate their own perspective on the nature of time?

TM: It's not easily explained. If I were to give an extremely brief résumé of it, I would say that the new view of time is that time is holographic, fractal, and moves toward a definitive conclusion, rather than the historical model of time, which is open-ended, trendlessly fluctuating, and in practical terms endless. What's being proposed is a spiral model of history that sees history as a process actually leading toward a conclusion. But the details of it are fairly complex.

DB: According to your timewave model, novelty reaches its peak expression and history appears to come to a close in the year 2012. Can you explain what you mean by this, and what the global or evolutionary implications are of what you refer to as the "end of time"?

TM: What I mean is this: The theory describes time with what are called novelty waves; because waves have wavelengths, one must assign an end point to the novelty wave, so the end of time is nothing more than the point on the historical continuum that is assigned as the end point of the novelty wave. Novelty is something that has been slowly maximized through the life of the universe, something that reaches infinite density, or infinite contraction at the point from which the wave is generated. Trying to imagine what time would be like near the temporal singularity is difficult because we are far from it, in another domain of physical law. There need to be more facts in play before we will be able to correctly envisage the end of time, but what we can say concerning the singularity is this: it is the obviation of life in three-dimensional space, everything that is familiar comes to an end, everything that can be described in Euclidian space is superseded by modes of being that require a more complicated description than is currently available.

DB: From your writings I have gleaned that you subscribe to the notion that psilocybin mushrooms are a species of high intelligence, that they arrived on this planet as spores that migrated through outer space and are attempting to establish a symbiotic relationship with human beings. In a more holistic perspective, how do you see this notion fitting into the context of Francis Crick's theory of directed pan-spermia, the hypothesis that all life on this planet and its directed evolution has been seeded, or perhaps fertilized, by spores designed by a higher intelligence?

TM: As I understand the Crick theory of pan-spermia, it's a theory of how life spread through the universe. What I was suggesting, and I don't believe it as strongly as you imply, but I entertain it as a possibility, is that intelligence, not life, but intelligence may have come here in this spore-bearing life form. This is a more radical version of the pan-spermia theory of Crick and Ponnamperuma. In fact, I think that theory will probably be vindicated. In a hundred years, if people do biology they will think it quite silly that people once thought that spores could not be blown from one star system to another by light pressure. As far as the role of the psilocybin mushroom, or its relationship to us and to intelligence, this is something that we need to consider. It really isn't important that I claim that it's an extraterrestrial; what we need is a body of people claiming this, or a body of people denying it, because what we're talking about is the experience of the mushroom. Few people are in a position to judge its extraterrestrial potential, because few people in the orthodox sciences have ever experienced the full spectrum of psychedelic effects that is unleashed. One cannot find out whether or not there's an extraterrestrial intelligence inside the mushroom unless one is willing to take the mushroom.

DB: You have a unique theory about the role that psilocybin mushrooms play in the process of human evolution. Can you tell us about this?

TM: Whether the mushrooms came from outer space or not, the presence of psychedelic substances in the diet of early human beings created a number of changes in our evolutionary situation. When a person takes small amounts of psilocybin their visual acuity improves. They can actually see slightly better, and this means that animals allowing psilocybin into their food chain would have increased hunting success, which means increased food supply, which means increased reproductive success, which is the name of the game in evolution. It is the organism that manages to propagate itself numerically that is successful. The presence of psilocybin in the diet of early pack-hunting primates caused the individuals that were ingesting the psilocybin to have increased visual acuity. At slightly higher doses of psilocybin there is sexual arousal and erection, and everything that goes with arousal of the central nervous system. Again, a factor that would increase reproductive success is reinforced.

DB: Isn't it true that psilocybin inhibits orgasm?

TM: No. I've never heard that. Not at the doses I'm talking about. At a psychedelic dose it might, but at just slightly above the "you can feel it" dose, it acts as a stimulant. Sexual arousal means paying attention, it means jumpiness, it indicates a certain energy level in the organism. And then, of course, at still higher doses psilocybin triggers this activity in the language-forming capacity of the brain that manifests as song and vision. It is as though it were an enzyme that stimulates eye-

sight, sexual interest, and imagination. And the three of these going together produce language-using primates. Psilocybin may have synergized the emergence of higher forms of psychic organization out of
primitive proto-human animals. It can be seen as a kind of evolutionary
enzyme, or evolutionary catalyst.

DB: During your shamanistic voyages how do you—or do
you—differentiate between the literal and the metaphorical I/thou dialogue that appears to occur in certain states of consciousness? In other
words, how do you differentiate between the possibility that you are
communicating with otherworldly independently existing entities and
the possibility that you are communicating with isolated unconscious
neuron clusters in your own brain?

TM: It's very hard to differentiate it. How can I make that same
distinction right now? How do I know I'm talking to you? It's just provi-
sionally assumed that you are ordinary enough that I don't question that
you're there, but if you had two heads, I would question whether you
were there. I would investigate to see if you were really what you appear to be. It's very hard to tell what this I/thou relationship is about,
because it's very difficult to define the "I" part of it, let alone the "thou"
part of it. I haven't found a way to tell, to trick it, as it were, into showing whether it is an extraterrestrial or the back side of my own head.

DB: But normally the way we can tell is we receive mutual veri-
fication from other people, and we get information from many senses.
You can touch me. You can see me. You can hear me.

TM: Well this is simply a voice, you know, so it's the issue of the
mysterious telephone call. If you're awakened in the middle of the night
by a telephone call, and you pick up the phone, and someone says
"Hello," it would not be your first inclination to ask "Is anybody there?"
because they just said "hello." That establishes that somebody is there,
but you can't see them, maybe they're aren't there, maybe you've been
called by a machine. I've been called by machines. You pick up the
phone and it says "Hello this is Sears, and we're calling to tell you that
your order 16312 is ready for pickup," and you say "Oh, thank you."
"Don't mention it." No, so this issue of identifying the other with certainty is tricky, even in ordinary intercourse.

RM: There is a lot of current interest in the ancient art of sound
technology. In a recent article you said that in certain states of consciousness you're able to create a kind of visual resonance and manipulate a

"topological manifold" using sound vibrations. Can you tell us more about this technique, its ethnic origins, and its potential applications?

TM: Yes, it has to do with shamanism that is based on the use of DMT in plants. DMT is a neurotransmitter that, when ingested and allowed to come to rest in unusually large amounts in the synapses of the brain, allows one to see sound, so that one can use the voice to produce not musical compositions, but pictorial and visual compositions. This, to my mind, indicates that we're on the cusp of some kind of evolutionary transition in the language-forming area, so that we are going to go from a language that is heard to a language that is seen, through a shift in interior processing. The language will still be made of sound, but it will be processed as the carrier of the visual impression. This is actually being done by shamans in the Amazon. The songs they sing sound as they do in order to look a certain way. They are not musical compositions as we're used to thinking of them. They are pictorial art that is caused by audio signals.

DB: Terence, you're recognized by many as one of the great explorers of the twentieth century. You've trekked through the Amazonian jungles and soared through the uncharted regions of the brain, but perhaps your ultimate voyages lie in the future, when humanity has mastered space technology and time travel. What possibilities for travel in these two areas do you foresee, and how do you think these new technologies will affect the future evolution of the human species?

TM: Some question. I suppose most people believe space travel is right around the corner. I certainly hope so. I think we should all learn Russian in anticipation of it, because apparently the U.S. government is incapable of sustaining a space program. The time travel question is more interesting. Possibly the world is experiencing a compression of technological novelty that is going to lead to developments that are very much like what we would imagine time travel to be. We may be closing in on the ability to transmit information forward into the future, and to create an informational domain of communication between various points in time. How this will be done is difficult to imagine, but things like fractal mathematics, superconductivity, and nanotechnology offer new and novel approaches to realizing these old dreams. We shouldn't assume time travel is impossible simply because it hasn't been done. There's plenty of latitude in the laws of quantum physics to allow for moving information through time in various ways. Apparently you can move information through time, as long as you don't move it through time faster than light.

DB: Why is that?

TM: I haven't the faintest idea. What am I, Einstein?

DB: Well, Terence, now I'm wondering what you think the ultimate goal of human evolution is?

TM: Oh, a good party.

DB: Have you ever had any experiences with lucid dreaming—the process by which one can become aware and conscious within a dream that one is dreaming—and if so, how do they compare with your other shamanic experiences?

TM: I really haven't had experiences with lucid dreaming. It's one of those things that I'm very interested in. I'm sort of skeptical of it. I hope it's true, because what a wonderful thing that would be.

DB: You've never had one?

TM: I've had lucid dreams, but I have no technique for repeating them on demand. The dream state is possibly anticipating this cultural frontier that we're moving toward. We are approaching something very much like eternal dreaming, going into the imagination, and staying there, and that would be like a lucid dream that knew no end—but what a tight, simple solution. One of the things that interests me about dreams is this: I have dreams in which I smoke DMT, and it works. To me that's extremely interesting, because it seems to imply that one does not have to smoke DMT to have the experience. You only have to convince your brain that you have done this, and it then delivers this staggering altered state.

DB: Wow.

TM: How many people who have had DMT dream occasionally of smoking it and have it happen? Do people who have never had DMT ever have that kind of an experience in a dream? I bet not. I bet you have to have done it in life to have established the knowledge of its existence, and the image of how it's possible, but then this thing can happen to you without any chemical intervention. It is more powerful than any yoga, so taking control of the dream state would certainly be an advantageous thing and carry us a great distance toward the kind of cultural transformation that we're talking about. How exactly to do it, I'm not sure. The

psychedelics, the near-death experience, the lucid dreaming, the medita-
tional reveries—all of these things are pieces of a puzzle about how to
create a new cultural dimension that we can all live in a little more sane-
ly than we're living in these dimensions.

DB: Do you have any thoughts on what happens to human consciousness after biological death?

TM: I've thought about it. When I think about it I feel like I'm on
my own. The Logos doesn't want to help here. The Logos has nothing to
say to me on the subject of biological death. What I imagine happens is
that for the self time begins to flow backward, even before death; the act
of dying is the act of reliving an entire life, and at the end of the dying
process consciousness divides into the consciousness of one's parents
and one's children, and then it moves through these modalities, and
then divides again. It's moving forward into the future through the people who come after you, and backward into the past through your ancestors. The further away from the moment of death it is, the faster it
moves, so that after a period of time, the Tibetans say 42 days, one is re-
connected to everything that ever lived, and the previous ego-pointed
existence is allowed to dissolve, returned to the ocean, the morphogenetic field, or the One of Plotinus—you choose your term. A person is a focused illusion of being, and death occurs when the illusion of being is no
longer sustained. Then everything flows out, and away from the disequilibrium state that is life. It is a state of disequilibrium, yet it is maintained for decades, but finally, like all disequilibrium states, it must
yield to the Second Law of Thermodynamics, and at that point it runs
down, its specific character disappears into the general character of the
world around it. It has returned then to the void/plenum.

DB: What if you don't have children?

TM: Well, then you flow backward into the past, into your parents, and their parents, and their parents, and eventually all life, and
back into the primal protozoa. It's very interesting that in the celebration
of the Eleusinian mysteries, when they took the sacrament, what the god
said was, "Procreate, procreate." It is uncanny the way history is determined by who sleeps with whom, who gets born, what lines are drawn
forward, what tendencies are accelerated. Most people experience what
they call magic only in the dimension of mate seeking, and this is where
even the dullest people have astonishing coincidences, and unbelievable
things go on—it's almost as though hidden strings were being pulled.
There's an esoteric tradition that the genes, the matings, are where it's

all being run from. It is how I think a superextraterrestrial would intervene. It wouldn't intervene at all; it would make us who it wanted us to be by controlling synchronicity and coincidence around mate choosing.

RM:　Rupert Sheldrake has recently refined the theory of the morphogenetic field—a nonmaterial organizing collective memory field that affects all biological systems. This field can be envisioned as a hyperspatial information reservoir that brims and spills over into a much larger region of influence when critical mass is reached—a point referred to as morphic resonance. Do you think this morphic resonance could be regarded as a possible explanation for the phenomena of spirits and other metaphysical entities, and can the method of evoking beings from the spirit world be simply a case of cracking the morphic code?

TM:　That sounds right. It's something like that. If what you're trying to get at is do I think morphogenetic fields are a good thing, or do they exist, yes I think some kind of theory like that is clearly becoming necessary, and that the next great step to be taken in the intellectual conquest of nature, if you will, is a theory about how out of the class of possible things, some things actually happen.

RM:　Do you think it could be related to the phenomena of spirits?

TM:　Spirits are the presence of the past, specifically expressed. When you go to ruins like Angkor Wat, or Tikal, the presence is there. You have to be pretty dull to not see how it was, where the market stalls were, the people and their animals, and the trade goods. It's quite weird. We're only conventionally bound in the present by our linguistic assumptions, but if we can still our linguistic machinery, the mind spreads out into time and behaves in very unconventional ways.

DB:　How do you view the increasing waves of designer psychedelics and brain-enhancement machines in the context of Rupert Sheldrake's theory of morphogenetic fields?

TM:　Well, I'm hopeful but somewhat suspicious. I think psychedelics should come from the natural world and be use-tested by shamanically oriented cultures; then they have a very deep morphogenetic field, because they've been used thousands and thousands of years in magical contexts. A drug produced in the laboratory and suddenly distributed worldwide simply amplifies the global noise present in the historical crisis. And then there's the very practical consideration that one cannot predict the long-term effects of a drug produced in a laboratory. Hashish, morning glories, and mushrooms have been used for vast stretches of time without detrimental social consequences. We know that. As far as the technological question is concerned, brain machines and all, I wish them luck. I'm willing to test anything that somebody will send me, but I'm skeptical. I think it's somehow like the speech-operated typewriter. It will recede ahead of us. The problems will be found to have been far more complex than first supposed.

DB: It's interesting the way you anticipate each question. The recent development of fractal images seems to imply that visions and hallucinations can be broken down into a precise mathematical code. With this in mind, do you think the abilities of the human imagination can be replicated in a supercomputer?

TM: Yes. Saying that the components of hallucinations can be broken down and duplicated by mathematical code isn't taking anything away from them. Reality can be taken apart and reduplicated with this same mathematical code—that's what makes the fractal idea so powerful. One can type in half a page of code and on the screen get river systems, mountain ranges, deserts, ferns, coral reefs, all being generated out of half a page of computer coding. This seems to imply that we are finally discovering really powerful mathematical rules that stand behind visual appearances. And yes, I think supercomputers, computer graphics, and simulated environments, this is very promising stuff. When the world's being run by machines, we'll all be at the movies. Oh boy.

RM: Or making movies.

TM: Or being movies.

RM: It seems that human language is evolving at a much slower rate than is the ability of human consciousness to navigate more complex and more profound levels of reality. How do you see language developing and evolving so as to become a more sensitive transceiving device for sharing conscious experience?

TM: Actually, consciousness can't evolve any faster than language. The rate at which language evolves determines how fast consciousness evolves; otherwise you're just lost in what Wittgenstein called the unspeakable. You can feel it, but you can't speak of it, so it's an entirely private reality. Notice how we have very few words for emotions? I love you, I hate you, and then basically we run a dial between those. I love you a lot, I hate you a lot.

RM: How do you feel? Fine.

TM: Yes, how do you feel, fine; and yet we have thousands and thousands of words about rugs, and widgets, and this and that, so we need to create a much richer language of emotion. There are times—and this would be a great study for somebody to do—there have been periods in English when there were emotions that don't exist anymore, because the words have been lost. This is getting very close to this business of how reality is made by language. Can we recover a lost emotion by creating a word for it? There are colors that don't exist anymore because the words have been lost. I'm thinking of the word *jacinth*. This is a certain kind of orange. Once you know the word *jacinth*, you always can recognize it, but if you don't have it, all you can say is it's a little darker orange than something else. We've never tried to consciously evolve our language, we've just let it evolve, but now we have this level of awareness, and this level of cultural need where we really must plan where the new words should be generated. There are areas where words should be gotten rid of that empower political wrong thinking. The propagandists for the fascists already understand this; they understand that if you make something unsayable, you've made it unthinkable. So it doesn't plague you anymore. So planned evolution of language is the way to speed it toward expressing the frontier of consciousness.

DB: I've thought at times that what you view as a symbiosis forming between humans and psychoactive plants may in fact be the plants taking over control of our lives and commanding us to do their bidding. Have you any thoughts on this?

TM: Well, symbiosis is not parasitism; symbiosis is a situation of mutual benefit to both parties, so we have to presume that the plants are getting as much out of this as we are. What we're getting is information from another spiritual level. They are giving us their point of view. What we're giving them is care, and feeding, and propagation, and survival, so they give us their very different point of view. We in turn respond by making the way easier for them in the physical world. And this seems a reasonable trade-off. Obviously they have difficulty in the physical world; plants don't move around much. You talk about Tao, a plant has the Tao. It doesn't *even* chop wood and carry water.

RM: Future predictions are often based upon the study of previous patterns and trends that are then extended like the contours of a map to extrapolate the shape of things to come. The future can also be seen as an ongoing dynamic creative interaction between the past and the present—the current interpretation of past events actively serves to formulate these future patterns and trends. Have you been able to reconcile these two perspectives so that humanity is able to learn from its experiences without being bound by the habits of history?

TM: The two are antithetical. You must not be bound by the habits of history if you want to learn from your experience. It was Ludwig von Bertalanffy, the inventor of general systems theory, who made the famous statement that "people are not machines, but in all situations where they are given the opportunity, they will act like machines," so you have to keep disturbing them, because they always settle down into a routine. So historical patterns are largely cyclical, but not entirely—there is ultimately a highest level of the pattern, which does not repeat, and that's the part that is responsible for the advance into true novelty.

RM: The part that doesn't repeat. Hmm. The positive futurists tend to fall into two groups. Some visualize the future as becoming progressively brighter every day and think that global illumination will occur as a result of this progression; others envision a period of actual devolution—a dark age—through which human consciousness must pass before more advanced stages are reached. Which scenario do you see as being the most likely to emerge, and why do you hold this view?

TM: I guess I'm a soft Dark Ager. I think there will be a mild dark age. I don't think it will be anything like the dark ages that lasted a thousand years; I think it will last more like five years and will be a time of economic retraction, religious fundamentalism, retreat into closed communities by certain segments of the society, feudal warfare among minor states, resource scarcity, and this sort of thing. But I think it will give way in the late nineties to the global future that we're all yearning for, and then there will be basically a fifteen-year period where all these things are drawn together with progressively greater and greater sophistication, much in the way that modern science and philosophies have grown with greater and greater sophistication in a single direction since the Renaissance. Sometime around the end of 2012 all of this will be boiled down into a kind of alchemical distillation of the historical experience that will be a doorway into the life of the imagination.

RM: Rupert Sheldrake's morphic resonance, Ralph Abraham's chaos theory, and your timewave model all appear to contain complementary patterns that operate on similar underlying principles—that energy systems store information until a certain level is reached and the information is then transduced into a larger frame of reference, like water in a tiered fountain. Have you worked these theories into an all-encompassing metatheory of how the universe functions and operates?

TM: No, but we're working on it. Well, it is true that the three of us—and I would add Frank Barr in there, who is less well known but has a piece of the puzzle as well—we're all complementary. Rupert's theory is, at this point, a hypothesis. There are no equations, there's no predictive machinery; it's a way of speaking about experimental approaches. My timewave theory is like an extremely formal and specific example of what he's talking about in a general way. And then what Ralph's doing is providing a bridge from the kind of things Rupert and I are doing back into the frontier branch of ordinary mathematics called dynamic modeling. And Frank is an expert in the repetition of fractal process. He can show you the same thing happening on many many levels, in many many different expressions. So I have named us Compressionists, or Psychedelic Compressionists. Compressionism holds that the world is growing more and more complex, compressed, knitted together, and therefore holographically complete at every point, and that's basically where the four of us stand, I think, but from different points of view.

DB: Can you tell us about Botanical Dimensions, and any current projects that you're working on?

TM: Botanical Dimensions is a nonprofit foundation that attempts to rescue plants with a history of shamanic and human usage in the warm tropics, and rescue the information about how they're used, store the information in computers, and move the plants to a nineteen-acre site in Hawaii, in a rain forest belt that reasonably replicates the Amazon situation. There we are keeping them toward the day when someone will want to do serious research on them. As a nonprofit foundation, we solicit donations, publish a newsletter, support a number of collectors in the field, and carry on this work, which nobody else is really doing. There's a lot of rain forest conservation going on, but very little effort to conserve the folk knowledge of native peoples. Amazonian people are going off to sawmills and learning to repair outboard motors, and this whole body of knowledge about plants is going to be lost in the next generation. We're saving it, and saving the plants in a botanical garden in Hawaii.

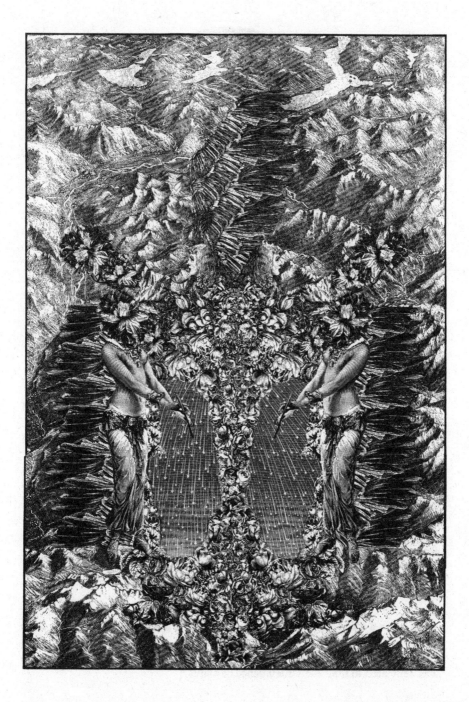

15

Plan/Plant/Planet

O UR PRESENT global crisis is more profound than any previous historical crises; hence our solutions must be equally drastic. I propose that we should adopt the plant as the organizational model for life in the twenty-first century, just as the computer seems to be the dominant mental/social model of the late twentieth century, and the steam engine was the guiding image of the nineteenth century.

This means reaching back in time to models that were successful fifteen thousand to twenty thousand years ago. When this is done it becomes possible to see plants as food, shelter, clothing, and sources of education and religion.

The process begins by declaring legitimate what we have denied for so long. Let us declare nature to be legitimate. All plants should be declared legal, and all animals for that matter. The notion of illegal plants and animals is obnoxious and ridiculous.

Reestablishing channels of direct communication with the planetary Other, the mind behind nature, through the use of hallucinogenic plants is the last best hope for dissolving the steep walls of cultural inflexibility that appear to be channeling us toward true ruin. We need a new set of lenses to see our way in the world. When the medieval world shifted its worldview, secularized European society sought salvation in the revivifying of classical Greek and Roman approaches to law, philos-

■■■

This essay appeared in the fall 1989 issue of *Whole Earth Review*. The entire issue was dedicated to the "alien intelligence of plants."

ophy, aesthetics, city planning, and agriculture. Our dilemma will cast us further back into time in a search for models and answers.

O

The solution to much of modern malaise, including chemical dependencies and repressed psychoses and neuroses, is direct exposure to the authentic dimensions of risk represented by the experience of psychedelic plants. The pro–psychedelic plant position is clearly an antidrug position. Drug dependencies are the result of habitual, unexamined, and obsessive behavior; these are precisely the tendencies in our psychological makeup that the psychedelics mitigate. The plant hallucinogens dissolve habits and hold motivations up to inspection by a wider, less egocentric, and more grounded point of view within the individual. It is foolish to suggest that there is no risk, but it is equally uninformed to suggest that the risk is not worth taking. What is needed is experiential validation of a new guiding image, an overarching metaphor able to serve as the basis for a new model of society and the individual.

The plant–human relationship has always been the foundation of our individual and group existence in the world. What I call the Archaic Revival is the process of reawakening awareness of traditional attitudes toward nature, including plants and our relationship to them. The Archaic Revival spells the eventual breakup of the pattern of male dominance and hierarchy based on animal organization, something that cannot be changed overnight by a sudden shift in collective awareness. Rather it will follow naturally upon the gradual recognition that the overarching theme that directs the Archaic Revival is the idea/ideal of a vegetation Goddess, the Earth herself as the much ballyhooed Gaia—a fact well documented by nineteenth-century anthropologists, most notably Frazer, but recently given a new respectability by Riane Eisler, Marija Gimbutas, James Mellaart, and others.

The closer a human group is to the gnosis of the vegetable mind—the Gaian collectivity of organic life—the closer their connection to the archetype of the Goddess and hence to the partnership style of social organization. The last time that the mainstream of Western thought was refreshed by the gnosis of the vegetable mind was at the close of the Hellenistic Era, before the Mystery religions were finally suppressed by enthusiastic Christian barbarians.

My conclusion is that taking the next evolutionary step toward the Archaic Revival, the rebirth of the Goddess, and the ending of profane history will require an agenda that includes the notion of our reinvolvement with and the emergence of the vegetable mind. That same mind that coaxed us into self-reflecting language now offers us the boundless landscapes of the imagination. Without such a relationship to psychedelic exopheromones regulating our symbiotic relationship with the plant kingdom, we stand outside of an understanding of planetary purpose. And an understanding of planetary purpose may be the major contribution that we can make to the evolutionary process. Returning to the bosom of the planetary partnership means trading the point of view of the history-created ego for a more maternal and intuitional style.

The widely felt intuition of the presence of the Other as a female companion to the human navigation of history can, I believe, be traced back to the immersion in the vegetable mind, which provided the ritual context in which human consciousness emerged into the light of self-awareness, self-reflection, and self-articulation: the light of the Great Goddess.

What does it mean to accept the solutions of vegetable forms of life as metaphors for the conduct of the affairs of the human world? Two important changes would follow from adopting this assumption:

• *The feminizing of culture.*   Culture would be feminized on a level that has yet to be fully explored. Green Consciousness means recognizing that the real division between the masculine and the feminine is not a division between men and women but rather a division between ourselves as conscious animals—omnivorous, land-clearing war makers, supreme expression of the yang—and the circumglobal mantle of vegetation—the ancient metastable yin element that constitutes by far the major portion of the biomass of the living earth.

• *An inward search for values.*   Inwardness is the characteristic feature of the vegetable rather than the animal approach to existence. The animals move, migrate, and swarm, while plants hold fast. Plants live in a dimension characterized by the solid state, the fixed, and the enduring. If there is movement in the consciousness of plants then it must be the movement of spirit and attention in the domain of the vegetal imagination. Perhaps this is what the reconnection to the vegetal Goddess through psychedelic plants, the Archaic Revival, actually points toward: that the life of the spirit is the life that gains access to the visionary realms resident in magical plant teachers. This is the truth that shamans have always known and practiced. Awareness of the green side of mind was called *Veriditas* by the twelfth-century visionary Hildegard von Bingen.

O

A new paradigm capable of offering hope of a path out of the cultural quicksand must provide a real-world agenda addressed to the escalating problems that the planet faces.

There are several domains in which the rise of awareness of *Veriditas* might help stave off Armageddon:

O

Detoxification of the natural environment. The process of detoxification is naturally carried out by the combined action of the atmosphere, the biological matrix, and the oceans. This planetwide process was able to take care of even urban industrial waste, until modern industrial technology became a truly global phenomenon. Planting species of datura, the plants once a part of the religious rites of the Indians of Southern California, and other plants that leach heavy metals from the earth and sequester them in their cellular tissue are examples of a natural process that could help clean up our environment. Recognizing the many ways in which the biological matrix of the earth functions to avert toxification, recognizing that nature is working to sustain life, might go a long way toward building a political consensus to actively participate in saving that same life.

O

Connectedness and symbiosis. Like plants, we need to maximize the qualities of connectedness and symbiosis. Plant-based approaches to modeling the world include awareness of the fractal and branching nature of community action. A treelike network of symbiotic relationships can now replace the model of evolution that we inherited from the nineteenth century. The earlier model, that of the tooth-and-claw struggle for existence, with the survivor taking the hindmost, is a model based on naive observation of animal behavior. Yet it was cheerfully extended into the realm of plants to explain the evolutionary interactions thought to cause speciation in the botanical world. Later, more sophisticated observers (C. H. Waddington and Erich Jantsch) found not the War in Nature that Darwinists reported but rather a situation in which it was not competitive ability but *ability to maximize cooperation with other species* that most directly contributed to an organism's being able to function and endure as a member of a biome. Plants interact with each other through the tangled mat of roots that connects them all to the source of their nutrition and to each other.

The matted floor of a tropical rain forest is an environment of great chemical diversity; the topology approaches that of brain tissue in its complexity. Within the network of interconnected roots, complex chemical signals are constantly being transmitted and received. Coadaptive evolution and symbiotic relationships regulate this entire system with a ubiquitousness that argues for the evolutionary primacy of these cooperative strategies. For example, mycorrhizal fungi live in symbiosis on the outside of plant roots and gently balance and buffer the mineral-laden water that is moving through them to the roots of their host.

O

Whole-system fine tuning.   If the phenomena associated with biological harmony and resonance could be understood, then such large-scale systems as global banking or global food production and distribution could be more properly managed. The Gaian biologists, Lovelock, Margulies, and others, have argued persuasively that the entire planet has been self-organized by microbial and planktonic life into a metastable regime favorable to biology and maintained there for over two billion years. Plant-based Gaia has kept a balance throughout time and space—and this in spite of the repeated bombardment of the earth by asteroidal material sufficient to severely disrupt the planetary equilibrium. We can only admire—and we should seek to imitate such a Tao-like sense of the planet's multidimensional homeostatic balance. But how? I suggest we look at plants—look more deeply, more closely, and with a more open mind than we have done before.

O

Recycling.   Like plants, we need to recycle. On a cosmic scale we are no more mobile than plants. Until this point in history we have modeled our more successful economic systems on animal predation. Animals can potentially move on to another resource when they exhaust the one at hand. Since they can move to new food sources, they potentially have unlimited resources. Plants are fixed. They cannot easily move to richer nutrients or leave an area if they foul or deplete it. They must recycle well. The fostering of a plant-based ethic that emulates the way in which the botanical world uses and replaces resources is a *sine qua non* for planetary survival. All capitalistic models presuppose unlimited exploitable resources and labor pools, yet neither should now be assumed. I do not know the methods, but I suggest that we start turning to the plant world to discover the right questions to ask.

O

Photovoltaic power.   Appreciation of photovoltaic power is part of the shift toward an appreciation of the elegance of the solid state that plants possess. Plants practice photosynthetic solutions to the problems of power acquisition. Compared to the water or animal-turned wheels, which are the Ur-metaphors for power production in the human world, the solid-state quantum-molecular miracle that involves dropping a photon of sunlight into a molecular device that will kick out an electron capable of energetically participating in the life of a cell seems like extravagant science fiction. Yet this is, in fact, the principle upon which photosynthesis operates. While the first solid-state devices arrived on the human cultural frontier in the late 1940s, solid-state engineering had been the preferred design approach of plants for some two thousand million years. High efficiency photovoltaics could today meet the daily needs of most people for electricity. It is the running of basic industries on solar energy that has proved difficult. Perhaps this is nature's way of telling us that we aspire to too much manufacturing.

O

A global atmosphere–based energy economy. The approach of vegetational life to energy production is called photosynthesis. This process could be modeled by the creation of a global economy based on using solar energy to obtain hydrogen from seawater. Solar electricity could supply most electricity needs, but the smelting of aluminum and steel and other energy-intensive industrial processes make demands that photovoltaic electricity is unlikely to be able to meet. However, there is a solution: plants split atmospheric carbon dioxide to release energy and oxygen as by-products. A similar but different process could use solar electricity to split water to obtain hydrogen. This hydrogen could be collected and concentrated for later distribution. Plants have been very successful at finding elegant solutions based on material present at hand; a hydrogen economy would emulate this same reliance on inexhaustible and recyclable materials.

The notion is a simple one really; it has long been realized by planners that hydrogen is the ideal resource to fuel a global economy. Hydrogen is clean: when burned it recombines with the water it was chemically derived from. Hydrogen is plentiful: one-third of all water is hydrogen. And all existing technologies—internal combustion engines, coal-, oil-, and nuclear-fired generators—could be retrofitted to run on hydrogen. Thus we are not talking about having to scrap the current standing crop of existing power production and distribution systems. Hydrogen could be "cracked" from seawater at a remote island location and then moved by the already existing technology that is used for the ocean transport of liquid natural gas from its production points to market. The objection that hydrogen is highly explosive and that proven technologies for handling it do not exist has largely been met by the

LNG industry and its excellent safety record. Hydrogen accidents could be extremely destructive, but they would be ordinary explosions—local, nontoxic, and without release of radioactivity. Like plant life itself, the hydrogen economy would be nonpolluting and self-sustaining; burned hydrogen recombines with oxygen to again become water.

An international effort of extraordinary scope would be necessary to begin to move toward a proof of concept demonstration of the feasibility of a hydrogen economy. Granted, there are many possible problems with such a scheme. But no plan for the production of energy sufficient to meet the needs of the twenty-first century is going to be without difficulties.

O

Nanotechnology. The era of molecular mechanism promises the most radical of the green visions, since it proposes that human-engineered quasibiological cells and organelles take over the manufacturing of products and culture. Nanotechnology takes seriously the notion that manufacturing techniques and methods of manipulating matter on the microphysical scale can affect the design process of the human-scale world. In the nanotech world, dwellings and machines can be "grown," and everything that is manufactured is closer to flesh than stone. The distinction between living and nonliving and organic and artificial is blurred in the electronic coral reef of human–machine symbiosis contemplated by the savants of nanotechnology.

O

Preservation of biological diversity. The life on this planet and the chemical diversity that it represents is likely to be the only source of biologically evolved compounds until the day that we discover another planet as teeming with life as our own. Yet we are destroying the living diversity of our world at an appalling rate. This must be stopped, not only through the preservation of ecosystems but also through the preservation of information about those ecosystems that has been accumulated over thousands of years by the people who live adjacent to them. It is impossible to underestimate the importance for human health of preservation of folk knowledge concerning healing plants. All the major healing drugs that have changed history have come from living plants and fungi. Quinine made conquest of the tropics possible, penicillin and birth control pills remade the social fabric of the twentieth century. All three of these are plant-derived pharmaceuticals. My partner Kat and I work in this area by managing Botanical Dimensions, a botanical garden in Hawaii that seeks to preserve the plants utilized in Amazonian shamanism, one of many such systems of knowledge that are fast disappearing.

The measures outlined above would tend to promote what might be called a sense of Gaian Holism, that is, a sense of the unity and balance of nature and of our own human position within that dynamic and evolving balance. It is a plant-based view. This return to a perspective on self and ego that places them within the larger context of planetary life and evolution is the essence of the Archaic Revival. Marshall McLuhan was correct to see that planetary human culture, the global village, would be tribal in character. The next great step toward a planetary holism is the partial merging of the technologically transformed human world with the archaic matrix of vegetable intelligence that is the Overmind of the planet.

I hesitate to call this dawning awareness religious, yet that is what it surely is. And it will involve a full exploration of the dimensions revealed by plant hallucinogens, especially those structurally related to neurotransmitters already present and functioning in the human brain. Careful exploration of the plant hallucinogens will probe the most archaic and sensitive level of the drama of the emergence of consciousness; it was in the plant–human symbiotic relationships that characterized archaic society and religion that the numinous mystery was originally experienced. And this experience is no less mysterious for us today, in spite of the general assumption that we have replaced the simple awe of our ancestors with philosophical and epistemic tools of the utmost sophistication and analytical power. Our choice as a planetary culture is a simple one: go Green or die.

16

Virtual Reality and Electronic Highs
(Or On Becoming Virtual Octopi)

LOOKING like a cross between a T'ai Chi master, a navy frogman, and the Terminator, a man harnessed to electronic leads and fitted with a strange piece of headgear slowly turns and gestures. The pointing hand and the ballet of sign language, combined with an air of intense concentration, give the unmistakable impression that the person is far, far away from the brightly lit San Francisco Bay area laboratory in which he stands. You might almost say that he seems as if he were in another world.

And you would be right. Before you stands a true astronaut of inner space, a researcher who is in the processes of going where few have gone before. But look quickly—what is today the visionary dream of the techie few will very soon be reality for the rest of us. Virtual reality, that is.

Is it mechanistic multimedia masturbation or a doorway swinging open on the flower-strewn fields of the romantic imagination? A tool for discovery and navigation in new aesthetic domains, or the final trivializing of the drive to be mindlessly entertained? These are the questions that I asked myself one morning recently as I drove toward a rendezvous with one of the mavens of virtual reality, the redoubtable Eric Gullichsen of Autodesk. Then of Autodesk, currently a free agent. For as I was to learn later that day, not even virtual reality is immune to corporate change and upheaval. Gullichsen and his associate Patrice Gelband

■■

This piece appeared in *Magical Blend*, no. 26, winter 1990 and was among the very first to examine the implications of this new technology.

are now virtual guns for hire. The status of Autodesk's future commitment to research and development in virtual reality is undecided.

Corporate intrigues aside, worlds are being created by such pioneers in the virtual reality (VR) field as Jaron Lanier and the Autodesk special design team Gullichsen headed. It was logical that Autodesk should be a leader in the VR field, for their AutoCAD software has based much of its appeal on the idea that the user can actually "walk around" in a high-resolution three-dimensional simulation of two-dimensional blueprints. Pursuit of this idea grew naturally into the idea of computer-generated worlds. And Lanier and VTL, his corporation, have been the persistent leaders in the field of body and hand imaging in the VR. The magical gloves and body stockings that are the keys to entry into virtual reality remain Lanier's speciality.

What is virtual reality? It is a technology currently under development by NASA and private companies in the San Francisco Bay area and on the East Coast. It began with the modest intent of simulating the experience of flying high-performance fighter aircraft under combat conditions. Think of it this way: You are the Defense Department. Would you turn over a fighter plane costing upward of one hundred million dollars to some apple-cheeked hayseed so he can learn to fly it? If you spend the cost of one plane on simulation and thereby prevent even one crash you are saving a lot of money and possibly human lives. And one hundred million dollars buys a lot of simulation!

What I saw at Autodesk was considerably more modest than the classified government efforts. Gullichsen estimated that the whole VR apparatus could be re-created for around fifty thousand dollars. Chicken feed in the world of high-tech research and development. The fifth-floor lab was a sparsely furnished office approximately fifteen by twenty feet with a humongous high-resolution color monitor and a quite ordinary computer workstation. Introduced around, I was asked if I had any questions. Figuring I had done my homework, I suggested we cut to the chase.

The glove, wonderfully redolent with all the associations that are carried by black silk gloves everywhere, was slipped onto my hand. I had found it difficult to visualize the motion sensors that I knew were stitched on to the back of the gloves on top of each flex point. They appeared to be small blue beads. The whole thing fitted smoothly. I was asked to close and open my hand while the software sensed and entered the flex values of my particular hand. Next came the helmet, looking like a fancy overweight scuba mask. Once on, it put a Sony Watchman color miniscreen about an inch from each eye; a slight discontinuity between the screens created the impression of three-dimensional space.

Once everything was in place I could see the fuzzy, but colored and recognizable, outlines of a cartoon version of an office. Hovering in space in front of me was what appeared to be a foreshortened spaghetti fork. This, I was told, was the virtual image of the glove I was wearing. Sure enough, wiggle thumb, leftmost tong of spaghetti fork wiggles. No Roger Rabbit appeared, but as I pondered the mechanics of the glove I burst noiselessly and effortlessly through a wall and into a burnt-sienna space that seemed to, and probably did, extend to infinity. Eric explained about pointing. I had been pointing without realizing it. Pointing is how you get around in VR, or cyberspace, as the true believers call it. When you point at something you move toward it. When you open your hand the motion ceases. It is that simple. The eye goes where the finger points, and the image of your gloved hand comes along and can be used to "pick up," by intersecting, objects in the VR. After a few moments the lag time in the refreshing of the images, the weightlessness, the newly insubstantial nature of objects, and the newfound power of my right index finger were all familiar enough to me that I could slowly make my way around the office without moving through walls and objects or taking off through the ceiling or the floor.

In short, I got it. Talking with Eric and his associate mathematician, Patrice Gelband, I had the eerie feeling that this might be what it would have been like to stop by the Wright brothers' bicycle shop to shoot the breeze with Wilbur and Orville about the latest ideas concerning lift ratios of airfoils. These folks are on to something. They know it and I will wager that soon the whole world will know it. We are on the brink of another leap in evolution, folks.

It is only a short step from fighter simulations to simulations of architectural models that you can literally "fly the client into," and it is only a slightly longer step from a 3-D blueprint of an imaginary office to the simulation of the Taj Mahal on a moonlight-flooded summer night—in virtual reality.

If all this sounds too far out to be true, or like a rehash of Philip K. Dick's novel *A God Named Jones*, then that is just the universe's way of telling you that you haven't been keeping up. Remember the feelies in Aldous Huxley's science fiction distopia *Brave New World?* Everyone went to the feelies and held on to a knob on each side of the velvet cushioned seat and was conveyed away to the latest risqué and ribald fantasy that the *schlockmeisters* of future pop culture had prepared for public consumption. Of course we have had the operational equivalent of the feelies since at least the introduction of television. And the effect of having vast narcotized masses of people hooked on a drug whose content is culturally sanctioned and institutionally controlled is certainly debatable. The creeping shit-for-brains disease that seems to have become endemic in America has been blamed on TV by some. However, on one level television and now virtual reality are nothing more than the latest instances of neoteny, the carrying over into adulthood of infantile physical or behavioral characteristics. Lets face it, the world is a complicated place; if millions of people choose to retreat into an electronically reinforced state of semiinfantilism it may end up making the total system ultimately easier to pilot into safe harbor.

Virtual reality is easy to denounce in the same breath with MTV and perhaps HDTV—upon which it will in some degree depend. But the fact is that VR is more than simply further movement down a primrose path strewn with *The Price of His Toys* catalogs. It is a technology that will not only allow us to make more and better art; potentially it is a technology that will dissolve the boundaries between us and allow us to see the contents of each other's minds. There is also the possibility that improved forms of communication, states of near telepathy among participating human beings, can be coaxed out of imaginative use of the technology. Because of what VR is intrinsically, there are several ways in which it could be the basis of an entirely new kind of communication between people.

Each age takes its self-image from the animal world. The nineteenth century, with its obsession with the power to reshape the earth and abolish distances through the new technology of the steam engine, took as its guiding image that of the thoroughbred race horse. The early twentieth century focused on speed, conquest of the air, and the integration of human beings and machines into an ever more lethal symbiosis. This process found its realization in high-performance fighter aircraft; the animal image was that of the raptor, the relentless bird of prey.

Jaron Lanier is fond of saying that in virtual reality one can choose to be anything: a piano, for example. Fine—having surveyed the smorgasbord of morphogenetic options offered by Mother Nature, I would choose to be a virtual octopus. Many people, once informed, would make the same choice. I believe that the totemic image for the future is the octopus. This is because the cephalopods, the squids and octopi, have perfected a form of communication that is both psychedelic and telepathic; a model for the human communications of the future. In the not-too-distant future men and women may shed the monkey body to become virtual octopi swimming in a silicon sea.

Consider: Nature offers the example of the octopus, a creature in which well-developed eyes and an ability to change the color, banding, and general appearance of the skin surface have favored a visual, and hence telepathic, form of communication. An octopus does not communicate with spoken words as we do, even though water is a good medium for acoustical signaling; rather, the octopus becomes its own linguistic intent. The octopus is like a naked nervous system, say rather a naked mind: the inner states, the thoughts, if you will, of the octopus are directly reflected in its outward appearance. It is as though the octopus were wearing its mind on its exterior. This is in fact the case. The octopus literally dances its thoughts through expression of a series of color changes and position changes that require no local linguistic conventions for understanding as do our words and sentences. In the world of the octopus to behold is to understand. Octopi have a large repertoire of color changes, dots, blushes, and traveling bars that move across their surfaces; this ability in combination with the soft-bodied physique of the creature allows it to obscure and reveal its linguistic intent simply by rapidly folding and unfolding different parts of its body. The octopus does not transmit its linguistic intent, it *becomes* its linguistic intent. The mind and the body of the octopus are the same and are equally visible. This means that the octopus wears its language like a kind of second skin; it appears to be and becomes what it seeks to mean. There is very little loss of definition or signal strength among communicating octopi. Indeed, their well-known use of "ink" clouds to conceal themselves may indicate that this is the only way that they can have anything like a private thought. The ink cloud may be a kind of correction fluid for voluble octopi who have misspoken themselves.

Like the octopus, our destiny is to become what we think, to have our thoughts become our bodies and our bodies become our thoughts. This is the essence of a more perfect Logos, a Logos not heard but beheld. VR can help here, for electronics can change vocal utterance into visually beheld colored output in the virtual reality. This output can then be manipulated, by tools still uncreated, tools to be found in the kit of the VR hacker/mechanic soon to be. This means that a three-dimensional syntax, one that is seen, not heard, becomes possible as an experience in VR. You may ask, What is the point of being able to see one's voice, even in virtual reality? The point is that others will be able to see it as well, that the ambiguity of invisible meanings that attends audio speech is replaced by the unambiguous topology of meanings beheld. At last we will truly *see* what we mean. And we will see what others mean too, for cyberspace will be a dimension where anything that can be imagined can be made to seem real.

When we are in the act of seeing what is meant, the communicator and the one communicated with become as one. In other words, the visible languages possible in VR will overcome the subject/object dualism as well as the Self/Other dualism.

In trying to imagine the futures onto which these doors open, let us not forget that culture and language were the first virtual realities. A child is born into a world of unspeakable wonder. Each part of the world is seen to glow with animate mystery and the beckoning light of the unknown. But quickly our parents and our siblings provide us with words. At first these are nouns; that shimmering pattern of sound and iridescence is a "bird," that cool, silky, undulating surface is "water." As young children we respond to our cultural programming and quickly replace mysterious things and feelings with culturally validated and familiar words. We tile over reality with a mosaic of interconnected words. Later, as we grow in ability and understanding, the culture in which we find ourselves provides conventionalized relationships for us to model. Lover, father, investor, property owner. Each role has its own rules and its own conventions. These roles, too, tile over and replace the amorphous wonder of simply being alive. As we learn our lines and the blocking that goes with them, we move out of the inchoate realm of the preverbal child and in to the realm of the first virtual reality, the VR of culture. Many of us never realize that this domain is virtual, and instead we assume that we are discovering the true nature of the real world.

Musing on this in a recent interview, Jaron Lanier observed: "I think virtual reality will have an effect of enhancing and, in a sense, completing the culture. My view is that our culture has been abnormally distorted by being incredibly molded by technology. . . . Virtual Reality, by creating a technology that's general enough to be rather like reality was before there was technology, sort of completes a cycle." Lanier's remarks concerning the field that he helped to create have a eerie aura of unfocused prescience. He is groping toward a bigger reason for doing all of this. He speaks in terms of a nonsymbolic language, and in terms of bifocal glasses with real reality on top, yesterday's VR on the bottom. He oscillates between the profound and the quirky. But the idea that VR completes a cycle of neurotic behavior that is as old as our use of tools is interesting. VR asks us to imagine a future in which there will be virtual realities within virtual realities. A man slept, and while asleep dreamed he was a butterfly. Upon awakening the man asked himself, "Am I a man who slept and dreamed he was a butterfly, or am I a butterfly who sleeps and is now dreaming he is a man?"

The promise of VR is that in the near future we will walk the beaches and byways of twice ten thousand planets, a virtual new galaxy to explore whose name will be Imagination. The rest of our lifetimes our busy mind's eye is culturally destined to peer out at thousands of shimmering realities: Angkor Wat and the volcanoes of Io, many of our own memories, and the memories of others who have shared this or that engineered vista or thrill.

My take on all this is different. I wish all these folks luck. I think that we can look forward to terrific pornography based on this technology, to simulations of fixing broken machinery in outer space and tidying up inside radioactive zones. Surgeons can already operate on virtual cadavers in one advanced medical teaching facility. But somehow I am haunted by a deeper hope for VR. After all, technology has already proven that it is the drug most palatable to the Western mind. Could not VR allow us to blaze a high trail into the wilderness of the human imagination? Then, where each went, would all be free to follow through the miracle of instant VR replay? Can the riches of the imagination be made a commodity that can be sold back to the consumer, who is also their producer? Selling the self should be the easiest of tasks in a society as narcissistic as our own.

And speaking of drugs, just where on the spectrum of the cultural pharmaphobia can public and governmental attitudes toward virtual reality be expected to fall? Is VR to be seen as a "safe and harmless substitute for drugs" or is it an "electronic illusion from hell"? It is a dreary comment on the current infantile state of public dialogue that there is little doubt that we will be subject to both claims in the debate ahead.

Certainly VR represents a technology of escapism that dwarfs the modest intent of the opium smoker or the video game addict. But on the other hand, so does modern film. Through color photography most people on earth have vicariously experienced sufficient data to allow them to create virtual reality fantasies based on imagination and media-fanned expectation. It seems highly unlikely that the development of VR will be treated as the spread of a new drug; rather, it is now seen as a new frontier for marketing and product development. Indeed, the nondestructive nature of VR means that the talent of many artists, designers, and engineers can be absorbed into VR projects with no impact whatsoever on ordinary reality. Finally, virtual reality, with its capacity for virtual replay of constructions of the imagination, may hold the key to accessing and mapping of the imagination. The dream of artists, to be able to show the fabric of their dreams and visions, may be fast approaching virtual reality.

The more extreme, inventive, and avant-garde of the VR constructions are likely to resemble experiences with psychedelic plants rather than more conventionalized forms of art. The doorway to the realms of dream and the unconscious will be opened, and what had been merely symbolic representations of eccentric individual experience will become that experience itself.

Does Lanier's "nonsymbolic communication" have anything to do with the visible languages of the DMT ecstasy? It was this less than obvious question that had got me interested in VR in the first place. My experiences with shamanic hallucinogens, especially *ayahuasca* use in the Upper Amazon Basin, had shown me the reality of vocal performances that are experienced as visual. The magical songs of the *ayahuasqueros*, the folk *medicos* of the Indians and mestizos of the jungle back rivers, are not song as we understand the term. Rather they are intended to be seen and to be judged primarily as visual works of art. To those intoxicated and adrift upon the visionary reveries unleashed by the brew, the singing voice of the shaman has become a magical airbrush of color and organized imagery that is breathtaking in its alien and cosmic grandeur. My hope is that virtual reality at its best may be the perfect mind space

in which to experimentally explore and entrain the higher forms of visual linguistic processing that accompany tryptamine intoxication. In other
words, the VR technology can be used to create a tool kit for the construction of objects made of visual language. These objects would be experienced in the VR mode as three-dimensional things; manifolds
devoid of ordinary verbal ambiguity. This phase shift is a move toward
a kind of telepathy. The shared beholding of the same linguistic intention in an objectified manifold is a true union. We become as one mind
with this style of communication. Language beheld could perhaps serve
as the basis for a deeper web of interlocking understandings between
human beings that would represent a kind of technically aided evolutionary forward leap of the species. The near future may hold a public
utility that will provide cable access to a hyperdimensional ocean of visi-
bly expressed public thoughts. This service will be delivered over cable
simply because the very large computers necessary to create moving,
real-time, high-resolution virtual realities will be state-of-the-art main-
frames for the next few years at least. A kind of informational network
that one can actually enter into and control through the use of visual
icons. Is this not true of cyberspace? I believe that it is, that it is what cy-
berpunk prophet William Gibson was thinking of in his novel
Neuromancer when he introduced the notion of cyberspace:

> [A] consensual hallucination experienced daily by billions of legitimate
> operators, in every nation. . . . A graphic representation of data abstract-
> ed from the banks of every computer in the human system. Unthinkable
> complexity. Lines of light ranged in the nonspace of the mind, clusters
> and constellations of data. Like city lights, receding. (1984, p. 3)

My hope for virtual reality would be that exploration of such new
frontiers of language and communication could be built into research
strategies from the start. Then the loop from the trivial to the archetypal
might be appreciably shorted as the VR option becomes well known.

A major career option of the near term is that of professional cyberspace architect/engineer. Such folks will design and direct the construction of virtual realities and scenarios. Gullichsen, in an article for
Nexus, wrote:

> The talents of a cyberspace architect will be akin to those of traditional
> architects, film directors, novelists, generals, coaches, playwrights, and
> video game designers. The job of the cyberspace engineer will be to make
> the experience seem real. This job is as artistic as it is technical, for expe-
> rience is something manufactured spontaneously in the mind and senses,
> not something that can be built, packaged, and sold like a car or a refrig-
> erator. (1989, p. 8)

Consciousness is no better than the quality of the codes that convey it. VR may hold the possibility of an icon-based visual language that could be universally understood while being much more wide spectrum in its portrayal of emotions and spatial relationships than is even theoretically possible for spoken language. But we will not find the fountain of pure visual poetry if we do not look for it.

17

Sacred Plants and Mystic Realities

D: COULD you describe the different phases of your spiritual quest—from the beginning?

TM: My original impetus was the shamanism of Central Asia, which, as an art historian in the late 1960s, interested me enormously. I went to Nepal to study the Tibetan language and got an insight not into Buddhism—which came to Tibet in the seventh century—but into the indigenous shamanism, Bon-Po, which has been there since earliest times. I quickly satisfied myself, comparing the experiences and the art that I was seeing in Nepal with the sort of experiences that I had as an undergraduate in the LSD culture of the mid-1960s, that there was no clear one-to-one mapping between the psychedelic experience and traditional systems of esoteric thought—even though Timothy Leary and Ralph Metzner had given great impetus to that idea by publishing a psychedelic guide based on *The Tibetan Book of the Dead.*

I practiced yoga when I lived in India and in the Seychelles, and I came to feel that either I was too lumpen to ever reach enlightenment by this means or this was essentially the repetition of historical formulas where the real object has long since been lost or forgotten. So I then looked at shamanic traditions in situations where there had been less acculturation to the ongoing sweep of civilization—that meant either the remote islands of Indonesia or the Amazon. And I visited both places—

■ ■

This interview with Nevill Drury appeared in the autumn 1990, vol. 11, no. 1, issue of the Australian magazine *Nature and Health.*

the Indonesian outer islands first, beginning with Sumatra. Over ten months, I walked myself south and east visiting Sumba, Sumbawa, Timor, Flores, the Moluccas, Ceram, and Ternate. I was supporting myself as a professional butterfly collector, having a wonderful time and confronting a puzzle that many, many botanists have commented upon, and that was the unexplained paucity of psychoactive plants in the Old World tropics.

For reasons that are not well understood, the South American tropics have a virtual monopoly on the plants that produce hallucinogenic indoles. Trying to construct an evolutionary scenario that would concentrate these compounds in one continent over all others is a thankless task, but having satisfied myself that there was no plant-based indigenous psychedelic shamanism in Indonesia, in 1970 I went to South America for the first time. I had made a thorough ethnographic study of the Amazon Basin before I went. Thanks to the work of Richard Evans Schultes at Harvard University, there is a compendious body of this sort of material. The principal hallucinogens of the Amazon Basin are tryptamines of some sort or another, usually activated by being taken in combination with harmine, a monoamine oxidase (MAO) inhibitor. This was very interesting because it seemed to imply a pharmacological sophistication among these indigenous people that was only surpassed in the West in the mid-1950s, when this MAO system was understood.

Anyway, we got down to South America and began experimenting with these plants—*ayahuasca*, the visionary vine that Richard Spruce had first encountered when he was there in 1853, and the tryptamine-containing snuffs of the Waika and Yanomamo people. It was very clear to me that the experience of LSD in a profane society was merely the edge of the psychedelic cosmos, and I realized that the conclusion that LSD was the most powerful of these compounds was really not well founded. What is happening with these tryptamine hallucinogens is a tremendous activation of the visual cortex, so that they are true hallucination-inducing drugs. The dominant motif is a flood of visual imagery that, try as one might, one cannot recognize as the contents of either the personal *or* the collective unconscious. This was truly fascinating to me. I had made a thorough study of Jung and therefore had the expectation that motifs and idea systems from the unconscious mind would prove to be reasonably homogeneous worldwide. What I found, instead, with the peak intoxication from these plants, was a world of ideas, visual images, and noetic insight that really could not be comapped on any tradition— even the esoteric tradition. All this seemed to go beyond it. This was so fascinating to me that I have made it the compass of my life.

ND: What impact have psychedelics had, in a creative sense, on Western culture?

TM: In the West the original contact with altered states of consciousness of any consequence would have to be opium. And opium was a major driving force on the Romantic imagination—Coleridge, De Quincy, Laurence Sterne, and a number of other writers were creating a world of darkened ruins, abandoned priories, black water sucking at desolate shores—clearly a gloss on the opium state. Then around 1820, Byron, Shelley, and others began experimenting with hashish as well. But strangely enough, presumably for cultural reasons, hashish never made inroads into the English literary imagination the way that opium had. It was left to an American—Fitz Hugh Ludlow—to detail his experiments as an undergraduate at Union College in 1853, eating large amounts of cannabis jelly. And comporting himself in a way that would be nearly unknown until a hundred years later!

There would come to be a fascination with what Baudelaire and Gautier called the "artificial paradise"—they saw these drugs as a tremendous spark plug to the literary imagination. That attitude was then passed on to people like Havelock Ellis, William James, and the Germans Klüver and Lewin in the matter of mescaline, which was the next compound to be isolated. In the late 1890s Lewin took peyote buttons to Germany and the pure substance was extracted. And there it was pretty much left until the LSD days of the sixties.

Now, what all these early researchers established when research was legal was that these substances did create a flood of eidetic imagery, they did seem to open up insight into what would have to be called "mystical landscapes." There was the sense that they were penetrating the world of gnosis.

When LSD was made illegal in the United States in the 1960s, as an afterthought so were all other known psychedelics. And consequently our description of what these compounds are capable of tends to be equated with a type of instant psychoanalysis. You would take these substances, and, through a recovery of childhood trauma and insight into your situation, you would shed neurotic attitudes. It was a type of wonder drug for psychological problems. And there it was left, because research became illegal—particularly research with human beings.

Nevertheless, there was a large underground community that continued to dabble in this area, and that community began to build up a picture of the activity of these substances that went well beyond the Freudian or the Jungian models. What gave particular impetus to this evolving point of view were the experiences people were having with psilocybin. Psilocybin is the active hallucinogenic compound in certain species of mushrooms that have been used for millennia in the central Mexican highlands. Under the influence of psilocybin there is an experience of contact with a speaking entity—an interior voice that I call the *Logos*. The Logos spoke the Truth—an incontrovertible Truth. Socrates had what he called his *deamon*—his informing "Other." And the ease with which psilocybin induces this phenomenon makes it, from the viewpoint of a materialist or reductionist rooted in the scientific tradition, almost miraculous.

So I set out to study this phenomenon and to try and determine for myself: Was this a deeper level of the psyche that could appear, somehow autonomously, to be a resident "Other" in the mind with whom one could have conversations? Was this the voice of Mother Nature? Or was it an extraterrestrial intelligence? These may seem like wild hypotheses, but you have to understand that I was pushed to them by evidence, by experience. This was not "blue sky" stuff. Here we had a "voice in the head" eager to reveal vast scenarios of esoteric history, the vast millennia unfolding in tlie human future.

ND: What did you make of it?

TM: Well, I still don't have the answer. I vacillate. It depends how close you are to actually having had the experience—it is hair-raisingly like dealing with an extraterrestrial! And yet once you put the experience behind you, your rational habits reassert themselves and you say to yourself "Surely it could not have been that . . ."

ND: You feel, don't you, that you are accessing quite different spiritual realms from those described by mystics and gurus from the Eastern traditions?

TM: Yes. Their stress on energy centers in the body, levels of consciousness, the moral perfection of spiritual dimensions—none of this I found to be reliable. What the psilocybin experience seems to argue is that there is a kind of parallel universe that is not at all like our universe, and yet it is inhabited by beings with an intentionality. It is not recognizably the universe of astral travel or of the Robert Monroe out-of-the-body experiments. What has always put me off about occultists is the humdrum nature of the other world. They talk about radiant people in flowing gowns—ascended masters and so on. My overwhelming impression of the other realm is its utter strangeness—its "Otherness." It is not even a universe of three-dimensional space and time. The other thing about it, which the esoteric traditions to my mind never confront directly, is the *reality* of it. I am not an occultist. I am spiritual only to the degree that I have been forced to be by experience. I came into it a reductionist, a rationalist, a materialist, an empiricist—and I say no reductionist, no empiricist could experience what I have experienced without having to seriously retool their philosophy. This is not a reality for the menopausal mystic, the self-hypnotized or the soft-headed. This is real. And the feeling that radiates out of the psychedelic experience is that it has a historical implication, that what has really happened in the twentieth century is that the cataloging of nature that began in the sixteenth century with Linnaeus has at last reached its culmination. And the cataloging of nature has revealed things that were totally unexpected—for example, the existence of a dimension that our entire language set, emotional set, and religious ontology deny.

What has happened in the twentieth century is that we have found out what the witch doctors are really doing, what the shaman really intends. This information cannot simply be placed in our museums and forgotten: it contains within it a nugget of incontrovertible experience that appears to argue that our vision of reality is sorely lacking. Somehow we have gone down a road of development that has hidden from us vast regions of reality—areas that we have originally dismissed as superstition and now don't mention at all.

ND: Do you feel that the shamanic reality is now the broadest paradigm available to us? Is it broader, say, than the Eastern mystical model?

TM: Oh, yes, I think so. What I think happened is that in the world of prehistory all religion was experiential, and it was based on the pursuit of ecstasy through plants. And at some time, very early, a group interposed itself between people and direct experience of the "Other." This created hierarchies, priesthoods, theological systems, castes, ritual, taboos. Shamanism, on the other hand, is an experiential science that deals with an area where we know nothing. It is important to remember that our epistemological tools have developed very unevenly in the West. We know a tremendous amount about what is going on in the heart of the atom, but we know absolutely nothing about the nature of the mind. We haven't a clue. If mathematical formulation is to be the bedrock of ideological certitude, then we have no certitude whatsoever in the realm of what is the mind. We *assume* all kinds of things unconsciously, but, when pressed, we can't defend our position.

I think what has happened—because of psychedelics on one level and quantum physics on another—is that the program of rationally understanding nature has at last been pushed so far that we have reached the irrational core of nature herself. Now we can see: My God, the tools that brought us here are utterly inadequate.

ND: Is the human potential movement currently reevaluating the role of psychedelics in understanding the nature of consciousness? Or do you find yourself somewhat out on a limb among your contemporaries?

TM: Well, it's a little of both. The human potential movement at times seems like a *flight* from the psychedelic experience. It will do anything provided there can be certain confidence that it won't work. Therapies have their place, but they are not addressing the question, What is the ground of Being?

I am not alone in advocating a revisioning of psychedelics, but my colleagues and I certainly represent a highly suspect and not entirely integrated faction of the human potential movement. In a way, you see, we are still reacting to what happened in the 1960s. One can say many things about one's personal psychedelic experiences—and they are always very personal—but if you try to look at ten thousand psychedelic experiences the generalized conclusion you reach about what these things do is: Number one, they dissolve boundaries *whatever the boundaries are.* And as a consequence of this they dissolve cultural programming. They are very democratic—they dissolve all cultural programming. So Marxist, shaman, fundamentalist Christian, and nuclear physicist will all find themselves deeply questioning their own beliefs, postpsychedelic. The thing about LSD that did mark it as different from all the other psychedelics was that a reasonably competent chemist could produce five million doses in a single day! Well, that was unique in human history. When you go to the Amazon or when you take peyote with the Huichol it is quite a chore to get sufficient material for twenty people. So the release of so much LSD into modern society caused the powers that be to assume that the whole social machine was being dissolved in acid—literally, before their very eyes. I think that this was a mistake, to go at it like this. There were many voices at that time, with many theories of how it should be handled. If Aldous Huxley had lived another ten years, it would have been very different. His idea was to get the psychedelic experience to artists, philosophers, city planners, architects—not every eighteen-year-old on earth.

ND: You focus especially on the tryptamines—but is there a cultural factor involved here also? Does a modern-day Westerner using these psychedelics access the same reality with these substance as a traditional South American shaman?

TM: Ultimately, I don't think that it is cultural. When you smoke DMT you have an experience that comes from the flesh and the bone of your humanness. However, this experience exists entirely as a private

reality until you pour it into a linguistic vessel. If you pour it into the linguistic vessel of English, it's going to look very different than if it is
poured into the linguistic vessel of Mazatecan. And this has to do with
the inevitable relativity of language. So part of what I have done is try to
create a phenomenological description of what actually happens. The
other thing about these psychedelic experiences is that they are so extraordinary that we have no way to anchor them in memory. If you visit
a city you haven't been to before you can always relate it to cities that
you *have* been to, but when you go to a place that has no comappable
point, then you have to create a new language almost from scratch.

Paradoxically, DMT seems to be about the language-forming activity in human beings. Interestingly, some tens of millennia ago the
African continent underwent a period of desiccation that continues into
the present. The great rain forests that covered most of Africa began to
retreat, leaving grasslands behind them. The primate populations that
were arboreal were forced by selective pressure to descend into the
grasslands and to abandon their previously vegetarian habits for an omnivorous diet. They already had a complex system of pack signals, as
monkeys do, but when they began to develop their hunting strategies on
the veldt, there was even more pressure to accelerate and develop this
signaling ability. Well, their omnivorous diet led them to focus on the
great herds of ungulate animals—wild cattle—that were evolving simultaneously. Now, in the dung of these ungulate animals the psilocybin
mushrooms make their natural home. They are "coprophilic"—that is to
say, "dung-loving" mushrooms. This is the only place that they grow. I
myself have observed the foraging habits of baboons in Kenya. Baboons
scrabble around in the dirt, and one of their favorite tricks is to flip over
cow pies looking for beetles and grubs. So the cow pie occupies an important position in their world. And yet the mushroom is a totally
anomalous object in the grassland environment—it stands out like a sore
thumb.

Roland Fischer, who did a lot of work with psilocybin before it
became illegal to give it to human beings, made a very interesting observation in the early 1960s. He gave very low doses to people—doses so
low that you would not have a psychedelic experience and in fact you
would not notice anything much at all, except a slight arousal. But he
gave these people visual acuity tests and he discovered that on small
does of psilocybin you can actually see more clearly than in your normal
state. You don't have to be an evolutionary biologist to understand that
if there is a plant in the environment that confers increased visual acuity
on an animal that has a hunting life-style, then those animals that accept
this item into their diet are going to be more successful hunters and
therefore have a more successful reproductive strategy than those ani-

mals not admitting the item into their diet. Well, if you take slightly higher doses of psilocybin this restless arousal turns into sexual arousal. And again, more successful copulations mean more successful impregnations, more successful births. This again favors those using the item in their breeding strategy. If you double the dose that causes this sexual arousal, then you have a full-fledged contact with something so bizarre, so mysterious, that to this day, fifty thousand years later, we still do not have the intellectual equipment to understand it. It appears in the minds of modern human beings with the same transcendental, awe-inspiring force that it must have aroused in the mind of an australopithecine.

ND: What then is your answer to people who continue to dismiss psychedelic experience as artificial? Surely your view is the exact reverse of that?

TM: Well, there's nothing artificial about it. These things were part of the human food chain from the very beginning. Where the misunderstanding comes is with the label—these are "drugs," and "drug" is a red-flag word. We are hysterical over the subject of drugs. Our whole society seems to be dissolving under the onslaught of criminally syndicated drug distribution systems. What we are going to have to do if we are to come to terms with this is to become a little more sophisticated in our definitions. I believe that what we really object to about "drugs" is that we are alarmed by unexamined, obsessive, self-destructive behavior. When we see someone acting in this way we draw back. That is what addiction to a drug such as cocaine or morphine results in. However, psychedelics actually break habits and patterns of thought. They actually cause individuals to inspect the structures of their lives and make judgments about them. Now, what psychedelics share with "drugs" is that they are physical compounds, often pressed into pills, and you do put them into your body. But I believe that a reasonable definition of drugs would have us legalize psilocybin and outlaw television!

Imagine if the Japanese had won World War II and had introduced into American life a drug so insidious that thirty years later the average American was spending five hours a day "loaded" on this drug. People would just view it as an outrageous atrocity. And yet, we in America do this to ourselves. And the horrifying thing about the "trip" that television gives you is that it's not your trip. It is a trip that comes down through the values systems of a society whose greatest god is the almighty dollar. So television is the opiate of the people. I think the tremendous governmental resistance to the psychedelic issue is not because psychedelics are multimillion-dollar criminal enterprises—they are trivial on that level. However, they inspire examination of values, and that is the most corrosive thing that can happen.

ND: Your idea is of the psychedelic pioneer as a type of alchemist who can make the soul tangible, as it were. Could you tell us more about this?

TM: Alchemy was the belief that spirit somehow resided at the heart of matter. The alchemists were the heirs to the great Hellenistic religious systems that are generally tagged as "gnostic." The central idea of Gnosticism is that the material of which "soul and true being" is composed is trapped through a series of cosmic misfortunes in a low-level universe that is alien to it. And the alchemists literalized these ideas to suggest that the spirit could somehow be distilled or coaxed from the dense matrix of matter. Well, this is also what the psychedelics reinforce, and it is interesting to see how alchemists at different times have contributed to the advancement of pharmacology. For instance, distilled alcohol was discovered by alchemists seeking the elixir of life, and Paracelsus popularized opium. This is not to fault the alchemical quest but to show that alchemy—the belief that there is spirit in matter—was a survival of an older, shamanic strata of belief that involved gaining the alliance of a plant. I think the notion that one can make spiritual progress by oneself is preposterous. It is virtually impossible to have the spiritual experiences that confirm a certain moral order and value system unless you resort to psychedelics or, alternatively, fasting or getting lost in the wilderness. I don't think people realize quite how efficacious the psychedelics are—these things work!

I wish people could be more catholic in their tastes. If you are an advocate of the virtues of yoga or natural diet or mantras—you really owe it to yourself to explore those concerns using psychedelics at the same time. I explored the possibilities I have just mentioned before settling on the golden road to the soul.

ND: So why is there such tremendous prejudice, both in the East and in the West, against psychedelics?

TM: I think people are in love with the journey. People love seeking answers. If you were to suggest to people that the time of seeking is over and that the chore is now to *face* the answer, that's more of a challenge! Anyone can sweep up around the ashram for a dozen years while congratulating themselves that they are following Baba into enlightenment. It takes courage to take psychedelics—*real courage*. Your stomach clenches, your palms grow damp, because you realize this is real—this is going to work. Not in twelve years, not in twenty years, but in an hour! What I see in the whole spiritual enterprise is a great number of people supporting themselves in one way or another on the basis of their lack of success. Were they ever to succeed, these enterprises would all be put out of business. But no one's in a hurry for that.

ND: In your scheme of things, is there any place for institutionalized religion, for orthodox religious beliefs?

TM: Yes. What I have found is that all of these systems that are offered as spiritual paths work splendidly in the presence of psychedelics. If you think mantras are effective, try a mantra on twenty milligrams of psilocybin and see what happens. All sincere religious motivation is illuminated by psychedelics. To put it perhaps in a trivial way, the religious quest is an automobile but psychedelics are the petrol that runs it. You go nowhere without the fuel no matter how finely crafted the upholstery, how flawlessly machined the engine.

ND: Where do you personally think the human potential movement is heading now, and where do you position yourself in the spectrum?

TM: I believe that the best idea will win. We are all under an obligation to ourselves and to the world to do our best—to place the best ideas on the table. Then all we have to do is stand back and watch. I have this Darwinian belief that the correct idea will emerge triumphant. To my way of thinking, psychedelics provide the only category that is authentic enough to be legislated out of existence. They're not going to make quartz crystals or wheat grass juice illegal—these things pose no problem. But I think that we are going to have to come to terms with the psychedelic possibility. We would have a long time ago in America except for the fact that, on this issue, the Government acts as the enforcing arm of Christian fundamentalism. Life, liberty, and pursuit of happiness are enshrined in the Constitution of the United States as *inalienable* rights. If the pursuit of happiness does not cover the psychedelic quest for enlightenment, then I don't know what it can mean. I think we are headed for a darker period before the light, because the self-deceiving cant of the Government on this issue is going to have to be exposed for what it is. I see the whole "hard drug" phenomenon as an enormous con game. Governments have always been the major purveyor of addictive drugs—right back to the sugar trade in England, the opium wars in China, the CIA's involvement in the heroin trade in Southeast Asia during the 1960s, and the current cocaine distribution coming out of South

America. We're going to have to abandon this Christian wish to legislate other people's behavior "for their own good."

Let's take two drugs for a moment and contrast them: Cocaine is ultrachic, costs $100 per gram, is utterly worthless as far as I can see, and doesn't get you as wired as a double espresso. Then there's airplane glue. It cost $1.20 a tube, and you can totally waste yourself with it and probably kill yourself no faster than you can with cocaine. So why aren't people in Dior gowns, driving Rolls Royces, honking up airplane glue? Because it's tatty, grotesque, déclassé. And this is what we have to put across about these hard drugs. The only way you can do that is to re-duce the price of cocaine to $1.25 per gram. Then it will be seen as a hor-rible, banal, destructive thing. Only when governments intervene by restricting access do things suddenly gain this astronomical worth. So it is a game that the government is playing.

ND: I do see signs in a number of countries that governments are at last heeding the environmental message. If we consider the concept of the Gaia hypothesis as a reflection of an emerging global awareness, it also seems to me that your concept of the "Oversoul" of the planet could also become important . . .

TM: These things are all part of the New Age, but I have aban-doned that term in favor of what I call the Archaic Revival—which places it all in a better historical perspective. When a culture loses its bearing, the traditional response is to go back in history to find the pre-vious "anchoring model." An example of this would be the breakup of the medieval world at the time of the Renaissance. They had lost their compass, so they went back to Greek and Roman models and created classicism—Roman law, Greek aesthetics, and so on.

In the twentieth century a global civilization has lost its bearing, and as we look back in time for a model to anchor us we have to go back before history to around twelve or fifteen thousand years ago. So the im-portant part of the human potential movement and the New Age, I be-lieve, is the reempowerment of ritual, the rediscovery of shamanism, the re-cognition of psychedelics, and the importance of the Goddess. There must also be an authentic religious mystery driving this. Psychedelics put you in touch with something that is both real and immediate—the mind of the planet. This is the Oversoul of all life on earth. It's the real thing. The Gaia hypothesis, which began by proposing that the entire planet is a self-regulating system, has now been brought to the level where some people are saying "It's almost alive." But I would go much further than that. Not only is it alive, but it is "minded."

I take very seriously the idea that the Logos is real, that there is a guiding Mind—an Oversoul—that inhabits the biome of the planet, and that human balance, dignity, and religiosity depend on having direct contact with this realm. That is what shamanism is providing. It was available in the West until the fall of Eleusis and the Mystery traditions—to some people—but then it was stamped out by barbarians who didn't understand what they had destroyed.

The soul of the planet is not neutral about the emerging direction of human history. We are part of a cosmic drama—I really believe that—and although the cosmic drama has lasted for untold ages, I don't think it's going to run for untold ages into the future.

ND: You see all this reaching some sort of climax in 2012 A.D. Could you explain that?

TM: I see some sort of culmination in 2012. The Maya also set 2012 as the end of a 5,128-year cycle. I believe that what we call historical existence is a self-limiting situation that cannot be projected centuries into the future. We are tearing the earth to pieces, we are spewing out toxins—and the entire planet is reacting. Psychedelics are going to play a major role in helping people to become aware of what is really happening.

ND: You have said that an important part of the mystical quest is to face up to death and recognize it as a rhythm of life. Would you like to enlarge on your view on the implications of the dying process?

TM: I take seriously the notion that these psychedelic states are an anticipation of the dying process—or, as the Tibetans refer to it, the *Bardo* level beyond physical death. It seems likely that our physical lives are a type of launching pad for the soul. As the esoteric traditions say, life is an opportunity to prepare for death, and we should learn to recognize the signposts along the way, so that when death comes, we can make the transition smoothly. I think the psychedelics show you the transcendental nature of reality. It would be hard to die gracefully as an atheist or existentialist. Why should you? Why not rage against the dying of the light? But if in fact this is not the dying of the light but the Dawning of the Great Light, then one should certainly not rage against that. There's a tendency in the New Age to deny death. We have people pursuing physical immortality and freezing their heads until the fifth millennium, when they can be thawed out. All of this indicates a lack of balance or equilibrium. The Tao flows through the realms of life and nonlife with equal ease.

ND: Do you personally regard the death process as a journey into one's own belief system?

TM: Like the psychedelic experience, death must be poured into the vessel of language. But dying is essentially physiological. It may be that there are certain compounds in the brain that are only released when it is impossible to reverse the dying process. And yet the near-death experience has a curious affinity to the shamanic voyage and the psychedelic experience.

I believe that the best map we have of consciousness is the shamanic map. According to this viewpoint, the world has a "center," and when you go to the center—which is inside yourself—there is a vertical axis that allows you to travel up or down. There are celestial worlds, there are infernal worlds, there are paradisiacal worlds. These are the worlds that open up to us on our shamanic journeys, and I feel we have an obligation to explore these domains and pass on that information to others interested in mapping the psyche. At this time in our history, it's perhaps the most awe-inspiring journey anyone could hope to make.

Bibliography

Allegro, John M. *The Sacred Mushroom and the Cross.* Garden City, NY: Doubleday, 1970.

Birks, Walter, and R. A. Gilbert. *The Treasure of Montsegur.* London: Aquarian Press, 1987.

Brumbaugh, Robert, ed. *The Most Mysterious Manuscript.* Carbondale, IL: Southern Illinois Univ. Press, 1978.

Carroll, Lewis. *The Annotated Alice: Alice's Adventures in Wonderland and Through the Looking Glass.* Introduction and notes by Martin Gardner. New York: Clarkson N. Potter, 1960.

D'Empirio, Mary. *The Voynich Manuscript: An Elegant Enigma.* Washington, DC: U.S. Department of Commerce, National Technical Information Service, 1978.

Duerr, Hans Peter. *Dreamtime.* Oxford: Basil Blackwell, 1985.

Eisler, Riane. *The Chalice and the Blade.* San Francisco: Harper & Row, 1987.

Eliade, Mircea. *Shamanism: Archaic Techniques of Ecstasy.* New York: Pantheon Books, 1964.

Gibson, William. *Neuromancer.* New York: Ace, 1984.

Graves, Robert. *Food For Centaurs.* Garden City, NY: Doubleday, 1960.

————. *Difficult Questions, Easy Answers.* Garden City, NY: Doubleday, 1964.

Guenther, Herbert V. *Tibetan Buddhism Without Mystification.* Leiden: E. J. Brill, 1966.

Gullichsen, Eric. "Cyberspace: Experiential Computing," *NEXUS '89 Science Fiction, Science Fact,* 1989.

Hofmann, Albert. *LSD: My Problem Child.* Los Angeles: Tarcher, 1983.

Jacobs, Barry L. *Hallucinogens: Neurochemical, Behavioral and Clinical Perspectives.* New York: Raven, 1984.

James, William. *The Varieties of Religious Experience.* Cambridge, MA, and London: Harvard Univ. Press, 1985.

Jaynes, Julian. *The Origin of Consciousness in the Breakdown of the Bicameral Mind.* Boston: Houghton Mifflin, 1977.

Lajoux, Jean-Dominique. *The Rock Paintings of Tassili.* Cleveland: World, 1963.

Levitov, Leo. *Solution of the Voynich Manuscript: A Liturgical Manual for the Endura Rite of the Cathari Heresy, The Cult of Isis.* Laguna Hills, CA: Aegean Park, 1987.

Lhote, Henri. *The Search for the Tassili Frescoes.* New York: E. P. Dutton, 1959.

Lloyd, John Uri. *Etidorhpa, or, The End of Earth.* Cincinnati: Authors Limited Edition, 1895.

————. *Etidorhpa, or, the End of Earth.* Albuquerque, NM: Sunn, 1976.

————. *Etidorhpa, or, the End of Earth.* New York: Pocket Books, 1978.

Magre, Maurice. *The Return of the Magi.* London: Philip Allan, 1931.

Maspero, Gaston. *The Dawn of Civilization—Egypt and Chaldaea.* London: Society for Promoting Christian Knowledge, 1894.

McKenna, Terence. *True Hallucinations.* Berkeley, CA: Lux Natura, 1984. An eight-tape "talking book."

McKenna, Terence, and Dennis McKenna. *The Invisible Landscape.* New York: Seabury, 1975.

Mellaart, James. *Earliest Civilizations of the Near East.* New York: McGraw-Hill, 1965.

—————. *Çatal Hüyük: A Neolithic Town in Anatolia.* New York: McGraw-Hill, 1967.

Merill, A. E. "The Narrative of Mr. W." *Science* 40, no. 1029 (September 18, 1914).

Munn, Henry. "The Mushrooms of Language." In Michael Harner, ed., *Shamanism and Hallucinogens.* London: Oxford Univ. Press, 1973.

Pim, Herbert Moore (Pseudonym A. Newman). "Monsieur Among the Mushrooms," *Irish Ecclestical Record* 5 (January–June 1915): 586–603.

Pim, Herbert Moore. "Monsieur Among the Mushrooms." Reprinted in *Unknown Immortals—In The Northern City of Success.* Dublin: Talbot, 1917.

Rodriguez, E., M. Aregullin, S. Uehara, T. Nishida, R. Wrangham, Z. Abramowski, A. Finlayson, and G. H. N. Towers. "Thiarubrine-A, A Bioactive Constituent of *Aspilia* (*Asteraceae*) Consumed by Wild Chimpanzees." *Experientia* 41 (1985): 419–420.

Runciman, S. *The Medieval Manichee: A Study of the Christian Dualist Heresy.* New York: Viking, 1961.

Saur, Carl. *Man's Impact on the Earth.* New York: Academic Press, 1973.

Schultes, R. E. "Some Impacts of Spruce's Amazon Explorations on Modern Phytochemical Research" *Rhodora: Journal of the New England Botanical Club,* 70, 783, July–September 1968.

Shah, Idris. *The Sufis.* Garden City, NY: Doubleday, 1964.

Vallee, Jacques. *The Invisible College.* New York: E. P. Dutton, 1975.

—————. *Messengers of Deception.* Berkeley, CA: And/Or Press, 1979.

Waddington, C. H. *The Nature of Life.* London: George Allen & Unwin, 1961.

Waite, A. E. *The Holy Grail.* New Hyde Park, NY: University Books, 1961.

Wakefield, W. L. *Heresy, Crusade and Inquisition in Southern France 1100–1250.* Berkeley: Univ. of California Press, 1974.

Warner, H. J. *The Albigensian Heresy.* New York: Macmillan, 1922, reprint 1978.

Wasson, R. Gordon. *Soma: Divine Mushroom of Immortality.* New York: Harcourt Brace Jovanovich, 1971.

—————. Foreword to *Phantastica: Rare and Important Psychoactive Drug Literature from 1700 to the Present.* Los Angeles: William and Victoria Dailey Antiquarian Books and Fine Prints, 1979.

Wasson, R. Gordon, Albert Hofmann, and Carl A. P. Ruck. *The Road to Eleusis: Unveiling the Secret of the Mysteries.* New York: Harcourt Brace Jovanovich, 1978.

Wasson, R. Gordon, S. Kramrish, J. Ott, and Carl A. P. Ruck. *Persephone's Quest: Entheogens and the Origins of Religion.* New Haven: Yale Univ. Press, 1986.

Wasson, V. P., and R. Gordon Wasson. *Mushrooms, Russia and History.* New York: Pantheon Books, 1957.

Wells, H. G. *Best Science Fiction Stories of H. G. Wells.* New York: Dover, 1966.

Whitehead, Alfred North. *Process and Reality.* New York: Free Press, 1969.

Index

This constitutes a continuation of the copyright page.

The author wishes to thank the following publishers and publications for permission to reprint articles that originally appeared in their pages:

Jay Levin (ed.) for permission to reprint *In Praise of Psychedelics*, which originally appeared in *L. A. Weekly*, May 20–26, 1988, vol. 10, no. 26. Allison Kennedy (ed.) at *Mondo 2000* (formerly *High Frontiers*) for permission to reprint the *High Frontiers* interview, originally printed in *High Frontiers*, vol. 1, no. 1, fall 1984. The Heldref Foundation for permission to reprint "A Conversation Over Saucers," which appeared in *Revision*, vol. 11, no. 3, winter 1989; "Temporal Resonance," which first appeared in *Revision*, vol. 10, no. 1, summer 1987; and "Hallucinogenic Mushrooms and Evolution," originally published in *Revision*, vol. 10, no. 4, spring 1988. The editors of *Magical Blend* magazine for permission to reprint "New Maps of Hyperspace," which appeared first in issue no. 22 of *Magical Blend*, April 1989, and "Virtual Reality and Electronic Highs," which appeared in *Magical Blend*, no. 26, April 1990. The Prism Unity Press of Great Britain for permission to reprint "Among *Ayahuasqueros*," which first appeared in their 1989 anthology *Gateway to Inner Space*, edited by Christian Ratsch. New Dimensions Radio (P. O. Box 410410, San Francisco, California 94141) for permission to transcribe "The New Dimensions Interview," no. 1243. Jay Kinney of *Gnosis* magazine for permission to reprint "The Voynich MS," portions of which appeared in *Gnosis*, no. 7, spring 1988. Dioscorides Press for permission to reprint "Wasson's Literary Precursors," which originally appeared in *The Sacred Mushroom Seeker*, edited by Thomas J. Riedlinger, copyright © 1990 by Dioscorides Press (an imprint of Timber Press, Inc.). David Jay Brown for permission to reprint the "*Critique* Interview," which originally appeared in the magazine *Critique*, summer 1989. *Whole Earth Review* for permission to reprint "Plan, Plant, Planet," which first appeared in the *Whole Earth Review*, fall 1989. Nevill Drury, editor of *Nature and Health*, for permission to reprint "Sacred Plants and Mystic Realities," which originally appeared in *Nature and Health*, vol. 11, no. 1, autumn 1990.

About the Illustrator

Satty (Wilfred Podriech), born in Bremen, Germany in 1939, began making pictorial collages in 1966, inspired by the openness and creativity of San Francisco's hippie era. He became a prolific artist, creating hundreds of black and white collages, many of them printed by the booming poster market and in the underground and establishment press. He produced two collage books, *The Cosmic Bicycle* and *Time Zone*, and his work has been exhibited in many galleries and museums, including the San Francisco Museum of Modern Art; the Museum of Modern Art, New York; and the National Museum, Warsaw. Satty died in San Francisco in 1982.

Some of the illustrations in this book first appeared in *The Cosmic Bicycle* and *Time Zone*. Most have never before been published.